Higher Education
and the Color Line

College Access, Racial Equity,
and Social Change

Higher Education and the Color Line

College Access, Racial Equity, and Social Change

Edited by
GARY ORFIELD
PATRICIA MARIN
and
CATHERINE L. HORN

Harvard Education Press
Cambridge, Massachusetts

Library of Congress Control Number 2004116556

Paperback ISBN 1-891792-59-8
Library Edition ISBN 1-891792-60-1

Published by Harvard Education Press,
an imprint of the Harvard Education Publishing Group

Harvard Education Press
8 Story Street
Cambridge, MA 02138

Cover Design: Alyssa Morris
Typography and Book Design: Sheila Walsh

The typeface used in this book is Sabon.

Contents

Dedication

*We dedicate this book to those
who are working to eliminate the color line
in higher education and to make equal opportunity
a reality for all.*

Acknowledgments

The idea for this book began at the 2003 Color Lines Conference at Harvard University. We are grateful to The Boston Foundation, the W. E. B. Du Bois Institute for African and African American Research, the Fannie Mae Foundation, the Foley Hoag Foundation, the Bill & Melinda Gates Foundation, The William and Flora Hewlett Foundation, the Hyams Foundation, and the Charles Stewart Mott Foundation for sponsoring that momentous event. We especially thank Lumina Foundation for Education for its generous support in making this book a reality. In particular, we thank Heather Wathington for all of her guidance.

We were fortunate to have such an impressive group of scholars committed to issues of equity agree to join us on this project. We thank them for keeping up with our timeline, responding quickly to our many communications, and working tirelessly to create this final product.

As always, we owe a great debt of gratitude to the staff at The Civil Rights Project, as well as Anthony Carnevale, Mitchell Chang, Jorge Chapa, Bridget Terry Long, Dennis Parker, and Julie Ruben, who offered their expertise to help shape these chapters. The Gevirtz Graduate School of Education at the University of California, Santa Barbara, also provided invaluable support through the process. In addition, we thank Carolyn Peele for her detailed editing whenever we called upon her.

Finally, we thank the Harvard Education Publishing Group for partnering with us on this endeavor, especially Caroline Chauncey, Dody Riggs, and Douglas Clayton. It is a pleasure to work with such dedicated and skilled colleagues.

The views expressed in this publication are the authors' and do not necessarily represent the views of Lumina Foundation for Education or its employees.

Higher Education and the Color Line

Introduction

GARY ORFIELD

At the turn of the 20th century, college was largely a white, middle-class experience. With the passage of the GI Bill following World War II, however, the United States created the first mass higher education system in the world, greatly expanding college enrollment and making it possible for millions of ex-soldiers, who otherwise would never have gone to college, to earn a college degree and experience the resultant social and economic mobility. The 1964 Civil Rights Act further expanded college access by outlawing racial/ethnic discrimination, and in 1965 the Higher Education Act and the College Work Study program extended greater assistance to less affluent students. In the 1960s, the civil rights revolution began desegregating public universities in the South, allowing black students to attend these newly interracial institutions. Other policies, which grew out of President Lyndon Johnson's War on Poverty, included federal efforts to identify and help promising low-income students who had not had adequate preparation for college, and provided the first need-based system of federal college aid. In the early 1970s this approach was extended and made permanent by the creation of Pell Grants, an important source of federal financial aid for low-income students.

During this period of expanding and affordable college access between World War II and the mid-1970s, the country witnessed an explosion of university attendance and completion, and for the first time attending college became a serious option for a significant percentage of nonwhite Americans. Between 1940 and 1958, total enrollment shot up from 1.49 million to 3.28 million, a 120 percent increase in just one generation (Bennett, 1996;

1

U.S. Census Bureau, 1961). The numbers reached 5.68 million by 1965, when federal financial aid was enacted, and soared to 9.70 million a decade later in 1975 (U.S. Census Bureau, 1981). Many small teachers colleges became universities, new campuses were opened, and the number of community colleges, which had changed little from 1940 to 1960, more than doubled—from 521 in 1960 to 1,128 (U.S. Census Bureau, 1961, 1981). Nonwhite college enrollment, which was 227,000 in 1960, exploded to more than 1,062,000 by 1976, an increase of 368 percent (U.S. Census Bureau, 1981). Black college enrollment climbed from just 18 percent of black high school graduates in 1960 to 32 percent in 1975 (U.S. Census Bureau, 1981). Public tuition costs were very low, and financial aid, which was mostly in the form of grants rather than loans, was rapidly growing. With the pressure of civil rights law, the resources that states and the federal government were spending to expand schools, the support of antipoverty programs, and the commitment of educational leaders, massive changes had been made to higher education. Although there was never a time when minorities or low-income students finished college at anything near the rate of whites, there was a brief period in the mid-1970s when it seemed that white and nonwhite students who finished high school had about an equal chance to *start* college.

There is a turning point in all policy cycles, however, and for higher education in the United States it can be narrowed down to the period between 1978 and 1981. In 1978 the U.S. Supreme Court was sharply divided on the issue of affirmative action, and left it hanging by narrow threads with a single vote in the *Bakke* decision. That summer, the national tax revolt began with the enactment of a radical tax-cutting measure, Proposition 13, in a California referendum. In Congress, the resurgent Republicans threatened to implement vouchers for higher education, and the Carter administration supported the Middle Income Student Assistance Act, which began the process of shifting aid from the poor to the middle class and changing from grants to federally subsidized loans.

The last two decades of the 20th century continued this reversal. The recession of the early 1980s brought a combination of soaring inflation and economic reverse. What ensued was radical tax cutting, a major reversal on civil rights, cuts in financial aid for college, state tax cuts, and decisions across the country to shift the cost of college increasingly to students, who would finance it more and more by loans. The War on Poverty was shut down and many of its programs constrained. As colleges faced rising costs and declining real aid from state and federal governments, they began increasing tuition faster than family income rose, something that continues today. By the 1990s, as a college education continued to become more important than ever for students' job and life prospects, the country was well into a period of serious decline in state efforts to support higher education. Politicians would get credit for aid programs for the middle class, with names like HOPE Scholarships (Georgia) or Bright Futures (Florida), despite the fact that money being spent on these programs had far surpassed that allocated for need-based aid. Entrance competition and requirements were rising, there was a massive increase in the use of tests to sort students, a serious attack on the remnants of affirmative action was taking shape, and the picture looked grim for minorities and low-income applicants. When affirmative action was eliminated in the two biggest states (Texas and California) in a single year, there appeared to be a serious risk that selective colleges and universities across the country would be resegregated if the Supreme Court were to decide that the kind of positive outreach required in the South in the 1970s and 1980s should be redefined as illegal discrimination against whites.

In 2003, proponents of affirmative action won a significant victory with the Supreme Court's *Grutter* decision. It is notable that even a very conservative Court rejected the effort of conservative law reform groups, such as the Center for Equal Opportunity and the Center for Individual Rights, to end affirmative action and, instead, explicitly recognized the educational and social value of diverse campuses. Important as this decision was in avoiding a further rollback, however, it merely maintained the status quo on campuses in terms of civil rights policy. In addition, members of the opposition, as well as the Bush administration, quickly began to interpret the decision narrowly and attempted to minimize the victory and attack race-conscious policies outside the admissions arena.

Ironically, then, the gains begun early in the 20th century were at risk of encountering severe limits and reversal in a society that was becoming more economically unequal and much less white. For many families, however, the human capital gained through higher education has become the most important source of wealth and security that families can give their children. With the loss of industrial jobs and union wages, and with international corporations imposing global competition and driving down the real wages of relatively unskilled work that could be transferred to other countries, educational credentials and skills are increasingly important determinants of life chances.

Higher education, a luxury for a tiny minority just a century ago, has now taken center stage in achieving the American dream. This great increase in the importance of college has coincided with a huge increase in the percentage of U.S. students who come from historically excluded minority groups, which had never had equal access to college and were concentrated in weak high schools, usually segregated by both race and poverty. Access to college has been increasingly threatened by large increases in tuition, reductions in state and federal resources, more intense competition for college spaces, and growing economic inequality in the country. Higher education has simultaneously become much more important in determining people's life success and much less accessible. Decisions about the evolution of higher education policy will be major factors in determining whether the U.S. moves toward a more or less equitable society.

The 21st century began with a massive reduction of public resources through tax cuts; a major increase in spending for defense, crime, and health care; and consolidated conservative control of all three branches of the federal government—conditions that seriously threaten access to higher education. The country may be on a path toward a higher education system that functions, in effect, as a reflection of the stratified society in which it operates. It could even serve to legitimate and perpetuate inequality. Affirmative action, need-based financial aid, support and transition programs for people from inferior schools, and other policies could be severely undermined, with some groups losing in the competition for limited funds and spaces. These shifts come in the midst of an extraordinary racial transformation destined to make the college-age population far more than half nonwhite by 2050.

This book continues a discussion about America's racial future begun at the Color Lines Conference held at Harvard University on Labor Day weekend in 2003. It was a historic coming together of 1,100 scholars and civil rights leaders from across the country to discuss the nature of multiracial America and its future. It brought an amazing outpouring of research—120 new studies—and an intense search for new understanding amid a rare crossing of lines among the disciplines and between the academy and those working in the political and legal systems.

One key issue discussed was whether higher education would play a role in opening up and creating equal opportunity for mobility in American society, or would reinforce the severe separation and inequality between white and nonwhite America. This book begins with that conversation, but it addresses far more than the current battles, focusing on what we really need to understand and deal with in a dramatically changing society. The book is not intended as a look back at old issues, except as they may inform the new, but instead looks directly into a future we can only begin to discern. It discusses evidence of persistent racial inequalities and what is known about the erosion of civil rights due to court decisions and legislation.

This book is built around three broad racial justice themes that will have an impact on higher education in the next generation: the racial transformation of higher education as the majority of public school enrollment becomes nonwhite; the evolving role of law and policy; and nontraditional paths to postsecondary success. Throughout the volume, the authors use multidisciplinary approaches and a multiracial understanding of American society. We believe that the new research included in this volume will help inform the discussions and decisions of federal and state policymakers, education providers, civil rights advocates, and other interested stakeholders about policy changes that could lead to equal opportunity in postsecondary education for minority and poor students.

The first chapter examines the racial transformation of higher education and the relative equality of access in various states. In "The Racial Transformation of Higher Education," Michal Kurlaender and Stella M. Flores lay out current demographic information on minority enrollment and completion, including changes in enrollment and the institutions students attend, all trends that policymakers must deal with. They also examine how opportunity is changing for minority students by educational sector, by state, and by race.

David Karen and Kevin J. Dougherty are the authors of "Necessary but Not Sufficient: Higher Education as a Strategy of Social Mobility." They discuss the key role of universities as instruments of social and economic mobility in the postindustrial society, consider why this function is so powerful yet invisible within the academy and the political world, and examine the social consequences for minority communities and for universities of continuing on the current path.

The third chapter, "Equity in Educational Attainment: Racial, Ethnic, and Gender Inequality in the 50 States" by Derek V. Price and Jill K. Wohlford, offers the Educational Attainment Parity Index (EAPI) as a tool to measure educational attainment and allow for comparisons of equity in attainment among different racial and ethnic groups.

Some studies have shown money to be the single biggest barrier to college access and completion for minority students. Obviously this is an intensifying problem as, once again, the cost of a college education is increasing sharply in a period of recession, something that happened in the early 1980s and early 1990s as well. Donald E. Heller, in "Can Minority Students Afford College in an Era of Skyrocketing Tuition?" provides the latest data on financial aid trends and research on their impact. While most work on financial aid focuses on one specific aspect and on social class, this chapter is an overview of the various elements including federal funds and merit scholarships, and explicitly examines the impact according to race. These issues, which seem likely to become much more severe if existing trends continue, are central to the future of access and success for minority and low-income students, given the enormous difference in family wealth and assets among racial groups.

With relatively little public attention, what seemed a promise of universal need-blind access to nonselective four-year public colleges has been replaced by increasing reliance on community colleges for access, particularly in the Sunbelt states. This pattern, first enshrined in the California 1960 Master Plan, reflects dubious assumptions about the fungibility of college credits and courses and the workability of transfer mechanisms. In "Illusions of Opportunity? From College Access to Job Access at Two-Year Colleges," Regina Deil-Amen, James E. Rosenbaum, and Ann E. Person analyze social mechanisms that affect opportunities and contribute to the color line, focusing on community and occupational colleges—institutions where large majorities of nonwhite students begin their education. The community college option is much less expensive and very popular with many state officials. As such, it is urgently important to understand how well this option works under various policies and conditions, how it could be more effective, and whether there are better and fairer options.

Recognizing the various roots of the equity crisis on campus leads to the question of whether or not there are good models for campus reforms that would change outcomes. In "Diversity on Campus: Exemplary Programs for Retaining and Supporting Students of Color," Dean K. Whitla, Carolyn Howard, Frank Tuitt, Richard J. Reddick, and Elizabeth Flanagan summarize the work of the National Campus Diversity Project at Harvard University's Graduate School of Education. This multiyear effort was designed to identify diversity programs that have been models for improving the racial climate on campuses, locate programs that have improved the academic achievement of underrepresented minorities, and examine the policies and practices of colleges that have been successful in increasing underrepresented students. Their description of what they found to be exemplary models can contribute to campus and state policy development and inform further research.

College test scores are strongly linked to family income, education, and race, making tests a major obstacle to access for historically excluded groups. Tests are, of course, commonly used as absolute barriers to college entry at various cut points, although they are not designed or recommended for use in this way. Catherine L. Horn, in "Potential or Peril: The Evolving Relationship between Large-Scale Standardized Assessment and Higher Education," examines accountability requirements for pass rates by graduates of teachers colleges and the negative impact practices requiring higher scores on teachers' exams have on minorities. She goes beyond analysis to discuss possible accountability considerations for higher education in the 21st century.

Returning to classic civil rights issues, Angelo N. Ancheta provides a legal analysis of the U.S. Supreme Court's 2003 *Gratz* and *Grutter* decisions and considers what is now at stake, where the next set of challenges lies, and what researchers and institutions need to consider in the future. In "After *Grutter* and *Gratz*: Higher Education, Race, and the Law," Ancheta explores the permissible, forbidden, and still unclear aspects of affirmative action and points to future risks and possibilities. His analysis will help administrators, policymakers, and advocates master a changed legal terrain. He shows that no important racial issue is ever permanently settled and that it would be dangerous to lose the strong focus on civil rights law and policy that helped save affirmative action in the Supreme Court.

Patricia Marin and John T. Yun bring the book to a close with "From Strict Scrutiny to Educational Scrutiny: A New Vision for Higher Education Policy and Research," presenting an evaluative framework, informed by a legal context, with which to consider higher education institutional policy. The knowledge gained by researchers during the affirmative action battle has had an impact on the law and on public debate, but now that that issue is resolved for a time, a much broader and more complex set of policy questions must be explored, some of which have been introduced in the prior chapters. The discussion includes ways of thinking about accountability, as well as strategies for evaluating Justice O'Connor's 25-year goal in the *Grutter* affirmative action decision, expressing the hope that educational preparation could become equal enough in 25 years to make the continuation of affirmative action unnecessary.

Taken as a whole, this book is not optimistic about the role of colleges and universities in the struggle for social justice. The authors in this book write from a variety of perspectives, but they join to present a dominant picture of institutions quietly implementing policies that will almost certainly increase social and economic stratification. It is important to note, however, that some leaders of higher education and social scientists would not share the interpretations of most of our authors. Leaders of colleges and universities see themselves struggling as best they can to meet a variety of goals in times of limited resources. They believe that they have fought hard and with some success to maintain some racial diversity on selective campuses, most notably in the Supreme Court victory of 2003, and they are trying to maintain access for low-income students. These leaders point to the escalating costs of providing a college education and note that students get such large benefits from college that it is a wonderful investment, even for those who must take on substantial debt burdens. They believe that it is valid to spend money to compete for high-scoring students who lend prestige to their campuses, not only on students who need aid, and they point to the limits of what they can do in the absence of decent levels of public support. They note that the vast majority of higher education institutions have managed to survive in hard times and are doing valuable educational work, and believe it is unfair that others hold them accountable for general social problems. Many say that it would be much better to address those inequalities in the elementary and high schools. Many of our authors work in universities and understand these arguments and problems, but also see other realities and responsibilities that higher education must be prepared to address.

Higher education has become more important in American life and work than could have been imagined a half century ago, but its mechanisms for assuring equal opportunity have been severely weakened. Recurrent serious fiscal constraints, particularly in the budgets of state governments, and the combination of major tax cuts with huge increases in the cost of criminal justice and health care have combined to create a crisis in public support for colleges and universities, which, in turn, have responded by raising costs to students. Although one basic threat to college opportunity was avoided when the U.S. Supreme Court narrowly upheld affirmative action in 2003, many more remain. Most states are implementing cutbacks in higher education that are likely to limit the opportunities for young black, Latino, and American Indian students—restricting capacity on four-year campuses, raising tuition faster than aid, shifting aid to more affluent students on the basis of test scores rather than need, cutting outreach programs, and increasing the importance of tests in college access.

No one can foresee all the issues that will shape higher education in the coming generations—issues affected by changes in American society, state and federal policies on higher education, the national labor market, and other significant factors. The authors in this book have not proposed, nor could they, a single policy or set of policies that would assure equity within this changing system serving a society in transformation. Instead they raise serious questions and interpretations that those in higher education must consider. Indeed, research in this area has been far too limited and there is a critical need for useful national longitudinal studies and detailed analyses of the flow of students through individual campuses and state higher education systems. Only a small handful of relevant longitudinal studies are produced in a generation, and many important variables are not included. There are too few serious state-level systemic studies and policy papers dealing with the often unnoticed impact of sets of policies and financial decisions. Few institutions critically analyze the impact of their own decisions. I strongly encourage scholars concerned about our educational and economic future, the structure and stratification of our society, the nature of politics in a knowledge-based economy, and, of course, questions of racial and ethnic justice and opportunity, to take up these questions. Higher education is at the center of the American future, and it must become much more attentive to social divisions and its role in creating a system of opportunity—or perpetuating one of stratification—if its potential is to be realized.

REFERENCES

Bennett, M. J. (1996). *When dreams came true: The GI Bill and the making of modern America*. Washington, DC: Brassey's.

Gratz v. Bollinger, 539 U.S. 244 (2003).

Grutter v. Bollinger, 539 U.S. 306 (2003).

Regents of the University of California v. Bakke, 438 U.S. 265 (1978).

U.S. Census Bureau. (1961). *Statistical abstract of the United States*. Washington, DC: Author.

U.S. Census Bureau. (1981). *Statistical abstract of the United States*. Washington, DC: Author.

1

The Racial Transformation of Higher Education

MICHAL KURLAENDER AND STELLA M. FLORES

As the United States becomes increasingly diverse and as the earnings gap between college- and high school-educated workers continues to grow, there is a critical need for researchers and policymakers to address the persisting racial/ethnic disparities in educational attainment. Over the last half-century, the U.S. educational system grew significantly, which coincided with dramatic demographic changes: 25 years ago, 74 percent of the school-age population was white, 15 percent African American, 9 percent Latino, and 2 percent Asian (Solmon, Solmon, & Schiff, 2002).[1] In 2000, whites were 63 percent of the population, Latinos 16 percent, African Americans 15 percent, and Asians 4 percent. It is at the intersection of demographic change and postsecondary educational attainment in the second half of the 20th century that we focus this chapter.

Although all groups in the United States have experienced improved educational attainment, disparities by race and social background continue to exist. On the one hand, there is evidence that the impact of race and social origin on years of secondary school completed has decreased over time (Featherman & Hauser, 1978; Hout, Raftery, & Bell, 1993). On the other hand, the relative rates of participation in college among minorities and lower socioeconomic students remain low (for additional discussion, see Price and Wohlford, this volume).

The overall increase in educational attainment in the U.S. has been paralleled by an expansion in the types of schooling opportunities available. The expansion of the community college and the growth in vocational training opened new postsecondary educational opportunities (Arum, 1998;

11

Brint & Karabel, 1989; Dougherty, 1994; Grubb, 1996). These opportunities generated new questions about the roles that different schooling options play in educational attainment, and whether they expand opportunity for groups historically underrepresented in higher education.

The purpose of this chapter is to provide the most current picture of racial/ethnic differences in higher education participation and to set the stage for subsequent chapters. In the first section, we document the race/ethnicity-specific rates of postsecondary enrollment and degree attainment using 2000 U.S. Census data by specific age groups and comment on the race-specific trends of postsecondary participation over the last half-century. In the second section we explore different postsecondary routes for college completion by race, using a national longitudinal dataset for students entering higher education after 1990. In the final section, we discuss how researchers and policymakers can most effectively address educational equity in the context of increasingly complex postsecondary participation, expanding schooling options, and rapidly changing demographics.

RACIAL AND ETHNIC DIFFERENCES IN POSTSECONDARY PARTICIPATION

Numerous authors have documented the increased racial diversity of the U.S. population and, in particular, the changing school- and college-age populations over the last half-century (see, e.g., Chapa & De La Rosa, 2004; San Miguel & Valencia, 1998; Solmon, Solmon, & Schiff, 2002; Vigil Laden, 2004). The 2000 Census illustrated the significant growth of non-white minority groups, and of self-identifying racial categories such as "other" and "mixed" (Vigil Laden, 2004). One of the most cited statistics of the 2000 Census was the spectacular growth of the Latino population since the 1990s (U.S. Census Bureau, 2004).

In order to understand racial and ethnic differences in rates of postsecondary participation in light of these demographic changes, it is important to note the historical context in which the first beneficiaries of racial integration entered higher education after the landmark 1954 *Brown v. Board of Education* decision. Both the legal framework and the political context in which African Americans gained access to public higher education led Latinos and other racial/ethnic groups to follow.[2] To some extent, however, these groups moved into different types of institutions, including Hispanic-serving institutions and tribal colleges and universities.[3] These institutions, along with historically black colleges and universities (HBCUs), continue to play an important role in providing postsecondary education to underrepresented minority groups.[4]

While the last half-century has been marked by an overall increase in high school completion across all racial and ethnic groups, there has been only a modest increase in college participation and, to an even lesser extent, college completion (Turner, 2004). Investigating the rates of postsecondary entry over the past three decades, Hauser (1993) finds that the chances that a Hispanic student would enter college peaked in the middle 1970s and have remained stable ever since. African Americans' chances of entering college rose during the 1970s, declined from 1979 to 1983, and then recovered. Whites' overall chances of entering college grew in this period, despite a period of decline in the 1970s.

Data from the Current Population Survey (see Figure 1) largely corroborate the postsecondary enrollment trends for racial/ethnic groups described by Hauser (1993) through the 1970s and 1980s. Furthermore, throughout the 1990s Hispanic postsecondary enrollment fluctuated, while there was a general increase in enrollment for African Americans. Whites generally experienced a steady increase in enrollment after 1985, followed by a slight decline between 1997 and 1999. However, Figure 2 reveals less variation in college completion rates over time for all racial/ethnic groups, particularly Latinos and blacks, as compared to college enrollment rates during this same period. Between the mid-1980s and 2000, there was a steady increase in the baccalaureate completion rate of white students, reaching about 34 percent in 2000. During this same period, completion rates for blacks rose steadily, but at a much slower pace, peaking in 2000 at approximately 18 percent. Hispanic completion rates rose between 1980 and 1985, decreased in the late 1980s, and then stabilized near 10 percent by 2000. Hispanics consistently had the lowest college completion rates between 1975 and 2000, although black rates were similarly low through the 1980s.

Solmon et al. (2002) examine higher education attainment by race/ethnicity and citizenship using the 1990 Census and the Current Population Survey, with a focus on California and Texas. This focus is timely and important, as these two states were barred from using race-conscious policies such as affirmative action in college admissions and financial aid in 1996.[5] We extend their analysis using Census data on educational attainment by race and ethnicity to the five states with the highest numbers of Latino and African American adults over the age of 18: California, Texas, New York, Florida, and Georgia.[6] We examine each major racial/ethnic group's educa-

FIGURE 1

Enrollment Rates of 18- to 24-Year-Olds in Degree-Granting Institutions, by Race/Ethnicity: 1972–2000

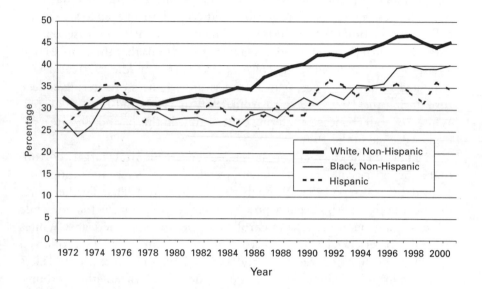

Source: U.S. Department of Commerce, Bureau of the Census, Current Population Survey, unpublished data.

tional attainment level, both at the national average and within each of these states.[7]

Although a portrait of educational attainment by race and ethnicity over the last few decades is informative, a detailed review of the most recent Census data allows for a more specific investigation of the current racial/ethnic differences in educational attainment. Furthermore, in light of changes and fluctuations in admissions and financial aid policies affecting minorities during the late 1990s (Horn & Flores, 2003; Marin & Lee, 2003; Tienda, Leicht, Sullivan, Maltese, & Lloyd, 2003), we provide a more detailed portrait of educational attainment by race and ethnicity in selected states. We chose these states because of their demographic significance in terms of the racial diversity of their college-age population. Together they represent the majority of black and Latino college-age participants in the United States. Their significance extends into the policy arena in that four of the five se-

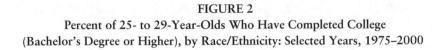

FIGURE 2

Percent of 25- to 29-Year-Olds Who Have Completed College
(Bachelor's Degree or Higher), by Race/Ethnicity: Selected Years, 1975–2000

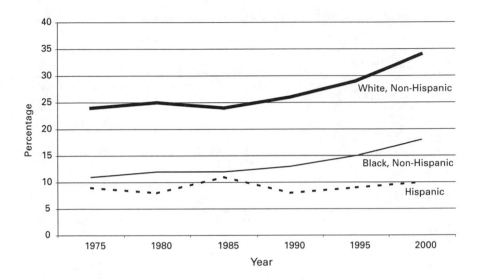

Source: U.S. Department of Education, National Center for Education Statistics, Digest of Education Statistics (2001), based on U.S. Department of Commerce, Bureau of the Census, March Current Population Surveys.

lected states were subject to changes in race-conscious higher education policies through various legal mechanisms in the late 1990s.

It is important to note that the U.S. Census collects data on the educational attainment of adults in their current state of residence and not in their state of origin, which may differ (Martinez, 2004). Additionally, to account for traditional, college-age entrance patterns with some flexibility and sufficient time to complete a degree, we examine the data for two age groups—18- to 24-year-olds to evaluate the "some college/no degree" level, and 25- to 34-year-olds to consider degree completion from the "associate degree" level to the "graduate/professional degree" level. We supplement the Census figures with the National Center for Education Statistics' most recent and complete cohort analysis, the 1988 National Education Longitudinal Study (NELS:88) 2000 follow-up. This cohort of students would have been approximately 26 years old at the time of the 2000 U.S. Census.

TABLE 1   Educational Attainment in 2000 by Respective Race and Ethnic Group in States with Highest Latino and Black Populations (by Adult Age Group)

	Less than 9th Grade (18–24)	HS Diploma or GED Equiv. (18–24)	Some College/ No Degree (18–24)	Associ- ate's Degree (25–34)	BA Degree (25–34)	Graduate or Profes- sional Degree (25–34)
All Individuals						
White Non-Hispanic	1.45	28.78	39.06	8.61	23.81	7.80
Latino	14.81	28.63	22.42	4.82	9.23	3.95
Black	2.33	33.66	32.05	6.95	12.33	3.89
Asian	2.17	21.46	39.82	6.13	30.01	22.74
American Indian	3.03	34.39	27.65	7.10	10.41	3.22
National Total	*3.15*	*29.27*	*35.49*	*7.99*	*20.35*	*6.71*
California						
White Non-Hispanic	1.21	26.55	41.92	8.00	28.62	10.14
Latino	15.01	27.92	21.84	4.07	5.83	1.94
Black	1.93	31.88	33.14	8.00	12.45	3.95
Asian	1.55	21.41	43.78	8.93	35.23	16.32
American Indian	2.35	32.83	30.01	7.20	9.62	2.93
State Total	*7.21*	*26.99*	*32.88*	*6.59*	*19.16*	*7.17*
Texas						
White Non-Hispanic	1.46	27.82	41.18	7.13	26.57	7.78
Latino	13.71	27.97	20.98	3.70	7.13	2.17
Black	2.39	34.01	30.74	5.93	12.83	2.89
Asian	1.84	19.68	41.51	6.10	33.69	24.52
American Indian	2.61	31.23	35.36	6.55	14.07	5.26
State Total	*6.50*	*28.42*	*31.82*	*5.68*	*17.92*	*5.74*
New York						
White Non-Hispanic	1.35	24.20	38.81	10.43	27.44	14.09
Latino	11.49	26.21	23.21	6.10	9.35	4.14
Black	2.96	29.30	27.73	8.75	13.43	4.91
Asian	2.80	20.04	37.84	5.82	33.70	19.95
American Indian	2.01	31.45	29.00	7.57	13.52	5.99
State Total	*3.81*	*25.29*	*33.60*	*8.94*	*22.20*	*11.14*
Florida						
White Non-Hispanic	1.78	29.64	32.77	10.28	20.59	6.78
Latino	11.98	27.07	24.22	8.22	12.11	6.01
Black	2.92	31.73	25.96	7.54	9.60	2.94
Asian	2.18	20.54	38.51	8.69	31.62	17.62
American Indian	4.15	30.26	25.57	9.05	14.27	1.88
State Total	*4.26*	*29.29*	*29.60*	*9.34*	*17.12*	*6.22*
Georgia						
White Non-Hispanic	1.80	29.50	34.52	6.20	25.34	8.34
Latino	31.72	23.76	11.47	2.95	8.06	3.09
Black	2.33	32.32	28.34	6.14	14.17	3.70
Asian	2.35	21.01	37.46	5.21	30.27	22.56
American Indian	2.31	29.76	29.05	6.19	15.32	3.93
State Total	*5.00*	*29.61*	*30.34*	*5.90*	*20.72*	*6.94*

Source: U.S. Census (2000), and authors' calculations.

Note: National totals include District of Columbia and Puerto Rico. Numbers do not add up to 100 percent since only select educational categories per age group were included.

Rates of Postsecondary Participation

Although the primary focus of this chapter is on college participation, evaluating the "less than 9th grade" Census category among college-age adults is an integral part of the U.S. educational pipeline story.[8] Table 1 illustrates that Latinos have the highest rate of no secondary schooling in the nation (14.81%, compared to 2.33% for blacks and 1.45% for whites) and in all of the specific states examined. In Georgia, for example, which was not identified as a significant Latino-origin immigration state until the 1990s, the proportion of 18- to 24-year-old Latinos with less than a ninth-grade education is 31.72 percent (Chapa & De La Rosa, 2004; U.S. Census Bureau, n.d.).[9] Comparatively, whites and blacks in Georgia have much lower proportions with no secondary schooling (1.80% and 2.33%, respectively). Although immigration most likely plays a role in the high percentage of Latinos with low educational attainment rates, other groups with steadily increasing immigration patterns do not exhibit similar patterns. The share of Asians with no secondary schooling, for example, does not exceed 3 percent across the states examined; however, the percentage for Latinos in the other states ranges from 11 to 32 percent for this specific age group.[10]

Average national figures by race and ethnicity show that whites, and to a greater extent Asians, within this age group are more likely to have attained at least "some college." There has been an overall rise in the college participation rates of all groups; however, Latinos, blacks, and American Indians in this age group are more likely to have obtained at most a high school degree or equivalent diploma than their white or Asian counterparts. Of the states examined, 18- to 24-year-old Latinos demonstrate a higher tendency to achieve no greater than a high school diploma or equivalent. For example, in Texas, the proportion of Latinos between 18 and 24 years old with no greater than a high school diploma is nearly 28 percent, compared to those who have not gone past ninth grade (13.71%), and some college/no degree (20.98%). Moreover, because Latinos are the group with the highest proportion of members who do not advance beyond the ninth grade, nationally and in each state, their postsecondary participation rates at subsequent levels are generally the lowest.

The data for African Americans indicate that they are also more likely than whites, on average, to have achieved no more than a high school degree or equivalent. However, there is some variation across the states in the participation rates of blacks with some college experience. For instance, in Florida, almost 26 percent of blacks reach the "some college/no degree" level, compared to just over 33 percent in California. California is the only state in which the proportion of African Americans who attain the level of "some college/no degree" (32.05%) exceeds the national average for this group. Nonetheless, the proportion of African Americans who have participated in some college is still well below that of whites and Asians, although higher than for Latinos and American Indians.

Rates of Postsecondary Degree Completion

Census data indicate that among 25- to 34-year-olds nationally, approximately 8 percent have an associate's degree; however, since many individuals obtain this degree in passing (as they work towards a BA), it is likely to be underreported or misreported in national and state statistics. Among all racial and ethnic groups, 25- to 34-year-old whites have the highest proportion who report obtaining an associate's degree (8.61%). American Indians have the second highest rate (7.10%), potentially revealing the important role of two-year tribal colleges in American Indian postsecondary attainment.[11] Across the states included in this discussion, Latinos consistently demonstrate the lowest shares of their 25- to 34-year-olds with associate's degree completion rates, except in Florida and New York. Nationally, the percentage of Latino 25- to 34-year-olds who have completed an associate's degree is, on average, 4.82 percent, compared to 8.61 percent for whites, 6.95 percent for blacks, 6.13 percent for Asians, and 7.10 percent for American Indians.

In examining baccalaureate attainment, 25- to 34-year-old whites and Asians have higher proportions of BA completers than their peers from other racial/ethnic backgrounds. This is true both nationally and within each of the states examined. For instance, the percentages of 25- to 34-year-old whites and Asians nationally who have received a BA degree are 23.81 and 30.01, respectively, compared to 9.23 percent for Latinos, 12.33 percent for blacks, and 10.41 percent for American Indians. In addition, the data reveal that the average proportion of Asians in this age range with a BA degree (30.01%), not disaggregated by Asian subgroups, is higher than that of whites across the nation and among the states. Latinos have the lowest shares of BA holders among all the racial and ethnic groups, except in Florida, where blacks in this age group have the lowest proportion. This figure is not surprising, given Florida's large Cuban population, which has consistently been the highest educated Latino subgroup population in the United States (Fry, 2002; Suárez-Orozco & Páez, 2002). The states with the highest percentage of Latinos between the ages of 24 and 35 who have BAs are Florida (12.11%) and New York (9.35%). However, BA attainment for

Latinos in this age group in California, Texas, and Georgia is below the national average of 9.23 percent, at 5.83, 7.13, and 8.06, respectively.

The proportion of 25- to 34-year-old African Americans with a BA is 12.33 percent nationally. The proportion of African Americans with a BA in the states with the highest black population exceeds the national average, with Georgia attaining the highest rates (14.17%), followed by New York (13.43%) and California (12.45%). Florida, however, has the lowest share of African Americans with a BA degree (9.60%). The disparities in BA completion for African Americans are particularly stark in Florida.

Table 1 illustrates that large gaps exist between whites and underrepresented minorities in graduate and professional degree attainment. This is true even in high-minority states such as California, Texas, and New York. The differences range from approximately six to eight percentage points in California, about five percentage points in Texas, and almost ten percentage points in New York. Asians have the highest proportions of 25- to 34-year-olds in the nation who hold a graduate or professional degree, and in all of the states examined. Given the high proportion of Latinos with less than a ninth-grade education and the overwhelming number of blacks and American Indians who do not make it past a high school diploma or GED equivalent, the disparities at the upper level of the higher education pipeline should not be a surprise. However, because the Census only measures a dichotomous outcome of degree attainment, it is less clear at what points these groups are most likely to discontinue their education with greater specificity. For this reason, it is useful to analyze longitudinal data on educational attainment.

Previous demographic analysis of decades leading up to the 2000 Census, and now this review, have provided a developing demographic portrait of educational attainment amid rapid demographic change. The present analysis provides a more current review of college enrollment and completion by race/ethnicity across the nation and for the states facing the largest demographic changes. However, an analysis of postsecondary participation at the *individual* level by specific cohort can provide another view of the racial/ethnic differences in college entrance and completion rates. Various authors have provided an analysis of individuals' postsecondary chances by income and racial/ethnic group (Ellwood & Kane, 2000; Massey, Charles, Lundy, & Fischer, 2003), while others have analyzed cohort groups from different decades to compare progression in completion (Turner, 2004). Employing cohort analysis allows us to examine what types of institutions students enter, when students withdraw from postsecondary studies, what types of postsecondary schooling they obtain, and whether they ever obtain a degree. Researchers can thus move beyond simply reporting disparities and analyze the origins and points in the educational attainment process that contribute to racial/ethnic inequality in educational outcomes. In the next section we provide a short cohort analysis of a segment of the college pipeline for each of the three largest racial/ethnic groups in the United States—whites, African Americans and Latinos.

THE COLLEGE COMPLETION PIPELINE:
MEASURING EDUCATIONAL ATTAINMENT

Broad demographic statistics of college participation and completion provide a very useful snapshot of racial/ethnic differences in higher education. To investigate the differences in postsecondary participation and baccalaureate attainment across racial/ethnic groups, we analyze data from the NELS:88. These data are nationally representative and include longitudinal data on individuals for eight years beyond intended high school completion. We use information from the fourth follow-up in 2000, administered when respondents were 26 years old. Our sample, therefore, includes students followed from 1988 through all four waves of data collection. While this is one of the most recent longitudinal datasets and it is rich with information on education participation, it is also a somewhat dated means by which to explore the current racial/ethnic transformation of higher education in the nation. (The NELS:88 cohort attended college primarily in the mid- to late 1990s.) Nevertheless, it provides an important tool for thinking about where the pipeline to baccalaureate attainment is particularly weak for minorities and can be a useful benchmark for future cohort studies.

Early investigations of educational attainment viewed attainment as the accumulation of years in school (Blau & Duncan, 1967; Hauser & Featherman, 1976; Sewell & Hauser, 1975), while more recent work measured educational attainment at identified levels of schooling, such as completion of high school or enrollment at the postsecondary level (Beattie, 2002; Grubb, 1996; Rivkin, 1995). One innovative approach to conceptualizing educational attainment views it as a sequence of transitions across educational levels. Conceptualizing educational attainment in this way is a natural extension of the traditional approach that measures total years of schooling, since the presence of a learner at any given level assumes a set of prior transitions through earlier levels. Thus, at each level of schooling, we can analyze the decisions of people in a given stage as to, first, whether they continue and, second, what level they achieve.

The College-Completion Pipeline

Figure 3 details a set of possible pathways from postsecondary entry to baccalaureate attainment for blacks, whites, and Latinos, respectively. The boxes in the left-hand column show the proportion of each group that graduates high school. From there, the arrows trace the pathways that each group follows to enter postsecondary education. Entry points include nonacademic technical or vocational institutions; two-year academic institutions, such as community colleges; and four-year institutions. The figure also indicates the proportion of students following each pathway who achieve baccalaureate status. For instance, we can examine the pathways followed by black high school graduates and compare the likelihood of baccalaureate attainment among those who enroll in two-year colleges versus those who enroll in four-year colleges.

Figure 3 reveals important differences in postsecondary participation and degree attainment between racial/ethnic groups in the United States. First, note that whites, on average, obtain high school diplomas at a higher rate (86%) than do blacks and Latinos (76.31% and 74.75%, respectively).[12] Second, among high school graduates, Latinos show the lowest rate of postsecondary entry into four-year institutions (29.83%), compared to whites and blacks (48.32% and 45.99%, respectively). Yet Latinos demonstrate the highest participation rates at academic two-year colleges (45.22%). In comparison, 26.84 percent of black high school graduates and 30.51 percent of white high school graduates attend two-year academic colleges. Looking at nonacademic postsecondary institutions, blacks and Latinos achieve similar rates of participation (10.71% and 10.20%, respectively), compared to only 5.73 percent among white high school graduates. Notably, although the differences are evident, there are remarkable similarities across race in rates of nonparticipation. Roughly 15 percent of white, black, and Latino high school graduates do not obtain any additional postsecondary schooling by the age of 26.

Looking at baccalaureate attainment, whites display the highest rates of degree completion, among both those that start their postsecondary schooling at four-year institutions and those that begin at two-year institutions. Whites have a BA completion rate of 33.79 percent among those that start at four-year institutions, compared to only 15.46 percent for Latinos and

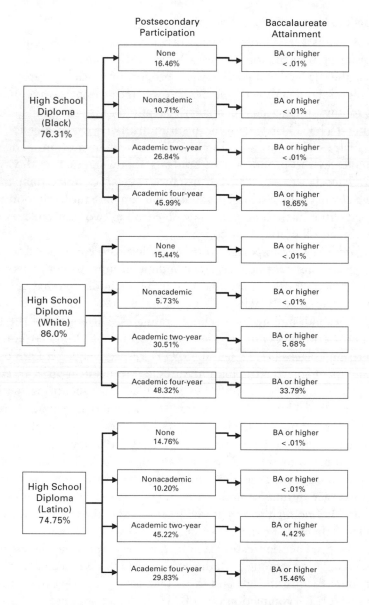

FIGURE 3
Race-Specific Rates of Postsecondary Participation and Attainment by Age 26

Note: Authors' calculations using the National Education Longitudinal Study 2000 follow-up (*n* = 10,153), applying survey weights and design effects; high school diploma holders do not include GEDs.

18.65 percent for blacks who start at four-year institutions. For those who start at two-year colleges, we see the greatest disparities between blacks, who have a BA completion rate of 1 percent, versus whites and Latinos, who have BA completion rates of 5.68 and 4.42 percent, respectively.

Another way to interpret these numbers is to consider how high school graduates from each respective racial/ethnic group are distributed across postsecondary participation. For example, among 100 African American high school graduates, about 16 would not go on to any form of higher education, about 11 would attend a technical or vocational school, about 27 would attend a community college, and nearly half, 46, would attend a four-year postsecondary institution. Of the 27 black students who initially enrolled in a community college, on average, less than one would obtain a BA by the age of 26, and of the 46 who began at a four-year school, only about 9 would obtain a BA by the age of 26. Among 100 white high school graduates, on average, about 15 would not go on to any form of higher education, about 6 would attend a technical or vocational school, about 31 would attend a community college, and nearly half, 48, would attend a four-year postsecondary institution. Of the 31 white students who initially enrolled in a community college, on average, only about 2 would obtain a BA by the age of 26, and of the 48 who began at a four-year school, about 16 would obtain a BA by the age of 26. Finally, among 100 Latino high school graduates, about 15 would not go on to any form of higher education, about 10 would attend a technical or vocational school, about 45 would attend a community college, and 30 would attend a four-year postsecondary institution. Of the 45 students who initially enrolled in a community college, on average, only about two would obtain a BA by the age of 26, and of the 30 who began at a four-year school, about five would obtain a BA by the age of 26.

It is important to note that these figures only provide a descriptive picture of postsecondary participation and baccalaureate attainment for different racial/ethnic groups. They do not permit us to draw any causal conclusions about the role of race in predicting postsecondary participation; however, they do allow us to examine the racial/ethnic disparities in degree completion more closely by providing a deeper look into the pathways of postsecondary entry and how they differ by race/ethnicity.

Different Pathways to Postsecondary Degree Attainment

From the descriptive look at the college completion pipeline it is clear that many students, but especially Latinos,[13] enter postsecondary studies through two-year community colleges rather than four-year institutions.[14] The growth of community colleges occurred as part of a larger process of higher education expansion in the post–World War II period, as high schools went from elite to mass institutions and equality of opportunity meant that nearly everyone could get some form of higher education (Brint & Karabel, 1989; Karabel, 1972). The role of community colleges as vehicles for moderating inequality in educational attainment or as a mechanism for sorting out particular students has become a subject of considerable attention over the last decade.

Research on the value of community colleges in increasing opportunities for underrepresented groups in higher education is mixed. Some might argue that if the goal were merely expansion, then community colleges are a success in that they provide noncompetitive and affordable entry into postsecondary education for all individuals (Rouse, 1995). In addition, these institutions can prepare or improve students' academic credentials in order to advance to a four-year degree-granting university. Others point out that increased access does not necessarily lead to a genuine expansion of educational opportunity (Brint & Karabel, 1989). Many researchers suggest that second-chance opportunities, such as community colleges, can actually exacerbate race and class inequalities in educational attainment. They argue that when the education system expands without narrowing economic and other differences between groups in society, or changing the opportunity structure, the result is educational inflation or "credentialism" (Karabel, 1972; Monk-Turner, 1998).

Community college students are more likely to have less academic preparation, lower achievement levels, and come from families of considerably lower educational attainment than those who begin postsecondary education at four-year institutions (Kane & Rouse, 1999). Grubb (1991) finds widespread declines in transfer rates among community college students and reports that among those completing the BA, a smaller fraction begin at the community college level. Overall, those who transfer from a community college to a four-year college are of a higher social class, less likely to be minority, and less likely to be female (Dougherty, 1994; Grubb, 1991; Whitaker & Pascarella, 1994). In fact, Dougherty (1994) found that the socioeconomic status of the transfer group closely resembled the composition of the original four-year college group.

Why should two-year colleges be regarded as just a starting point? It is certainly reasonable to conclude that many community college students do not desire more than a technical or associate's degree, and thus even some college is better than not attending at all. Evaluating community colleges from this perspective would suggest that merely enrolling in any postsecondary schooling is better than not attending at all. While this is true for individuals who are experimenting with college or acquiring a technical degree only available at a two-year institution, a far greater number of community college students indicate a strong desire to transfer and to obtain a BA (Monk-Turner, 1998). In this regard, two-year institutions achieve only limited success. Nevertheless, community college clearly offers a substantial labor market payoff. Kane and Rouse (1995) find that the average person who attended a two-year college earned about 10 percent more than those without any college did. This was true even for those who did not obtain an associate's degree. Even more interesting, the wage differentials between individuals with no college and those with 30 completed credits (roughly one year) was similar, regardless of whether the units were completed at a two- or four-year institution.

As Figure 3 details, while community colleges may offer wide access to postsecondary education for a diverse group of students, for most the entryway is as far as they go. In fact, those who eventually succeed in obtaining a BA are those who upon entry possess the better academic credentials and who come from a more advantaged social class (Cabrera, La Nasa, & Burkum, 2001; Lee & Frank, 1990). In addition, different community colleges have very different rates of success in transferring students, a difference that is often associated with their racial composition. Moreover, these descriptive figures suggest that both researchers and policymakers need to pay more attention to the expanding set of educational pathways for postsecondary schooling, and the extent to which these pathways are utilized by and provide opportunities for individuals from different racial/ethnic groups.

IMPLICATIONS FOR POLICY AND FOR FUTURE RESEARCH

By 1990 the earnings differential between a college and high school education was at an all-time high of about 65 percent (Murphy & Welch, 2001; Turner, 2004). Individuals with a college degree are, among other things, more likely to participate in civic activities, have greater occupational prestige, and are less likely to be unemployed than those who earn a high school diploma (Cabrera et al., 2001). Moreover, the type of college destination affects both career opportunities and income (Dale & Krueger, 1999). Despite substantial progress in equalizing opportunities for all students, large disparities in educational attainment remain between different racial/ethnic groups, and the need to account for and address such disparities is great.

There are several possible explanations for the persistent gaps in educational attainment between the races, many of which are further explored in other chapters in this volume. One explanation for the disparities in college enrollment and completion rates is an economic one. For many minority students, the opportunity costs (e.g., missed wages and/or tuition and fees) for attending college are too great, and thus they choose to work rather than attend college, or they opt for both and ultimately are unable to sustain the demands of school on top of full-time work. This is further compounded by financial aid policies that have not kept pace with the widespread rise in tuition at all public institutions (Advisory Committee on Student Financial Assistance, 2002; College Board, 2002).

A second explanation is the unequal preparation many African American and Latino students receive in their K–12 schooling. We know that these students are more likely to attend racially and economically segregated, low-performing schools with weaker resources, such as fewer qualified teachers, a less rigorous curriculum, and worse facilities (Entwisle, Alexander, & Olson, 1997; Orfield & Lee, 2005). Beyond standard measures of school quality, secondary school resources also prove to be an important determinant of college success (Adelman, 1999). Differences in K–12 schooling, coupled with persistent racial gaps on standardized tests—a primary tool for college admissions—contribute to the disparities we witness in college attainment. Unfortunately, the increasing reliance on standardized tests, many of which are attached to high stakes for students, can further discourage minority students, who historically do not perform as well on these tests as their white peers (Orfield & Kornhaber, 2001; Valenzuela, 2004).

A third explanation is the changing policies regarding race in college admissions. Prior to the U.S. Supreme Court *Grutter v. Bollinger* decision upholding affirmative action, higher education experienced nearly a decade of rollbacks in affirmative action in college admissions, recruitment, and financial aid. For example, California ended race-conscious affirmative action with Proposition 209 in 1996, and Texas ended affirmative action admissions policies with the Fifth Circuit Court of Appeals' *Hopwood* decision that same year. While the direct impact of those changes on enrollment and completion rates has been difficult to measure, several indirect effects have been identified, such as the "chilling effect" on admissions for minority students, who perceive that they will no longer be accepted by certain universities so they do not apply or they set their sights lower (Orfield & Miller, 1998).

Finally, a host of factors that may be difficult to observe and to measure contribute to racial disparities in college attainment, even among those who start at four-year degree-granting institutions. Chief among them are academic support, encouragement, and a positive collegiate experience. Such factors have been found to be associated with college persistence and degree completion (Astin, 1993; Cabrera et al., 2001).

Whites are consistently better off across a range of factors that determine college entry and completion. They are less likely to be poor, less likely to come from single-parent households, and more likely to come from better educated families (Hauser, 1993). Financial or academic issues may lead many minority students to the community college or other subbaccalaureate institutions, which are nonselective and often offer a less expensive option for postsecondary schooling. Many policymakers hail community colleges as viable alternatives for students not successful in the traditional routes. Yet the evidence is not clear on whether these colleges are really successful at meeting students' needs, or on what rewards they offer.

Policies aimed at improving access to postsecondary schooling will need to be multifaceted if they are to reduce stratification in educational attainment among different racial/ethnic groups. The increasing costs of higher education will remain a barrier to participation for poor students (for further discussion, see Heller, this volume), many of whom are African American and Latino. Addressing disparities in K–12 schooling will need to become a priority of the higher education community if they are committed to increasing eligibility and changing the college pipeline. As race-conscious policies for admissions become more clearly defined, with guidance from the recent Supreme Court decisions, colleges will also need to rethink admissions policies in order to attract, admit, and retain a diverse student body. Finally, policies also need to address improving mobility within higher education.

As we look ahead, the continuing demographic changes in the nation's K–12 population could lead to a real transformation of higher education in many states and across the country. Population trends and projections suggest that the Latino population will continue to grow at a much faster rate than the U.S. population overall (Chapa & De La Rosa, 2004). The demographic changes facing the nation and the changing policies in higher education require a new wave of research on equity in educational attainment. The nation's changing demographics also call for great urgency in addressing the higher education color line at all levels of American education and within all types of postsecondary institutions.

NOTES

1. Throughout the chapter we use African American and black, and Hispanic and Latino interchangeably. Our discussion on American Indians refers only to this group as defined by the U.S. Census, and not to all Native American groups in the U.S. Therefore, we restrict the discussion only to individuals who identified as American Indian on the 2000 U.S. Census.
2. American Indians have, of course, a unique history with education access in the United States (see Swisher & Tippeconic, 1999).
3. For an explanation of Hispanic-serving institutions and tribal colleges and universities, as well as other institutions serving minorities, see Vigil Laden (2004).
4. We define underrepresented minorities in postsecondary education as African American or black, Hispanic or Latino, and American Indian.
5. For a detailed discussion, see Horn and Flores (2003); Orfield and Kurlaender (2001); Tienda, Leicht, Sullivan, Maltese, and Lloyd (2003). In 2003, with the *Grutter* decision, Texas regained its ability to use race-conscious policies.
6. The figures refer to states with the highest number of blacks and Latinos over the age of 18, and not the total population over age 18.
7. Due to space limitations, we do not include data disaggregated by Asian and Latino subgroups, which would likely enrich this analysis and highlight important demographic patterns.
8. When reporting high school completion rates, recent research has contested even the slight progress made in diploma receipt as reported in federal datasets, such as the Current Population Survey, noting that dropout statistics from these databases are often underreported due to the fact that they are measured cross-sectionally rather than tracked longitudinally (Orfield, 2004). Swanson (2004), for instance, reports a high school graduation rate for all students of 68 percent, versus a rate of 83 percent reported by the Current Population Survey (Folger & Nam, 2004).
9. We speculate that this figure is unusually high due to the more recent Hispanic immigration patterns facing the South (see Chapa & De La Rosa, 2004).
10. Although not presented in this analysis, Latino subgroup social characteristics have historically differed according to migration incorporation and majority Latino status in the United States. For example, Latino history in Florida has traditionally been one of Cuban origin, while the history of California and Texas has been one of Mexican origin (Portes & Rumbaut, 1996; Suárez-Orozco & Páez, 2002).
11. For a more detailed discussion on the role of tribal colleges and student outcomes, see Boyer (1998, 2002); Ortiz and Boyer (2003).
12. This analysis is most useful for evaluating the proportional differences among racial/ethnic groups; the absolute numbers of high school diploma holders and degree attainment vary somewhat from those presented in Census data and by some other national datasets. For example, the high school completion rate, which is often calculated differently across studies and datasets, may be overstated in the NELS:88 data.

13. One reason there may be such low community college participation rates among blacks is that a high majority of HBCUs, 88 percent, are four-year institutions. Latinos, on the other hand, are more likely to attend Hispanic-serving institutions, 53 percent of which are two-year colleges (see Benitez & DeAro, 2004). However, only 12.9 percent of all black enrollment is at HBCUs, so further research on the issue of blacks and community college attendance is required (Provasnik & Shafer, 2004).

12. As might be expected, there are important differences in college enrollment destinations by socioeconomic status; however, we chose to present these figures with a primary focus on race.

REFERENCES

Adelman, C. (1999). *Answers in the tool box: Academic intensity, attendance patterns, and bachelor's degree attainment* (Document No. PLLI 1999-8021). Washington, DC: U.S. Department of Education, Office of Educational Research and Improvement.

Advisory Committee on Student Financial Assistance. (2002). *Empty promises: The myth of college access in America.* Washington, DC: U.S. Department of Education.

Arum, R. (1998). Invested dollars or diverted dreams: The effect of resources on vocational students' educational outcomes. *Sociology of Education, 71,* 130–151.

Astin, A. W. (1993). *What matters in college?* San Francisco: Jossey-Bass.

Beattie, I. (2002). Are all "adolescent econometricians" created equal? Racial, class, and gender differences in college enrollment. *Sociology of Education, 75,* 19–43.

Benitez, M., & DeAro, J. (2004). Realizing student success at Hispanic serving institutions. In B. Vigil Laden (Ed.), *Serving minority populations* (pp. 35–49). San Francisco: Jossey-Bass.

Blau, P. M., & Duncan, O. D. (1967). *The American occupational structure.* New York: Wiley.

Boyer, P. (1998). Many colleges, one vision: A history of the American Indian higher education consortium. *Tribal College, 9*(4), 16–22.

Boyer, P. (2002). Defying the odds: Tribal colleges conquer skepticism but still face persistent challenges. *Tribal College, 14*(2), 12–19.

Brint, S., & Karabel, J. (1989). *The diverted dream: Community colleges and the promise of educational opportunity in America, 1900–1985.* New York: Oxford University Press.

Brown v. Board of Education, 347 U.S. 483 (1954).

Cabrera, A. F., La Nasa, S. M., & Burkum, K. R. (2001). *On the right path: The higher education story of one generation.* University Park: Pennsylvania State University, Center for the Study of Higher Education.

Chapa, J., & De La Rosa, B. (2004). Latino population growth, socioeconomic and demographic characteristics, and implications for educational attainment. *Education and Urban Society, 36,* 130–149.

College Board. (2002). *Trends in college pricing, 2002.* Washington, DC: Author.

Dale, S. B., & Krueger, A. B. (1999). *Estimating the payroll to attending a more selective college: An application of selection on observables and unobservables* (Working Paper No. W7322). Cambridge: National Bureau of Economic Research.

Dougherty, K. (1994). *The contradictory college: The conflicting origins, impacts, and futures of the community college.* Albany: State University of New York Press.

Ellwood, D. T., & Kane, T. J. (2000). Who is getting a college education? Family background and the growing gaps in enrollment. In S. Danziger & J. Waldfogel (Eds.), *Securing the future* (pp. 283–324). New York: Russell Sage.

Entwisle, D. R., Alexander, K. L., & Olson, L. S. (1997). *Children, schools, and inequality.* Boulder, CO: Westview Press.

Featherman, D. L., & Hauser, R. M. (1978). *Opportunity and change.* New York: Academic Press.

Folger, J. K., & Nam, C. B. (2000). *Education of the American population.* Washington, DC: U.S. Department of Commerce, Bureau of the Census.

Fry, R. (2002). *Latinos in higher education: Many enroll, too few graduate.* Washington, DC: Pew Hispanic Center.

Grubb, W. N. (1991). The decline of community college transfer rates: Evidence from national longitudinal surveys. *Journal of Higher Education, 62,* 194–222.

Grubb, W. N. (1996). *Working in the middle: Strengthening education and training for the mid skilled labor force.* San Francisco: Jossey-Bass.

Grutter v. Bollinger, U.S. 288 F.3d 732 (2002).

Hauser, R. M. (1993). Trends in college entry among whites, blacks, and Hispanics. In C. T. Clotfelter & M. Rothschild (Eds.), *Studies of supply and demand in higher education* (pp. 64–104). Chicago: University of Chicago Press.

Hauser, R. M., & Featherman, D. L. (1976). Equality of schooling: Trends and prospects. *Sociology of Education, 49,* 99–120.

Hopwood v. Texas, 861 F. Supp. 551 (W.D. Tex. 1994); 78 F. 3d 932 (5th Cir. 1996), *cert. denied,* 116 S. Ct. 2580 (1996).

Horn, C. L., & Flores, S. M. (2003). *Percent plans in college admissions: A comparative analysis of three states' experiences.* Cambridge, MA: Civil Rights Project at Harvard University.

Hout, M., Raftery, A. E., & Bell, E. O. (1993). Making the grade: Educational stratification in the United States, 1925–1989. In Y. Shavit & H. P. Blossfeld (Eds.), *Persistent inequality: Changing educational attainment in thirteen countries* (pp. 25–49). Boulder, CO: Westview Press.

Kane, T. J., & Rouse, C. E. (1995, June). Labor-market returns to two- and four-year colleges. *American Economic Review, 85,* 600–614.

Kane, T. J., & Rouse, C. E. (1999). The community college: Educating students at the margin between college and work. *Journal of Economic Perspectives, 13*(3), 63–84.

Karabel, J. (1972). Community colleges and social stratification. *Harvard Educational Review, 42,* 521–562.

Lee, V., & Frank, K. (1990). Students' characteristics that facilitate the transfer from two-year to four-year colleges. *Sociology of Education, 63,* 178–193.

Marin, P., & Lee, E. K. (2003). *Appearance and reality in the sunshine state: The Talented 20 Program in Florida.* Cambridge, MA: Civil Rights Project at Harvard University.

Martinez, M. C. (2004). *Postsecondary participation and state policy: Meeting the future demand.* Sterling, VA: Stylus.

Massey, D. S., Charles, C. Z., Lundy, G. F., & Fischer, M. J. (2003). *The source of the river: The social origins of freshmen at America's selective colleges and universities.* Princeton, NJ: Princeton University Press.

Monk-Turner, E. (1998). Community college education and its impact on socioeconomic status attainment. *Mellen Studies in Education, 41.*

Murphy, K., & Welch, F. (2001). Wage differentials in the 1990s: Is the glass half-full or half-empty? In F. Welch (Ed.), *The causes and consequences of increasing inequality* (pp. 341–364). Chicago: University of Chicago Press.

National Center for Education Statistics. (2001). *Dropout rates in the United States.* Washington, DC: U.S Department of Education.

Orfield, G. (Ed.). (2004). *Dropouts in America: Confronting the graduation rate crisis.* Cambridge, MA: Harvard Education Press.

Orfield, G., & Kornhaber, M. (Eds.). (2001). *Raising standards or raising barriers? Inequality and high stakes testing in public education.* New York: Century Foundation Press.

Orfield, G. (with Kurlaender, M.). (Ed.). (2001). *Diversity challenged: Evidence on the impact of affirmative action.* Cambridge, MA: Harvard Education Publishing Group.

Orfield, G., & Lee, C. (2005). *Why segregation matters: Poverty and educational inequality.* Cambridge, MA: Civil Rights Project at Harvard University.

Orfield, G., & Miller, E. (Eds.). (1998). *Chilling admissions: The affirmative action crisis and the search for alternatives.* Cambridge, MA: Harvard Education Publishing Group.

Ortiz, A. M., & Boyer, P. (2003). *New Directions for Institutional Research, 118,* 41–49.

Portes, A., & Rumbaut, R. (1996). *Immigrant America: A portrait.* Berkeley: University of California Press.

Provasnik, S., & Shafer, L. L. (2004). *Historically black colleges and universities, 1976 to 2001* (NCES 2004–062). Washington, DC: Government Printing Office.

Rivkin, S. G. (1995). Black/white differences in schooling and employment. *Journal of Human Resources, 30,* 826–852.

Rouse, C. E. (1995). Democratization or diversion? The effect of community colleges on educational attainment. *Journal of Business and Economic Statistics, 13,* 217–224.

San Miguel, G., & Valencia, R. R. (1998). From the treaty of Guadalupe Hidalgo to *Hopwood*: The educational plight and struggle of Mexican Americans in the southwest. *Harvard Educational Review, 68,* 353–412.

Sewell, W. H., & Hauser, R. M. (1975). *Education, occupation, and earnings: Achievement in the early career.* New York: Academic Press.

Solmon, L. C., Solmon, M. S., & Schiff, T. W. (2002). The changing demographics: Problems and opportunities. In W. A. Smith, P. Altbach, & K. Lomotey (Eds.), *The racial crisis in American higher education: Continuing challenges for the twenty-first century.* Albany: State University of New York Press.

Suárez-Orozco, M., & Páez, M. M. (Eds.). (2002). *Latinos remaking America.* Berkeley: University of California Press.

Swanson, C. B. (2004). Sketching a portrait of public high school graduation: Who graduates? Who doesn't? In G. Orfield (Ed.), *Dropouts in America: Confronting the graduation rate crisis* (pp. 13–40). Cambridge, MA: Harvard Education Press.

Swisher, K. G., & Tippeconic, J. W. (1999). *Next steps, research and practice to advance Indian education.* Charleston, WV: ERIC Clearinghouse on Rural Education and Small Schools.

Tienda, M., Leicht, K., Sullivan, T., Maltese, M., & Lloyd, K. (2003). *Closing the gap? Admissions and enrollments at the Texas public flagships before and after affirmative action.* Princeton, NJ: Texas Top 10 Percent Project.

Turner, S. E. (2004). Going to college and finishing college: Explaining different educational outcomes. In C. M. Hoxby (Ed.), *College choices: The economics of where to go, when to go, and how to pay for it* (pp. 13–61). Chicago: University of Chicago Press.

U.S. Census Bureau. (n.d.). *The population profile of the United States: 2000.* Washington, DC: U.S. Government Printing Office. Retrieved February 20, 2005, from http://www.census.gov/population/www/pop-profile/profile2000.html

U.S. Census Bureau. (2004). *Newsroom: Hispanic origin population.* Retrieved January 31, 2005, from http://www.census.gov/Pressrelease/www/releases/archives/hispanic_origin_population/index.htm

Valenzuela, A. (Ed.). (2004). *Leaving children behind: Why Texas-style accountability fails Latino youth.* Albany: State University of New York Press.

Vigil Laden, B. (2004). Serving emerging majority students. In B. Vigil Laden (Ed.), *Serving minority populations* (pp. 1–19). San Francisco: Jossey-Bass.

Whitaker, D., & Pascarella, E. (1994). Two-year college attendance and socioeconomic attainment: Some additional evidence. *Journal of Higher Education, 65,* 194–210.

2

Necessary but Not Sufficient
Higher Education as a Strategy
of Social Mobility

DAVID KAREN AND KEVIN J. DOUGHERTY

In the last 40 years, higher education has virtually become the necessary passport to middle-class success, as the value of the high school degree has sharply dropped. Being aware of this, many more high school students now go on to college. But despite a large increase in the overall number of students going to college, differences by race and social class are actually increasing. To understand this conundrum, we must better comprehend the politics of college access and how the larger patterns of inequality in the United States are reproduced through education. At the same time, we must appreciate that a major political reaction has undermined the legitimacy and effectiveness of policies for achieving educational equality.

In this chapter, we examine the role of higher education in providing opportunities for social and economic mobility in the United States. We consider the specific benefits associated with higher education, who has access to those benefits, and why those benefits are conferred. We ask why and how higher education has expanded and whether such expansion has facilitated more equal outcomes. We focus especially on the *politics* of access: We see higher education as a scarce and valuable resource, the prize in a struggle among competing groups. Dominant and subordinate groups, state officials, and higher education officials are all involved in negotiating the color and class lines in higher education, often under the guise of meritocracy.[1] When these officials establish particular definitions of "merit" in admitting or funding students, they are making decisions not only about who gets ahead but about who we are as a society (Bowen & Bok, 1998). As we will show, decisions about "merit" are not politically innocent, in either origin or consequence. Such decisions play an important part in whether higher education can effectively support the effort to create equality of opportunity across race and class. We finish by considering what can be done within the present context to increase opportunity, noting that such efforts are most successful when part of a broader movement for social and economic justice.

THE IMPORTANCE OF HIGHER EDUCATION

Access to higher education has taken on crucial importance in debates about social mobility and equality because there is clear evidence that a college education is associated with significant economic and noneconomic benefits.

Economic Benefits

The economic benefits of higher education include higher pay, job satisfaction, and employment stability. As shown in Table 1, in 2002, adults without a high school degree on average, earned less than $19,000 per year, while those with degrees beyond the BA averaged between $60,000 and $74,000, depending on their racial background. To be sure, these figures do not control for the fact that people who differ in educational level also differ in other characteristics that affect income, such as family social-class background, test scores, marital status, labor force experience, location, etc. But even when we control for these differences, we find that those holding an associate's degree enjoy average earnings 20 to 30 percent higher than high school graduates; for those holding a BA, the earnings advantage is 30 to 50 percent (Grubb, 2002).

Since we are specifically interested in race here, it is worth examining the earnings differences among whites, blacks, and Latinos who have a given level of education. These data show clearly that equalizing education doesn't close earnings gaps between races. For example, among those with a BA, whites earn 24 percent more than blacks and 28 percent more than Latinos.

Beyond their income advantages, college-educated people also enjoy a small but statistically significant advantage in job satisfaction. This is due in large part to the fact that they tend to earn more and hold jobs that provide more challenge and greater autonomy (Pascarella & Terenzini, 1991). Edu-

TABLE 1
Average Income for Workers Age 18 and Over: 2002

Race	Did Not Complete High School	High School Graduate	Some College	BA	Advanced Degree
White	$19,300	$28,100	$31,900	$52,500	$73,900
Black	16,500	22,800	27,600	42,300	59,900
Latino	19,000	24,200	27,800	40,900	67,700

Source: U.S. Census Bureau (2004).

TABLE 2
Racial and Socioeconomic Differences in College Access and Choice

Race/SES	College Access (percentage of 1992 high school completers who entered post-secondary education by fall 1994)	College Choice (percentage of college students who enter a four-year versus a two-year institution or below)
White	66	59
Black	53	55
Hispanic	51	41
Asian	81	62
Top 1/4 SES*	88	74
Middle 1/2 SES	63	51
Bottom 1/4 SES	36	37

Note: National Education Longitudinal Study of Eighth Graders in 1988. The figures are for those graduating high school in 1992 and entering postsecondary education by fall 1994.

Source: U.S. Department of Education (1996, p. 12).

* SES is an index of socioeconomic status. The variable was based on five equally weighted, standardized components: father's education, mother's education, family income, father's occupation, and mother's occupation.

cational attainment also reduces the likelihood of being unemployed. In 2003, among those 25 years and older, the unemployment rate for college graduates or more was 3.1 percent, but was 8.8 percent for those who had not graduated from high school (Bureau of Labor Statistics, 2003).

Noneconomic Benefits

Beyond the economic benefits, higher education also results in improved health, civic involvement, and support for equality and civil liberties. Controlling for family background and intellectual ability, the more college education someone has, the better their later health status and the longer their life expectancy. College-educated people also have been found to have a greater general interest in politics and political activism than high school–educated people of similar social origins and personality characteristics. Finally, there is evidence that college-educated people—controlling for age and background characteristics—show higher levels of humanitarianism and social conscience, support for equal opportunity for minorities and women, support for civil liberties and freedom of speech for nonconformists, and openness and tolerance (Pascarella & Terenzini, 1991).[2]

CONTINUED INEQUALITY

These large advantages enjoyed by college graduates have been made palatable by the fact that college attendance has risen greatly over the past 50 years, making it seem as if college attendance is becoming more equal. In 2001, just over 60 percent of all high school completers went on to some form of postsecondary education within one year of leaving high school, up from 49 percent in 1980. However, although the higher education system has greatly expanded, big differences in college attendance still remain according to race and class—in fact, those differences are getting *larger*.

Table 2 illustrates the sharp differences in college access and choice by race and class. African American and Latino students are significantly less likely to enter postsecondary education than white students, and if they do attend they are considerably more likely to end up in two-year rather than four-year colleges. And if racial differences are marked, socioeconomic differences are even larger. Seven out of eight high school graduates attended college within the two years following high school graduation if they were in the top quartile of socioeconomic status (SES); fewer than 3 in 8 did so if they were in the bottom quartile of SES. And while almost 3 out of 4 of those who went to college from the top SES quartile attended a four-year college, fewer than 3 in 8 from the bottom quartile did so. In fact, "[a] student from the highest socioeconomic quartile and the lowest test score quartile was as likely to have enrolled in college as a student from the lowest socioeconomic quartile and the highest aptitude quartile" (Gladieux, 2004, p. 24).

TABLE 3
Changes in College Entrance

College Entrance Rate, by Percentage

Race/Ethnicity: College entrance within one year of high school graduation	1972	1980	2001
White, non-Hispanic	49.7	49.8	64.2
Black	44.8	42.7	54.8
Hispanic	45.0	52.3	51.7
Maximum Difference (percentage points)	4.9	9.6	12.5

Social Class: College entrance within 2.5 years of high school graduation	1972		1992
Top 1/4 SES*	78.0		88.3
Middle 1/2 SES	43.1		63.0
Bottom 1/4 SES	26.7		36.0
Maximum Difference (percentage points)	51.3		52.3

Sources: U.S. Department of Education (2002, p. 222); U.S. Department of Education (1981, p. 58; 1996, pp. 12, 21).

* SES is an index of socioeconomic status. The variable was based on five equally weighted, standardized components: father's education, mother's education, family income, father's occupation, and mother's occupation.

It may seem that further increases in college attendance would reduce these racial and socioeconomic disparities. But in fact, as shown in Table 3, the racial gap in college access got larger and the class gap did not shrink during the 1980s and 1990s, despite the fact that the rate of college attendance rose sharply. Over the last few decades, while there have been notable increases in the percentage of black, Latino, and low-SES high school graduates attending college, whites and high-SES students have increased their college attendance as well, so the gaps have, at best, stayed the same.

In considering equality of college opportunity, we need to keep in mind that the type of college—two-year versus four-year, less selective versus more selective—has a major impact on students' educational and economic attainment. For example, all other things being equal, community college entrants attain fewer years of education and fewer BA degrees than students of comparable social background, educational aspirations, and high school preparation who enter four-year colleges (Dougherty, 1994). And, as the selectivity of the institution increases, graduation rates also increase, as do the likelihood of educational attainment beyond the BA and economic payoffs (Bowen & Bok, 1998; Brewer, Eide, & Ehrenberg, 1999; Carnevale & Rose, 2004). It is therefore distressing to see, as demonstrated in Tables 4a and 4b, that the increasing class and racial gaps in college access have been accompanied by an increasing gap in access to more selective institutions. Two distinct patterns emerge from these tables. First, it is clear that an increasing percentage of college entrants are attending two-year colleges; this increase is particularly apparent among blacks and those with lowest SES. Second, students from the most affluent backgrounds have become increasingly likely to attend the most selective colleges.

There are a number of cases around the world where college access has expanded quite markedly but educational gaps in college attendance between advantaged and disadvantaged groups were not closed (Hout, Raftery, & Bell, 1993). Hout and others refer to this pattern as maximally maintained inequality (MMI). One common pattern is for a society to increase the college attendance rate of its high school graduates over time. But since this pattern would occur for all social groups, the gap in the rates of movement into higher education between dominant and subordinate groups will have remained the same. Only when the elite group reaches close to 100 percent and cannot raise its likelihood of college attendance will we see a decline in the difference between groups in their rates of transition from high school graduation to college. But even then, the top group may well establish a new, more exclusive credential.

As things stand now, our system of educational and occupational allocation is characterized by strong associations between social origins and whether one goes to college, where one goes to college, and whether one completes college. Moreover, those associations have not shrunk, despite the large increase in college attendance over the last 50 years. Why has equality of opportunity eluded us? To answer this question, we need to consider the politics of college access.

THE POLITICS OF COLLEGE ACCESS

If higher education expansion is to become a way to expand equality of opportunity, we need to understand its dynamics. To what degree is it driven by the needs and demands of disadvantaged students, and to what degree is it driven by other and even contrary interests? Our thinking here has been

TABLE 4a
Changes in Access to Four-Year vs. Two-Year Colleges,
by Percentage

Race/Ethnicity	*1972*	*1992*	*Diff.*
White	69.2	59.3	−9.9
Black	73.7	55.1	−18.6
Hispanic	46.5	41.4	−5.1
Asian	N/A	61.7	

Social Class	*1972*	*1992*	*Diff.*
Top 1/4 SES	76.4	73.7	−2.7
Middle 1/2 SES	63.5	50.7	−12.8
Bottom 1/4 SES	60.5	36.8	−23.7

Source: U.S. Department of Education (1981, p. 61; 1996, pp. 12, 21).

TABLE 4b
Changes in Access to Highly Selective Four-Year Colleges,
by Percentage

Social Class	*1981*	*1998*	*Diff.*
Richest (> $200K)	20.5	27.9	7.4
Upper ($100–200K)	14.8	17.3	2.5
Upper Middle ($60–100K)	8.1	8.8	0.7
Middle ($30–60K)	4.8	5.1	0.3
Lower Middle ($20–30K)	3.7	4.5	0.8
Lowest (< $20K)	3.0	4.7	1.7

Source: McPherson & Schapiro (1999, pp. 22–23).

Note: The income figures are inflation-adjusted income defined by what they were in 1998.

shaped by a "neo-institutional perspective," elaborated most explicitly by DiMaggio and Powell (1983). As we consider the dynamics of higher education expansion, we need to consider the entire organizational field: "key suppliers, resource and product consumers, regulatory agencies, and other organizations that produce similar services or products" (DiMaggio & Powell, 1983, p. 148). We need to consider, then, not only the students, but also the role of government (especially its financing and regulating roles), competition among institutions of higher education, and the interests of individual institutions.

The Discourse of Higher Education Democratization

The expansion of higher education has often been viewed as a process of democratization. Such a discourse focuses on the role of the free market and of the federal and state governments in creating and expanding the system of public higher education in ways that enable individuals to fulfill their aspirations for gaining the skills necessary for increasingly technical occupations (Trow, 1962). In the 19th century, through the Morrill Acts (1862 and 1890), the federal government provided states with land grants to finance the establishment of public universities. In the early 20th century, state governments supported the widespread establishment of local community colleges (Cohen & Brawer, 2003). This accelerated after World War II, at which time the federal government passed a series of laws—from the 1944 GI Bill to the Higher Education Act (HEA) of 1965—that dramatically increased college access. According to President Lyndon Johnson, "The HEA of 1965 means that a high school senior in this great land of ours can apply to any college or university in any of the 50 states and not be turned away because his family is poor" (American Council on Education, 2004). Passed as one of the Great Society programs, the HEA was part of a larger initiative to provide a "hand up" to equalize opportunity to access the American Dream.

The continued prospects for this democratizing movement appear strong. With the increased gap between the incomes of high school and college graduates the economic incentives to complete college have never been stronger, and it appears that the public is quite conscious of this. In a 1999 nationwide poll of adults, Carnevale and Rose (2004) found that "not getting a college education" was considered a disadvantage in life by 87 percent of respondents, higher than the 78 percent who rated "growing up in a low-income black family" as a disadvantage. By far, the public chose educational institutions as having primary responsibility in helping young people get ahead, and aspirations for higher education have become very common among high school students. High school seniors with aspirations for at least a BA increased from 50 percent in 1972 to 69 percent in 1992, a rise of 19 percentage points. During that same period, black high school seniors with aspirations for at least a college degree rose from 51 percent to 72 percent (21 percentage points), and students in the bottom quartile in socioeconomic status with similar aspirations increased from 18 percent to 47 percent (29 percentage points; U.S. Department of Education, 1995).

The demand for access to higher education, however, has occurred at a collective level as well. Subordinate groups of various types mobilized to gain greater access to higher education, either through expanded student aid or changes in admissions practices. The civil rights and women's movements, both nationally and on individual campuses, produced impressive changes in recruitment and admissions practices. For example, at the City University of New York (CUNY), the mobilization of the black and Puerto Rican communities in 1969 led to the implementation of an open admissions program that resulted in a guarantee of access to a college in the CUNY system for every New York City high school graduate (Lavin & Hyllegard, 1996).[3] Furthermore, mobilization by minority and women's groups opened up access even at the most selective institutions. Notably, however, working-class students, who did not mobilize, made no such inroads into these institutions (Karen, 1991b).

The discourse of higher education policy as a process of democratization involving public officials responding to popular demand captures an important part of the politics of college access in the United States. But it also misses a lot. For one, the governmental response not infrequently has been motivated less by commitment to equality than to a desire to maintain political control in a period of popular mobilization. Just as in the 1930s, when large segments of the population were questioning the legitimacy of the promise of equal opportunity, the claims on the state made by subordinate groups in the 1960s led to a similar expansion of universalistic social programs as a means of containing social conflict (Piven & Cloward, 1977).[4] In addition, the discourse of higher education policy as democratization misses the fact that college expansion has been fueled as well by nondemocratic desires and that there have been powerful efforts to blunt the democratizing thrust of higher education expansion.

Nondemocratizing Sources of Expansion

Government officials have supported policies to increase access to higher education in response to group demands for equalizing opportunity. However, consistent with neo-institutional theory, they have also supported college expansion because supplying college seats fits the values and interests of government officials operating within the constraints of direct business pressure, capitalist culture, and the power of business to invest or disinvest in an area's economy (Block, 1987). For example, as or more important than expanding college opportunity for the development of the Morrill Act was the desire to further economic growth. A key component of the Morrill Act was the creation of the Agricultural Extension Service by which university expertise and research could be applied to the problems of farmers operating in a global market in agricultural products (Geiger, 1986).

At private institutions as well, despite their desire to become more national institutions and the obvious benefit of increasing the number of paying customers, many Ivy League colleges, during the first few decades of the 20th century, instituted selective admissions plans by limiting the size of the entering class so that they could more easily restrict the number of Jews. Free of government regulation, these institutions were, nevertheless, certainly constrained by their powerful elite Protestant benefactors and their desire to maintain their relationship with the elite (Karabel, in press).

Nondemocratizing interests also played a role in the rise of the community college. The state universities supported the founding of community colleges not just to expand college opportunity, but also to keep the universities academically selective by channeling less prepared students away from their doors (Brint & Karabel, 1989; Dougherty, 1994). At the local level, school superintendents and high school principals—who were the prime instigators of local drives to found community colleges—were certainly moved by evidence of student need for college opportunity. But they were also moved by their desires to earn prestige as college founders and to secure jobs as presidents of the new colleges (Dougherty, 1994). In addition, state governors, legislators, and education departments strongly pushed the expansion of community colleges not only to provide college opportunity, but also because they were mindful that building more community colleges, rather than expanding existing four-year colleges, would cost state governments far less. Finally, community colleges, because of their strong commitment to occupational education, could help stimulate the growth of state economies by attracting business firms with the carrot of publicly subsidized employee training (Brint & Karabel, 1989; Dougherty, 1994). In the end, the mix of democratizing and nondemocratizing motives created a contradictory community college system that provides enhanced opportunity for higher education but also diverts students from pursuing a BA (Brint & Karabel, 1989; Dougherty, 1994; Rouse, 1998).

Resistance to Democratization

Finally, the democratization thesis ignores the fact that there have been two related processes that undermine tendencies toward the democratization of higher education. The first tendency is structural; it is part and parcel of our system of inequality. The second involves efforts by elites to counterbalance the successes of subordinate groups in increasing access to higher education.

The first tendency is that, almost "naturally," those already advantaged by family background secure other advantages as well, including advanced education and more attractive jobs. The hope would be that employment decisions would overcome this by hiring on the basis of skill requirements and ability, regardless of background. But, in fact, education requirements for specific jobs are often only vaguely related to skills. The most highly re-munerated jobs often require extensive education *not* because of the highly technical nature of the positions; after all, many skills can be and are learned on the job. Instead, high-status jobs have high educational requirements because employers are looking for people well socialized into the dominant culture, and elite colleges and universities provide that. So even as higher education opens its doors to the previously excluded, the reproduction of class and racial inequality is maintained (Bourdieu, 1977; Collins, 1979).

Beyond its "normal" workings, the system of inequality is augmented by specific instances of counter-mobilization against democratizing efforts. In response to mobilization by excluded groups and a subsequent democratization of access, especially with respect to race-conscious affirmative action, a massive counter-mobilization appeared, especially in the GOP, during the Carter presidency and even more so under Reagan, and has been a continual presence since.

Three different ideological frames have been used to justify and encourage this political reaction. The first was the branding of affirmative action as a deviation from equal treatment, that is, as reverse discrimination. To the extent that a person's accomplishments were weighed differently because they were a member of a particular ethnic or racial group, this was seen either as a violation of an individual's rights or as engaging in undeserved preferential treatment. The second frame involved claims that those who benefited from the democratization of access were not worthy or meritorious. Such claims usually focused on virtually any changes in higher education institutions, from "new" student orientations to providing services to students that, heretofore, had been deemed unnecessary (everything from remediation to additional counseling to "theme" houses). The ideological foundation for these two frames was the focus on the individual, on hard work, on the achievement ideology, on meritocracy and a nostalgic claim of how current practices deviated from "proper" institutional behavior. The third key ideological frame was the political and social construction of the fiscal crisis of the state. In the context of tax cuts and other priorities, it is often argued that fiscal constraints simply and objectively *dictate* that higher education expenditures must be cut and educational opportunity curtailed.

These ideological frames have provided the cover for a number of specific counter-mobilization attempts by the advantaged, who feel that they are struggling to preserve their lead in an increasingly difficult race. The most prominent counter-mobilization attempts have involved court cases and state referenda against affirmative action. But, historically, the counter-mobilization has also included alumni revolts at selective colleges against declining "legacy" privileges, state and local decisions to remove remediation from four-year colleges, and federal and state undermining of the principle of need-based student aid (Karabel, in press; Mazzeo, 2002; Schrag, 1999)

Beginning with the *DeFunis* (1974) and *Bakke* (1978) cases, attacks on affirmative action focused attention on the very few slots in highly selective institutions—perhaps 10 percent of all the places in higher education—that were going to African Americans. The larger issue of access to the remaining slots in institutions that are barely selective or nonselective (Fallows, 2003) fell off the policy table. Though anti-affirmative action measures failed in Congress (e.g., the ideologically named Equal Opportunity Act of 1995 and the Civil Rights Act of 1997), opponents of affirmative action enjoyed success in two state referenda. Finally, although the U.S. Supreme Court reaffirmed, in the *Gratz* (2003) and *Grutter* (2003) Michigan cases, the use of race as one of many factors that may affect admission, attempts continue to undermine affirmative action at the state level (Schmidt, 2003).

Historically, the democratization of access at very selective institutions—with increases in minorities and women—has led to alumni revolts and the return of relatively large legacy advantages (Karabel, in press). Similarly, the rise of early admission plans has tended to disadvantage those from noncollege backgrounds. Upper-class and white students make much greater use of early admissions than less advantaged students, and this confers a significant admissions advantage. Whether due to institutions' desire to increase their yield rates, the higher percentage of students in this pool who don't need financial aid, etc., early admissions applicants are accepted at a much higher rate, even controlling for test scores, etc., than are regular applicants (Avery, Fairbanks, & Zeckhauser, 2003).

Meanwhile, again in the name of "maintaining standards," 44 states have moved to eliminate remedial courses in public four-year institutions (D. Lavin, personal communication, August 12, 2004; Mazzeo, 2002; Schrag, 1999). As a result, a much larger percentage of postsecondary students—

especially those who are from areas with poor schools and/or are immigrants and have language difficulties—begin their college careers in two-year institutions, with lower prospects of BA attainment. Such restrictions are often made in economic/fiscal crisis terms, suggesting that remediation is too expensive at four-year institutions, yet this argument is specious. There is no compelling evidence that the proportion of students requiring remediation was rising sharply, but there is compelling evidence that political, business, and educational elites were getting concerned that educational standards were eroding (Mazzeo, 2002).

Another important part of this counter-mobilization has been the weakening of government commitment to need-based student aid, marked by a failure to raise Pell Grants at the same rate as college costs and by shifts toward loans, tax credits, and merit aid (see Heller, this volume). Attacks on grant aid for higher education began as Carter came into office. Federal expenditures on Pell Grants, which were the heart of the federal government's attempt to help low-income students overcome the barriers to postsecondary education, have never again reached the levels (in constant dollars) of 1976, and they less and less offset the costs of tuition at institutions of higher education. Whereas in 1979–80, a low-income family would have had to come up with one-fifth of its income to pay for the remaining costs of attending a four-year public institution after receiving its Pell Grant, in 2001–02 it had to pay 37 percent of its income (King, 2003). While Pell Grants have shrunk in their relative contribution to paying for college, the role of loans has expanded. Today, loans make up 69 percent of federal student aid financing (and 54% of aid from all sources; College Board, 2003). This is problematic because a number of studies find that loans are less effective than grants in boosting access (St. John, 1990). Working-class students, but especially African Americans, are reluctant to take out loans for fear they will fail to secure well-paying, stable jobs and be unable to pay them back (Heller, 1999; Terenzini, Cabrera, & Bernal, 2001).

Meanwhile, state support for higher education has shifted toward merit aid, further complicating the quest for equality of higher educational opportunity. In 1993, Georgia established the HOPE (Helping Outstanding Pupils Educationally) Scholarship program, which is entirely "merit based": that is, it is awarded on the basis not of need but of high school grades and test scores.[5] It set off a large movement toward merit-based programs among the states. Whereas in 1982 merit aid represented 9 percent of state undergraduate aid dollars, that figure had climbed to 22 percent by 1999 (Heller, 2002). Though states differ in how they define merit, many of the state awards go to high-income families and/or go disproportionately to white and Asian American students (Heller, 2002). In the context of competition over college ranking in *U.S. News and World Report*, such merit aid increases yield rates and, by rewarding standardized test performance, results in the further exclusion of subordinate groups.

Seizing the name for different purposes, the federal government introduced the Hope Scholarship tax credit in 1998 to offset the taxes of middle- and upper-income families who pay tuition (not room and board) during the first two years of college. The Lifetime Learning Tax Credit applies to tuition costs beyond the first two years of college. Because the tax credits only apply to *offsetting* taxes (they can't be used for refunds) and since the tax credit is reduced for every dollar of grant money received (primarily by low-income students), these tax credits primarily benefit higher income students. Further, tax credits are not as successful as grants in encouraging college attendance because the higher income beneficiaries would likely have attended college anyway (McPherson & Schapiro, 2002).

Overall, the structural tendencies toward the reproduction of inequality and the counter-mobilization against higher educational equality over the last three decades—waged under the ideological cover of fiscal crisis and meritocracy—have moved U.S. policies away from the aims set by the HEA of 1965 and has led to increasing inequality of college access and choice by race and class. What can be done?

WAYS TO REDUCE INEQUALITY

As we have shown above, there is sharp, important, and increasing inequality by race and class in opportunity to attend college. This inequality needs to be reduced if we wish to lessen race and class inequality in the larger society. At the same time, it is important not to overestimate the importance of college inequality, as it is only one of several important causes of overall social inequality. Moreover, the political viability of efforts to increase educational equality depends in good part on the political strength of democratizing movements in society as a whole. Therefore, in analyzing what needs to be done, we will focus not only on educational solutions but also on extra-educational solutions.

Educational Solutions

The educational solutions must recognize that the issue is no longer just equalizing college access but also college choice and college success. Though we believe that massive social movements of subordinate groups focused on issues of general social inequality would be *most* helpful, there are some individual-level solutions that would aid the process as well, including heating up aspirations, providing better financing and information about financing, and improving academic performance.

Equalizing Access to College

Despite the large increase in college-going rates over the last 20 years, race and class inequalities in access to college have persisted and even grown. What should we do?

Increasing Aspirations

To get to college, it is important that one want to do so and expect to be able to do so. But there are large racial and social-class gaps in aspirations. For example, there is a 50-point difference between the bottom and top SES quartiles in the percentage of 1992 high school seniors expecting to earn at least a BA. The racial gaps are much smaller, but still show lower aspirations for blacks and Latinos than for whites and especially for Asians (U.S. Department of Education, 1996).

A variety of suggestions have been offered to reduce these racial and class differences. A major one is to give students more encouragement and information as early as elementary school. Parents, peers, schoolteachers, and counselors need to provide more convincing evidence that there is an economic payoff to college, for example, by showcasing college graduates of color who have achieved high-paying jobs. An important part of this is increasing the number of counselors in high schools serving minority and low-income students, where student/counselor ratios tend to be large and counselors have many other responsibilities, making college counseling often perfunctory. These efforts in high school are being supplemented by federal, state, and private efforts, such as GEAR UP and I Have a Dream, to reach disadvantaged elementary and middle school students well before they decide about college. These programs provide mentoring, tutoring, and a guarantee of college access and financial aid if they meet specific requirements, such as completing a college-prep curriculum and maintaining a certain minimum GPA (Freeman, 1997; Gladieux & Swail, 2000; McDonough, 1998).[6]

Of course, these individual-level efforts work even better in the context of social movements that demand concrete change. When institutions respond positively to movement demands for educational and occupational opportunity, aspirations follow suit.

Improving Academic Preparation

Minority and working-class students emerge from high school less well prepared academically than more advantaged students, which strongly affects college attendance. For example, among eighth graders in 1988, 88 percent of students who were in the top quartile of SES reported postsecondary participation by 1994, but only 36 percent of those in the bottom SES quartile did so (a 52 percentage point difference; U.S. Department of Education, 1996). When you remove the impact of differences among students in their academic preparation by restricting the comparison to students in the top quartile in tested twelfth-grade achievement, the gap drops to 20 percentage points (97% versus 77%). Similarly, in the top test quartile, racial differences in postsecondary attendance between whites and blacks disappear and the white-Latino difference in attending college is only five percentage points (U.S. Department of Education, 1996).[7]

A wide variety of solutions have been offered to reduce these racial and class differences in academic preparation. They include more rigorous coursework in high school, particularly in math, less tracking (especially by class and race), racial and class desegregation of schools, developing a climate of high teacher expectations for all students, better financed and staffed schools, and more provision of good preschooling (Dougherty, 1996; Entwisle, Alexander, & Olson, 1997; Freeman, 1997; Gladieux & Swail, 2000; Roscigno, 1998). Outside of school, children's academic performance would be improved by greater family and residential stability and greater availability of health care, all of which would be greatly aided by an incomes policy, a national health care plan, and housing subsidies (Rothstein, 2004).

Reducing the Information Gap

Minority and low-income students often lack the information—about where and how to apply or how to finance college—to be able to turn college ambitions into reality (Terenzini, Cabrera, & Bernal, 2001; U.S. Department of Education, 2003b). The solutions to these inequalities of information are much the same as those for reducing inequalities in expectations. However, for minority and low-income students, high school counselors may play a particularly important role in reducing inequality of information. They are better placed to secure and distribute information on SAT and ACT tests (dates, costs, financing), test-preparation courses and materials (and how to pay for them), financial aid sources for college, and what the academic requirements really are at different colleges. Therefore, it is particularly important to increase greatly the number of well-trained counselors in high schools with many minority and low-income students (McDonough, 1998).

Financial Aid

Rising tuition and inadequate financial aid are two of the main causes for the growing racial and class gap in college access (Heller, 1999; McPherson & Schapiro, 1999; Terenzini et al., 2001; U.S. Department of Education, 2002). A recommitment to funding Pell Grants more adequately—as well as focusing state and institutional aid on needy students and reducing the percentage of aid from loans and tax credits—will return us to striving toward LBJ's goal of not allowing finances to get in the way of being able to attend any college or university.

Equalizing College Choice

As noted above, access to four-year colleges, especially to the most selective ones, varies greatly by race and social class, and the inequalities have grown over time. As much as half of the explained variation is due to differences in educational expectations and academic preparation (Karen, 2002). The solutions offered above for increasing access to higher education generally would also help increase access to more selective colleges. But there is another factor that needs to be added: admissions barriers at selective four-year colleges. Though the admissions process of selective colleges is presented as meritocratic, we have seen that this is not entirely the case. Even seemingly meritocratic admissions criteria such as test scores and high school grades build in class and racial advantages. But there are also many nonmeritocratic criteria, such as the advantage given to children of alumni. A variety of proposals have been made to reduce the racial and class advantages built into the admissions processes of selective colleges. These include reducing or eliminating the admissions advantage of alumni's children, cutting back on early admission/decision plans, continuation of race-conscious affirmative action with the addition of class as a factor, deemphasizing standardized tests and putting more emphasis on high school GPA and class rank, and using a disadvantage index based on parental education and income as one admissions criterion (Avery, Fairbanks, & Zeckhauser, 2003; Carnevale & Rose, 2004; Hurtado, Milem, Clayton-Pedersen, & Allen, 1998; Karen, 1991a).

Equalizing College Success

As important as it is for minority and low-income students to go to college, it is perhaps equally important for them to attain a degree, especially a four-year degree. As it is, there are significant racial and class differences in persistence and graduation. While 32 percent of whites and 40 percent of Asian Americans attained a BA within six years after entering college in 1995–96, only 17 percent of blacks and 19 percent of Latinos did so. Similarly, students whose parents had a high school diploma or less earned four-year degrees at a rate of 16 percent, while 61 percent of those whose parents had advanced degrees completed a BA (U.S. Department of Education, 2003a).

Increasing Retention to a Degree

To improve retention, we need to raise students' aspirations, improve their academic skills, and better integrate them into the academic and social life of the college. Many students enter college without clear degree aspirations. These "experimenters" (Grubb, 1996) should be encouraged to develop clearer and more deeply held degree aspirations through better academic and personal advising (Dougherty, 2002).

In order to improve the academic skills of entering students, it is important to work with students both before and after they enter college. Effective remediation in college requires that colleges know which students need help (through mandatory assessment at entrance) and ensure that those students indeed get remediation (through mandatory placement in remedial courses). While engaged in remediation, students should be allowed to take regular college-level courses in order to bolster their academic motivation by giving them a sense of progress and, perhaps, to integrate them into learning communities (see below). Finally, remedial courses should be infused to the maximum degree possible with higher-order thinking skills, thus preparing students for transition to regular academic courses. More important, colleges should focus on increasing their retention rates; a commitment to admit a student should be seen as a commitment to do what is necessary to help that student graduate (Grubb, 2001; Levin, 1999; Phipps, 1998; Shaw, 2001; Tinto, 1998).

However effective remedial education in college might become, it is important as well to align high school students' academic skills more closely with colleges' academic expectations. The most important proactive policy is establishing a closer alignment between high school and college curricula. There are a number of states that have moved from a K–12 toward a P–16 educational system, with all the attention to alignment that such a system implies. Short of this, some states have established programs to inform high schools on how well their graduates are doing in college.

Beyond raising the hopes and aligning the skills of entering students, it is important to integrate them better academically and socially into their college. This is particularly true for minority and low-income students, who often enter colleges where they are a distinct minority and in which they may feel marginalized. Useful devices are first-year seminars for freshmen that help students and faculty bond and providing semester- or year-long counseling. Learning communities, which are sets of courses taken in common by students, usually with an overarching theme, are also very useful. By sharing knowledge and learning, they can generate supportive peer groups that provide academic and social integration (Tinto, 1998). In order to further the social integration of minority students, it is also important to take strong steps to create a more inclusive community. This would entail a formal and strong commitment to identifying and confronting racial and ethnic stereotypes and embedded white advantages; formal processes for resolving conflicts; regular assessments of the campus climate for diversity; support for ethnic student organizations; formal mentoring for minority students; cooperative learning methods in classes; and more minority faculty and staff, as well as faculty and staff generally who welcome interaction with minority and low-income students (Hurtado et al., 1998; Massey, Charles, Lundy, & Fischer, 2003).

Facilitating Transfer and the Pursuit of the Baccalaureate Degree

For many minority and low-income students, the path toward higher degrees begins in the community college. Though a few community colleges are beginning to offer baccalaureate degrees (Dougherty, 2002), the main path to the BA still requires transfer to a four-year college. It is important, therefore, to increase the interest of community college students in transferring and to facilitate that process. To raise transfer aspirations, community colleges need to establish transfer centers and other means to encourage and support transfer students. Transfer must then be facilitated by targeting aid to transfer students and by helping them persist in the four-year college through more efficient credit articulation and better pretransfer preparation for the more rigorous posttransfer curriculum. At the same time, we should strive for an even more seamless process by encouraging universities to offer baccalaureate courses at community colleges and community colleges to offer baccalaureate degrees themselves (Dougherty, 2002).

Though the efforts above are very much worth pursuing, they are unlikely to be fully implemented or to realize their full potential in the absence
of political will. The forces blunting efforts to democratize higher education
are powerful. One means of building this political will lies in developing
new political discourses that tie the further democratization of higher education to the interests of the already privileged. A striking case is in Texas,
where the state is making a major effort to close racial and ethnic gaps in
college access because state policymakers came to realize that the economic
and fiscal future of the state lies in adequately educating the state's rapidly
growing Latino population (Texas Higher Education Coordinating Board,
2003).

Noneducational Solutions

Based on our analysis thus far, it should be clear that we do not believe that
a sole focus on increasing college access and even increasing access to the
most selective institutions will alone lead to equal outcomes. First, expanding the number of places in the educational system so that the least advantaged can gain access to higher levels does not necessarily close the gap with
the already advantaged. When the gap begins to close, we generally witness
an attempt via counter-mobilization, as described above, to reopen that
gap in the form of changing admissions requirements or creating a new credential level. Moreover, the conversion of educational degrees into labor-
market outcomes is related to the graduate's access to economic and social
capital, both of which are unequally distributed. Second, and more fundamentally, even if opportunity for educational success were made more
equal, those holding credentials would still be allocated to an unequal set of
positions. Furthermore, given the historic avoidance in the United States of
full-employment policies or guaranteed minimum incomes, our citizens are
always subject to the vicissitudes of industrial contraction and expansion,
outsourcing, increasing employer reluctance to take on health care obliga-
tions, etc.

In such an environment, we suggest that we focus directly on changing
what Fischer and his coauthors (1996) call our unusually narrow and extended economic ladder. Compared to many other societies, the United
States has created a social structure that is radically unequal. We have far
more poverty and greater income inequality than comparable industrialized
societies (Smeeding, Rainwater, & Burtless, 2001). These inequalities are
fostered in considerable part by a less progressive taxation system, greater
hostility to the formation of unions, and a weaker welfare state.

CONCLUSION

We have offered some specific proposals for increasing the representation and success of students of color and working-class students in our colleges and universities. The long decade of the 1960s—characterized by massive protests of subordinate groups—yielded, perhaps, our greatest push toward increasing equality of opportunity in college access. The circumstances—as they always are—were unique but, even under conditions of war and a stagnant economy, our most selective institutions opened themselves to women and people of color, our largest city guaranteed a place in college to every high school graduate, and the federal government enacted the Basic Educational Opportunity Grant (a.k.a. Pell Grants). In the current context, then, we again need to mobilize to compel the federal and state governments to increase support for higher education, push all institutions of higher education to broaden their conceptions of who their students are, and pressure them to provide the resources and support necessary to graduate those they admit. But beyond this mobilization around higher education, perhaps it is time for a broad movement of subordinate groups to challenge the structure of inequality in the larger society.

NOTES

1. These terms draw on Parkin's (1979) explication of Weber's notion of social closure. "Dominant" groups engage in exclusionary social closure, attempting to monopolize rewards and privileges for themselves. "Subordinate" groups, denied access to societal rewards, attempt to usurp them and engage in usurpationary social closure. A dual closure situation is possible, in which a middle group attempts to usurp from above and exclude those below. The advantage of this formulation is that the struggles themselves define the positions rather than requiring an *a priori* group definition that, inevitably, raises "boundary problems." For example, while Asian Americans, generally, would not be regarded as a subordinate group with regard to college access, working class Asian Americans certainly would be.

2. It should be noted that this finding of the positive impact of higher education on sociopolitical attitudes has been forcefully challenged by several scholars (Jackman & Muha, 1984; Phelan et al., 1995).

3. Only six years later, during the New York City fiscal crisis, these gains were substantially rolled back. This illustrates a point we make later in the chapter about how fiscal crises provide the opportunity for counter-mobilization against egalitarian movements.

4. But in the United States, as opposed to many countries in Western Europe, such programs have focused much more on providing the appearance of equal opportunity for education than on providing anything approaching a guaranteed safety net (Heidenheimer, 1981).

5. It should be noted that those invoking the use of merit in financial aid decisions sometimes use that term very loosely (McPherson & Schapiro, 1999).

6. A federal fiscal crisis (created in part by a combination of tax cuts for the wealthy and increased defense expenditures) has precipitated calls for cuts in social programs. At press time, President Bush proposes to increase slightly the amount of money that students may obtain from Pell Grants, financing this in part by eliminating the Perkins loan program. At the same time, specific programs that focus on bringing low-income students into higher education, such as GEAR UP, Talent Search, and Upward Bound, are slated for elimination.

7. Cabrera and La Nasa (2001) document similarly large differences by race and, especially, class.

REFERENCES

American Council on Education. (2004). What is the Higher Education Act? Answers and issues. Retrieved December 15, 2004, from http://www.acenet.edu/hena/read Article.cfm?articleID'499

Avery, C., Fairbanks, A., & Zeckhauser, R. (2003). *The early admissions game*. Cambridge, MA: Harvard University Press.

Block, F. (1987). *Revising state theory*. Philadelphia: Temple University Press.

Bourdieu, P. (1977). Cultural reproduction and social reproduction. In J. Karabel & A. H. Halsey (Eds.), *Power and ideology in education* (pp. 487–511). New York: Oxford University Press.

Bowen, W., & Bok, D. (1998). *The shape of the river: Long-term consequences of considering race in college and university admissions*. Princeton, NJ: Princeton University Press.

Brewer, D. J., Eide, E. R., & Ehrenberg, R. G. (1999). Does it pay to attend an elite private college? *Journal of Human Resources, 34,* 104–123.

Brint, S., & Karabel, J. (1989). *The diverted dream: Community colleges and the promise of educational opportunity in America, 1900–1985*. New York: Oxford University Press.

Bureau of Labor Statistics. (2003). Employment status of the civilian noninstitutional population 25 years and over by educational attainment, sex, race, and Hispanic or Latino ethnicity for 2002 and 2003. Retrieved December 12, 2004 from ftp://ftp.bls.gov/pub/special.requests/lf/aat7.txt

Cabrera, A. F., & La Nasa, S. M. (2001). On the path to college. *Research in Higher Education, 42,* 119–149.

Carnevale, A. P., & Rose, S. J. (2004). Socioeconomic status, race/ethnicity, and selective college admissions. In R. J. Kahlenberg (Ed.), *America's untapped resource: Low-income students in higher education* (pp. 101-156). New York: The Century Foundation Press.

Cohen, A. M., & Brawer, F. B. (2003). *The American community college* (4th ed.). San Francisco: Jossey-Bass.

College Board. (2003). *Trends in college pricing, 2003*. New York: Author.

Collins, R. (1979). *The credential society: An historical sociology of education and stratification*. New York: Academic Press.

DeFunis v. Odegaard, 416 U.S. 312 (1974).

DiMaggio, P., & Powell, W. W. (1983). The iron cage revisited: Institutional isomorphism and collective rationality in organizational fields. *American Sociological Review, 48*, 147–160.

Dougherty, K. J. (1994). *The contradictory college: The origins, impacts, and futures of the community college.* Albany: State University of New York Press.

Dougherty, K. J. (1996). Opportunity to learn standards: A sociological critique. *Sociology of Education* [special issue], 40–65.

Dougherty, K. J. (2002). The evolving role of community college: Policy issues and research questions. In J. Smart & W. Tierney (Eds.), *Higher education: Handbook of theory and research* (vol. 17, pp. 295–348). New York: Kluwer.

Entwisle, D. R., Alexander, K. L., & Olson, L. S. (1997). *Children, schools, and inequality.* Boulder, CO: Westview Press.

Fallows, J. (2003, November). The new college chaos. *Atlantic Monthly,* pp. 106, 108–110, 112–114.

Fischer, C. S., Hout, M., Jankowski, M. S., Lucas, S. R., Swidler, A., & Voss, K. (1996). *Inequality by design: Cracking the bell curve myth.* Berkeley: University of California Press.

Freeman, K. (1997). Increasing African Americans' participation in higher education. *Journal of Higher Education, 68*, 523–550.

Geiger, R. (1986). *To advance knowledge: The growth of American research universities, 1900–1940.* New York: Oxford University Press.

Gladieux, L. E. (2004). Low-income students and the affordability of higher education. In R. J. Kahlenberg (Ed.), *America's untapped resource: Low-income students in higher education* (pp. 17–57). New York: Century Foundation Press.

Gladieux, T., & Swail, W. S. (2000). Beyond access: Improving the odds of college success. *Phi Delta Kappan, 81*, 688–692.

Gratz v. Bollinger, 539 U.S. 244 (2003).

Grubb, W. N. (1996). *Working in the middle.* San Francisco: Jossey-Bass.

Grubb, W. N. (2001). *From black box to Pandora's box: Evaluating remedial/developmental education.* New York: Community College Research Center, Teachers College, Columbia University. Retrieved December 11, 2004, from http://www.tc.columbia.edu/~iee/ccrc/public.htm

Grubb, W. N. (2002). Learning and earning in the middle, part one: National studies of pre-baccalaureate education. *Economics of Education Review, 21*, 299–321.

Grutter v. Bollinger, 539 U.S. 306 (2003).

Heidenheimer, A. (1981). Education and social entitlements in Europe and America. In P. Flora & A. Heidenheimer (Eds.), *The development of welfare states in Europe and America* (pp. 269–304). New Brunswick, NJ: Transaction Books.

Heller, D. (1999). The effects of tuition and state financial aid on public college enrollment. *Review of Higher Education, 23*, 65–89.

Heller, D. (2002). State aid and student access: The changing picture. In D. Heller (Ed.), *Condition of access: Higher education for lower income students* (pp. 59–72). Westport, CT: American Council on Education and Praeger.

Hout, M., Raftery, A. E., & Bell, E. O. (1993). Making the grade: Educational stratification in the United States, 1925–1989. In Y. Shavit & H. Blossfeld (Eds.), *Persistent inequality: Changing educational attainment in thirteen countries* (pp. 25–49). Boulder, CO: Westview Press.

Hurtado, S., Milem, J. F., Clayton-Pedersen, A. R., & Allen, W. R. (1998). Enhancing campus climates for racial/ethnic diversity: Educational policy and practice. *Review of Higher Education, 21*, 279–302.

Jackman, M., & Muha, M. (1984). Education and intergroup attitudes. *American Sociological Review, 49*, 751–769.

Karabel, J. (in press). *The chosen.* Boston: Houghton Mifflin.

Karen, D. (1991a). "Achievement" and "ascription" in admission to an elite college. *Sociological Forum, 4*, 349–380.

Karen, D. (1991b). The politics of class, race, and gender access to higher education in the United States, 1960–1986. *American Journal of Education, 99*, 208–237.

Karen, D. (2002). Changes in access to higher education in the United States, 1980–1992. *Sociology of Education, 75*, 191–210.

King, J. E. (2003). *2003 status report on the Pell Grant Program.* American Council on Education Center for Policy Analysis. Retrieved on December 13, 2004 from http://www.acenet.edu/bookstore/pdf/2003_pell_grant.pdf

Lavin, D. E., & Hyllegard, D. (1996). *Changing the odds: Open admissions and the life chances of the disadvantaged.* New Haven: Yale University Press.

Levin, H. M. (1999, February). *Remediation in the community college.* Paper presented to the Social Science Research Council Workshop on the Multiple and Changing Roles of Community Colleges, New York.

Massey, D., Charles, C. Z., Lundy, G., & Fischer, M. J. (2003). *The source of the river: The social origins of freshmen at America's selective colleges and universities.* Princeton, NJ: Princeton University Press.

Mazzeo, C. (2002). Stakes for students: Agenda setting and remedial education. *Review of Higher Education 26*, 19–39.

McDonough, P. (1998). Structuring college opportunities. In C. A. Torres & T. R. Mitchell (Eds.), *Sociology of education* (pp. 181–210). Albany: State University of New York Press.

McPherson, M. S., & Schapiro, M. O. (1999). *Reinforcing stratification in American higher education.* Stanford, CA: Stanford University, National Center for Postsecondary Improvement.

McPherson, M. S., & Schapiro, M. O. (2002). Changing patterns of institutional aid: Impact on access and educational policy. In D. Heller (Ed.), *Condition of access: Higher education for lower income students* (pp. 73–94). Westport, CT: American Council on Education and Praeger.

Parkin, F. (1979). *Marxism and class theory: A bourgeois critique.* New York: Columbia University Press.

Pascarella, E., & Terenzini, P. T. (1991). *How college affects students: Findings and insights from twenty years of research.* San Francisco: Jossey-Bass.

Phelan, J., Link, B. G., Stueve, A., & Moore, R. E. (1995). Education, social liberalism, and economic conservatism. *American Sociological Review, 60*, 126–140.

Phipps, R. A. (1998). *College remediation: What it is, what it costs, what's at stake.* Washington, DC: Institute for Higher Education Policy.

Piven, F. F., & Cloward, R. A. (1977). *Poor people's movements.* New York: Vintage.

Regents of the University of California v. Bakke, 438 U.S. 265 (1978).

Roscigno, V. (1998). Race and the reproduction of educational disadvantage. *Social Forces, 76*, 1033–1060.

Rothstein, R. (2004). Class and the classroom. *American School Board Journal, 191*(10), 17–21.

Rouse, C. E. (1998). Do two-year colleges increase overall educational attainment? Evidence from the states. *Journal of Policy Analysis and Management, 17*, 595–620.

St. John, E. P. (1990). Price response in enrollment decisions. *Research in Higher Education, 31*, 161–176.

Schmidt, P. (2003, April 4). Behind the fight over race-conscious admissions, *Chronicle of Higher Education*, A22.

Schrag, P. (1999). End of the second chance? The crusade against remedial education. *American Prospect, 10*(44), 68–74.

Shaw, K. M. (2001). Reframing remediation as a systemic phenomenon: A comparative analysis of remediation in two states. In B. K. Townsend & S. K. Twombly (Eds.), *Community colleges: policy in the future context* (pp. 193–221). Westport, CT: Ablex.

Smeeding, T., Rainwater, L., & Burtless, G. (2001). U.S. poverty in a cross-national context. In S. Danziger & R. H. Haveman (Eds.), *Understanding poverty* (pp. 162–192). Cambridge, MA: Harvard University Press.

Terenzini, P. T., Cabrera, A. G., & Bernal, E. M. (2001). *Swimming against the tide: Poor in American higher education.* New York: College Board.

Texas Higher Education Coordinating Board. (2003). *Closing the gaps: Higher education plan.* Austin: Author. Retrieved December 8, 2004, from www.thecb.state.tx.us/advisorycommittees/hep/heplanfinal.pdf

Tinto, V. (1998). Colleges as communities. *Review of Higher Education, 21*(2), 167–177.

Trow, M. (1962). The democratization of higher education in America. *European Journal of Sociology, 3*, 231–262.

U.S. Census Bureau. (2004). *Mean earnings of workers 18 years and older by educational attainment, race, Hispanic origin, and sex: 1975 to 2002.* Washington, DC: Author. Retrieved December 13, 2004 from http://www.census.gov/population/socdemo/education/tabA-3.pdf

U.S. Department of Education. (1981). *College attainment four years after high school.* Raleigh, NC: Research Triangle Institute.

U.S. Department of Education. (1995). *Trends among high school seniors, 1972–1992.* NCES 95-380. Washington, DC: Author.

U.S. Department of Education. (1996). *National education longitudinal survey, 1988–1994, descriptive summary report.* NCES 96-175. Washington, DC: Author.

U.S. Department of Education. (2002). *Digest of education statistics, 2002.* Washington, DC: Author.

U.S. Department of Education. (2003a). *Descriptive summary of 1995–96 beginning postsecondary students: Six years later.* NCES 2003-151. Washington, DC: Author.

U.S. Department of Education. (2003b). *Getting ready to pay for college.* NCES 2003-030. Washington, DC: Author.

3

Equity in
Educational Attainment
Racial, Ethnic, and Gender Inequality
in the 50 States

DEREK V. PRICE AND JILL K. WOHLFORD

Access to postsecondary education represents the gateway to individual opportunity and the vehicle for expanding social benefits such as long-term economic growth, a healthier population, and increased civic participation. For the United States, expanding access to higher education has been an explicit priority since the passage of the Higher Education Act in 1965. This watershed legislation created federal grants and subsidized loans that gave many students who had been historically denied access to college the financial means to enroll. During the last 40 years, the results have been remarkable. But while access and attainment have increased for all racial, ethnic, and gender groups, the educational attainment gaps between racial and ethnic groups have grown larger (Price, 2004a).

This paradox is often overlooked because of the traditional way that educational attainment is measured and analyzed. Most analysts use national statistics from the U.S. Census that disaggregate educational attainment by racial and ethnic characteristics to explain the changes within each racial and ethnic category over time. These simple longitudinal comparisons, however, do not provide an adequate measure of educational attainment for three reasons.

First, the statistics do not account for changes in population growth over time. Therefore, a larger percentage of a group with a bachelor's degree could be a function of declining populations within that group rather than increasing educational attainment of that group. Second, national statistics obscure significant variations in educational attainment rates across the 50 states. Third, these figures do not allow for easy comparisons of educational attainment between different racial and ethnic groups, an important consideration from an equity perspective. To address these limitations, we created an Educational Attainment Parity Indicator (EAPI).

The EAPI measures a state's share of adults age 25 and older with at least a BA for each race and gender group relative to the group's share of the population in the state. In other words, it accounts for changes in population over time, as well as changes in educational attainment. The EAPI allows for easy comparisons of equity in educational attainment among different racial, ethnic, and gender groups and can be used by state policy-makers as an indicator of how well they are closing the educational attainment gap in their states. This type of comparison is important because of the rapidly changing demographics of the nation's future college-going population. Closing the educational attainment gap is also vital because the future workforce of most states will consist of increasing pluralities of African Americans, Hispanics, Asians, and people of other races, and fewer whites.

We begin with a presentation of the demographic trends of the college-eligible population, followed by a description of the pipeline to a college degree. Successful completion through this pipeline requires accurate information, academic preparation, financial resources, and a diverse and tolerant college campus climate. We then review the emergent research on equity indicators and introduce the EAPI. After a discussion of the national picture of educational attainment equity using the EAPI, we conclude with a brief overview of the public policy context of higher education access, including recommendations for a policy agenda to address the educational attainment paradox.

THE NEW MOSAIC OF COLLEGE-ELIGIBLE STUDENTS

According to the National Center for Education Statistics (NCES), the percentage of high school graduates immediately enrolling in postsecondary education in the October after completing high school increased from 49.2 percent in 1972 to 63.3 percent in 2000. In raw numbers, total undergraduate enrollment in degree-granting postsecondary institutions increased from 7.4 million students in 1970 to almost 12.7 million students in 1999 (NCES, 2002). This growth in enrollment occurred across all institutional types:

public four-year enrollments increased by 39 percent, private four-year enrollments by 66 percent, and public and private two-year enrollments by
138 percent. In 1970, only 11 percent of adults age 25 years and older had
at least four years of college; by 2000, 25 percent of adults had a bachelor's
degree or more.[1]

Demographic projections show that most of the increase in the traditional college-eligible population during the next decade will consist of students of color and students from low-income backgrounds.[2] According to
the U.S. Census Bureau, between 2000 and 2010, 63 percent of the growth
in the 18- to 24-year-old resident population will be people of color. As
Table 1 shows, in comparative terms, the traditional college-age Hispanic
population will grow by 18 percent, compared to 20 percent for blacks, 11
percent for Asians, and 35 percent for other races, including multirace individuals—in contrast, the white, non-Hispanic college-age population will
grow by 7 percent. According to the Western Interstate Commission on
Higher Education, by 2006 almost half of public high school graduates in
the United States will be from families with incomes less than $50,000;
more than 16 percent will be from families with incomes less than $20,000
(WICHE, 2003).

The population projection for adults age 25–54 is more dramatic—the
core of the future workforce and potential nontraditional adult students
will become increasingly blacks, Hispanics, Asians, and people of other
races (See Table 1). The population of white, non-Hispanic men and women
age 25–54 is expected to decrease by more than four million by 2010; in
contrast, the Hispanic population age 25–54 will increase by 5.3 million
and the black population will increase by 1.6 million. Indeed, *all* of the
growth in the adult population age 25–54 between 2000 and 2010 will be
among Hispanics, blacks, Asians, and people of other races. By 2010, 41
percent of the 18- to 24-year-old population will be people of color, as will
37 percent of the 25- to 54-year-old population. The increasing multicultural mosaic of the U.S. population could not be more striking.

Given these projections, it is imperative that the United States address
the significant differences in college enrollments and educational attainment that exist among racial, ethnic, and income groups. According to the
U.S. Census Bureau, 39 percent of all white 18- to 24-year-olds were enrolled in a degree-granting institution in 1999. The comparable rates for African Americans and Hispanics were 30 percent and 19 percent, respectively. Public two-year colleges are more likely to have majority enrollments
of students of color than are four-year schools. In fact, 88 percent of the 206

TABLE 1
Projected Population Changes of Potential Adult and
Traditional-Age College Students, 2000–10

| Race/ | 18–24 Years Old | | | | 25–54 Years Old | | | |
Ethnicity	2000	2010	Difference	% Change	2000	2010	Difference	% Change
Asian	1,179,523	1,307,028	127,505	10.9	5,272,582	6,836,180	1,563,598	29.7
Black	3,971,659	4,768,030	796,371	20.1	15,261,504	16,911,314	1,649,810	10.8
Other Races	832,643	1,125,387	292,744	35.2	2,614,043	3,255,685	641,642	24.5
Hispanic	4,761,673	5,611,019	849,346	17.8	14,936,269	20,272,458	5,336,189	35.7
White, Non-Hispanic	16,921,934	18,142,017	1,220,083	7.2	85,981,744	81,818,560	–4,163,184	–4.8

Source: U.S. Census Bureau (2000), Population Projections of the United States, updated to reflect the 2000 Census (author calculations).

public two- and four-year colleges and universities that have 50 percent or more minority enrollments are community colleges (Price, 2004b). Enrollment gaps also remain between lower- and higher-income groups. In 2000, the college participation gap between low- and high-income students age 18 to 24 was almost 30 percent—the same level recorded in 1970 (College Board, 2002). In the 1999–2000 school year, 55 percent of dependent students from families with incomes below $30,000 and 65 percent of independent students with incomes below $20,000 were in community colleges as first-time undergraduates (Federico Cunningham, 2002).

Educational attainment gaps among various racial and ethnic groups are also growing. The U.S. Census reported in 1974 that 18 percent of white men had completed at least four years of college, which was nine percentage points higher than Hispanic men and 12 percentage points higher than African American men. Similarly, 11 percent of white women had completed at least four years of college, which was seven percentage points higher than Hispanic women and six percentage points higher than African American women. Between 1974 and 2000, the attainment gap between white and Hispanic men more than doubled, from nine percentage points to 20 percentage points; the attainment gap between white and black men also increased from 12 to 15 percentage points. The attainment gaps among white, black, and Hispanic women also increased over the last 25 years. Between 1974 and 2000, the attainment gap between white and Hispanic women doubled, from seven to 15 percentage points; the attainment gap between white and black women increased, from six to nine percentage points.

These gaps increased considerably, despite significant growth in educational attainment for all racial and ethnic groups over the previous three decades. In 2000, 31 percent of white men had completed at least four years of college—an increase of 13 percentage points since 1974. The percentage of African American men with at least a BA more than doubled to 16 percent, Hispanic men increased to 11 percent. Similarly, the percentage of white and Hispanic women who completed at least a BA more than doubled, to 26 percent and 11 percent, respectively, while the percentage of African American women with a BA more than tripled, to 17 percent.

Two important facts—that the vast majority of the growth of future college-eligible students will be students of color, and that students of color are disproportionately from lower-income households—highlight the demographic challenge that underscores the educational attainment paradox. For example, the Current Population Survey (U.S. Census Bureau, 2002a) indicates that 50 percent of Hispanic and 55 percent of black households (together comprising 23% of total households) had incomes in the lowest two quintiles. Comparatively, only 37 percent of white households, which make up about two-thirds of the total, had similarly low incomes. If equity in educational attainment is an important public value, then public policy must develop and implement strategies to expand access to higher education with an emphasis on Hispanics, African Americans, American Indians, and other low-income students (including whites).

The pathway to educational attainment is complex, and it requires personal and social resources including adequate financial investments, rigorous secondary school curriculum, broad dissemination of information about college admission requirements, and the availability of financial aid. Equally important is a welcoming campus culture that celebrates student diversity. The next section briefly summarizes the research describing the pipeline to a college degree and outlines the disadvantages facing students of color and low-income students.

THE PATHWAY TO A COLLEGE DEGREE

The pathway to a college degree requires significant personal and public financial investments. An important component of public investment in educational attainment is financial aid. According to the Advisory Committee on Student Financial Assistance (2002), more than 150,000 college-qualified students each year do not enroll in any postsecondary institution due to inadequate financial aid. Furthermore, the research and policy literatures indicate that an "affordability crisis" for low-income students and racial and ethnic minorities has affected the decision to enroll in college, the choice of postsecondary institution, and the ability to persist and attain a bachelor's degree (Cofer & Somers, 1999, 2000; Davis, 1997; Heller, 1997, 2002; Kane, 1999; Kipp, Price, & Wohlford, 2002; McPherson & Schapiro, 1998; National Center for Public Policy and Higher Education, 2002; Price, 2004a; St. John, 2003).

Yet educational attainment is not only about financial resources—it also reflects students' academic preparation and awareness of higher education opportunity, as well as whether or not a postsecondary campus environment effuses a culture of success (Lumina Foundation for Education, 2005). For example, the intensity and quality of secondary school curriculum have strong effects on bachelor's degree attainment, and these effects are more pronounced for African American and Latino students (Adelman, 1999). Unfortunately, low-income students and racial and ethnic minorities overwhelmingly attend secondary schools with significantly fewer resources than wealthier (and predominantly white) suburban schools (Frankenberg & Lee, 2002; NCES, 1998). Only 21 percent of high school graduates from families with incomes less than $25,000 were highly or very highly qualified for college, based on their secondary school curriculum, compared to 56 percent of high school graduates from families with incomes greater than $75,000 (NCES, 2001).

It is also widely understood by researchers and higher education leaders that information about postsecondary opportunities is unevenly available to students. For instance, low-income students rely almost exclusively on high school counselors for information about college while upper-income students report having a variety of sources—including parents, students, catalogues, college representatives, and private guidance counselors (Cabrera & La Nasa, 2000). Even when students and parents are aware of the importance of college, they often remain poorly informed about the actual price of college—a 2002 survey of adults indicated that the public significantly overestimates tuition and fees (American Council on Education, 2002). Moreover, more than two-thirds of students in sixth through twelfth grades (and 46% of their parents) are unable to hazard any guess about the price of college (NCES, 2001).

Finally, after students gain admission to college, the campus environment can also affect persistence and attainment. At a minimum, colleges and universities can provide student support services, such as engaging students in active learning, building supportive and inclusive communities, and setting high expectations to improve student retention (Gardner, Siegel, & Cutright, 2001; Woodard, Mallory, & De Luca, 2001). Segregation in public and private primary and secondary education may contribute to a "subtle, covert and blatant racism" that continues to permeate many U.S. colleges (Feagin, Vera, & Imani, 1996). Indeed, campuses can be intimidating for racial and ethnic minorities who enter predominantly white postsecondary institutions from almost exclusively nonwhite K–12 schools (Freeman, 1997). Put another way, colleges and universities that recruit and admit students of color inherit a "racial malaise" that must be addressed (Wathington, 2004). Higher education needs to both accommodate the reality that many white, black, Hispanic, and Native American students are not prepared for the diversity on college campuses, and also challenge the racially segregated backgrounds of their students by expanding knowledge for all students about diverse groups and their experiences (Wathington, 2004).

EQUITY INDICATORS AND THE ATTAINMENT GAP

A first step toward effectively closing the postsecondary educational attainment gap and addressing the many factors that contribute to it is to better understand the extent to which educational attainment equity remains an unaccomplished goal. The use of equity indicators to examine the progress of underserved students in postsecondary education is still quite rare. The scarcity of equity indicators is not because of a lack of data; rather, it is because data often are not disaggregated by race and ethnicity, and even when they are, they are not reported in accessible ways (Bensimon, Hao, & Bustillos, in press). Two of the few scholars who use equity indicators in their research are Estela Bensimon and Jeanne Oakes.

In 2000, Bensimon and her colleagues at the Center for Urban Education at the University of Southern California developed the Diversity Scorecard to examine inequities in educational outcomes for students of color in higher education and to close the achievement gap. From this perspective, educational inequity is a problem of institutional performance rather than a function of individual weaknesses or deficits (Bensimon, 2003). The key assumption of the Diversity Scorecard is that "evidence about equity in educational outcomes for underrepresented students presented in the form of graphically displayed quantitative data can have a powerful effect in mobilizing institutional attention and action" (Bensimon, 2004, p. 44). The Diversity Scorecard is thus an *intervention* through which college and university presidents, vice presidents, deans, counselors, and faculty use existing data to develop equity indicators, and then create a scorecard for their own campus. The purpose of this process is for leaders across a campus community to better understand inequity in educational outcomes by creating the tools that lead to self-recognition of the issues and subsequently inspire a widespread commitment to address them (Bensimon, 2004).

Oakes's project, the University of California All Campus Consortium on Research and Diversity (UC ACCORD), is also focused on equity in opportunity for underrepresented students. As part of her project, Oakes created the College Opportunities Ratio to measure the effectiveness of high schools in producing college-ready graduates. This equity indicator illustrates the relative preparedness of high school students from different racial and ethnic groups according to the high schools from which they graduated (Oakes, 2003). The goal for the UC ACCORD project is to help policymakers better understand barriers to equity in achievement and college-going, to encourage interventions to overcome these barriers, and to monitor a state's progress in removing them (Oakes, 2003).

Our aim for our Educational Attainment Parity Indicator (EAPI) is to contribute to the equity agenda in research by providing easy comparisons of educational attainment between and within states. In this way, the EAPI can raise awareness about the ongoing inequities in educational attainment among different racial and ethnic groups. We believe that closing the educational attainment gap and achieving equity for all requires new policy structures at the federal, state, and institutional levels. We offer the EAPI as an exploratory tool to bring to the attention of policymakers, educators, business and civic leaders, researchers, and community activists those situations where barriers to equity in educational attainment should be examined more closely. The next section introduces the Educational Attainment Parity Indicator, describes how it changes, and explains how policymakers and other stakeholders can use it.

THE EDUCATIONAL ATTAINMENT PARITY INDICATOR

The Educational Attainment Parity Indicator is a broad index that measures how men's and women's educational attainment compare across racial and ethnic groups. The EAPI measures a state's population 25 years and older who have obtained at least a BA relative to each racial, ethnic, and gender groups' share of the total population. An EAPI of 1.0 for any race-and-gender group (e.g., black females) indicates that the group has achieved educational attainment parity—an EAPI greater than 1.0 for a particular race-and-gender group indicates overrepresentation in educational attainment within the state. Conversely, an EAPI less than 1.0 signifies that a particular race-and-gender group is underrepresented in educational attainment within the state. Thus, the EAPI represents a simple index that measures the extent to which equity in educational attainment is present. The EAPI equation is as follows:

$$\frac{\text{Race-and-Gender BA / Total BA}}{\text{Race-and-Gender Population / Total Population}}$$

For example, the EAPI equation for black females, age 25 years and older, in Indiana, would look like this:

$$\frac{\text{Black Females in Indiana with at least BA / Total Population in Indiana with at least a BA}}{\text{Total Population of Black Females in Indiana / Total Population of Indiana}}$$

Mathematically, educational attainment parity among all groups requires that each group's EAPI converge to 1.0. If any group has an EAPI above 1.0, then it is evident that another group within the state has an EAPI below 1.0. Because this measure is centered on 1.0, comparisons of EAPI among states within race-and-gender groups *and* within states across race-and-gender groups are permissible.[3]

Data Sources and Limitations

Data for the EAPI come from the U.S. Decennial Census, 1960–2000. Although this measure succeeds at controlling for changes in the population of different race-and-gender groups nationally and by state, and further creates an indicator that is both comparative and standardized, it is nonetheless constrained due to data limitations. Specifically, the way the U.S. Census categorizes race and ethnicity increases in detail over time. In 1960, for example, educational attainment by state was aggregated only for "white" and "non-white" categories.[4] In the years prior to 1980, the Census Bureau used "4 or more years of college" rather than "bachelor's degree" as their measure of educational attainment. Thus, for the years prior to 1980 our measure considers "4 or more years of college" to be the equivalent of obtaining at least a bachelor's degree.

Despite these data limitations, longitudinal calculations of the EAPI can be useful tools for researchers and policymakers alike because they provide a simple relational measure of educational attainment among race-and-gender groups, accounting for population changes over time, and therefore allow for easy comparisons of educational attainment between states and within states.[5] In order for the EAPI to contribute to the public policy discourse on state trends in educational attainment, it is important to understand how a particular race-and-gender group's EAPI can change over time. Three different events can account for an increasing EAPI:

1. The percentage of a race-and-gender group with a BA increases faster than the group's total population. This is precisely the mark of a race-and-gender group making real educational attainment progress.
2. The percentage of a race-and-gender group with a BA declines but the total group's population declines faster. Although the EAPI will increase under this circumstance, it would not indicate a real closing of the educational attainment gap over time.
3. The percentage of a race-and-gender group with at least a BA increases faster than the total increase in bachelor's degrees for all groups combined. This circumstance also indicates progress for the particular race-and-gender group, but is not necessarily good for a state's overall goal of increasing educational attainment for all groups.

Similarly, three different events can account for a decreasing EAPI:

1. The percentage of a race-and-gender group with a BA increases, but not as fast as the total increase in bachelor's degrees for all groups combined. In this circumstance, the declining EAPI actually masks real progress in educational attainment for the particular race-and-gender group. At the same time, because other groups' attainment is increasing at a faster rate than the particular group, the gaps in educational attainment between race-and-gender groups are also increasing, thus perpetuating the educational attainment paradox. However, if a group experiences a decreasing EAPI, this is the best of the three possible situations for it to occur in.
2. The percentage of a race-and-gender group with a BA declines faster than the group's total population.
3. The group's total population increases faster than the group's BA population.

As an indicator, the EAPI can be used to measure progress for a particular race or ethnic group. From a policy perspective, however, it is insufficient to use the EAPI without examining further the causes of the changes in the indicator. As described above, the reasons for changes in the Educational Attainment Parity Indicator can reflect both population changes (in terms of shares for each race or ethnic group) as well as educational attainment gains (in terms of the proportion of adults age 25 years and older with at least a BA). Therefore, it is important to understand whether increases in the EAPI for any group are a function of declining shares of a state's population or, more favorably, of a faster increase in the proportion of any race or ethnic group with at least a BA compared to their general population growth.

States should explore several questions regarding their EAPI scores, which may be influenced by the in- and out-migration of educated populations, or by changes in the total population of less educated adults. For the former, states might examine their policies related to economic development, as well as other policies that influence the likelihood of attracting and retaining college-educated populations, particularly among blacks, Hispanics, and Native Americans. For the latter, states might consider enacting specific programs and policies targeted to increase these groups' college preparation, awareness, participation, and attainment.

Because the EAPI is also affected by real gains in educational attainment (i.e., a group's proportion of overall college graduates is increasing faster than the group's share of the overall population), states have an opportunity to learn about policies that work to increase educational attainment. For example, states could determine which policies and practices they have enacted that might account for a group's increasing (or decreasing) EAPI and expand or contract such programs accordingly. In short, because the EAPI is an indicator, it is a useful measure of a state's progress in producing and retaining college graduates. However, the real value of the measure comes when states and other stakeholders take the initiative to determine the root causes of their EAPI scores. While the EAPI is intended for state-level action, for the purposes of this chapter and introducing the indicator, the next section provides a national perspective of the changes in EAPI since 1960.

THE NATIONAL TREND IN EDUCATIONAL ATTAINMENT PARITY

The broadest picture of the national trend in educational attainment parity suggests that racial and ethnic minorities made considerable progress between 1960 and 1980, but that this progress has slowed and, for some groups, even reversed since 1980 (see Figure 1). For example, the growth in educational attainment for nonwhite women increased significantly from 1960 to 1980 (especially between 1970 and 1980), but has slowed considerably since 1980. Similarly, nonwhite men saw gains in educational attainment between 1960 and 1980, but the EAPI has declined consistently since 1980. In contrast, the growth in educational attainment for white women was quite modest from 1960 to 1980 and accelerated after 1980. In fact, the national EAPI for white women in 2000 indicates that they have achieved educational attainment parity based on the share of white women in the population.

The trend in the EAPI for white men is a slow and steady decline. Even with a declining EAPI, white men remained the largest single group with BAs in 2000, and their EAPI of 1.20 indicates that white men remained overrepresented among adults with at least a BA. In fact, this EAPI decline is not because fewer white men are earning a bachelor's degree; rather, the decline in the EAPI is largely a function of white men becoming a smaller share of the population with a BA and a smaller share of the total population.

Examining Educational Attainment Parity among the 50 States, 1980–2000 [6]

Because a shift in educational attainment trends occurred after 1980 and because the U.S. Census began collecting better data on race and ethnicity after 1974, we examine the EAPI for blacks, Hispanics, and Native Americans as defined in the 1980 U.S. Census. Figure 2 illustrates the national trend in the EAPI from 1980 to 2000. The disaggregated data are generally consistent with the national picture during the last four decades. For example, non-Hispanic white men remain overrepresented among adults with at least a BA, but because they are becoming a smaller share of the population with a BA and a smaller share of the total population, the EAPI for non-Hispanic white men is declining. In addition, the EAPI trajectory for non-Hispanic white women indicates significant gains in educational attainment, especially since 1980, and also suggests that non-Hispanic white women have achieved educational attainment parity.

The trend in the EAPI for black, Hispanic, and Native American men and women is not very positive. In simple terms, educational attainment equity is not present for Hispanics, blacks, and Native Americans. In fact, in 2000 educational attainment was between 38 and 56 percentage points below parity for racial and ethnic minorities. At the same time, there is a con-

FIGURE 1
National Trends in Educational Attainment Equity, 1960–2000

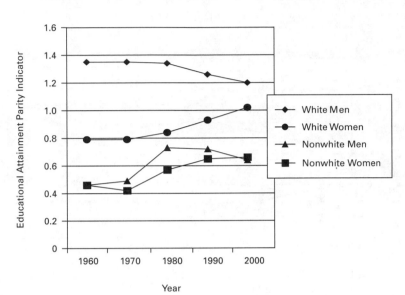

Source: U.S. Census Bureau (1960, 1970, 1980, 1990, 2000; author calculations).

siderable and discouraging gender gap among racial and ethnic minorities. On the one hand, the EAPI improved for Native American, Hispanic, and black women between 1980 and 2000. In contrast, the EAPI declined for Hispanic and Native American men during this period, and was essentially flat for black men. In the following sections, we describe the changes in EAPI for black, Hispanic, and Native American men and women between 1980 and 2000.

African Americans
Despite the growth in educational attainment nationally, there remains a significant gap in educational attainment for black men and women. Nationally, despite modest gains in the EAPI for nonwhite men and women between 1960 and 1980, black men have experienced very little progress in educational attainment parity during the past two decades—the EAPI was basically flat, increasing only two percentage points between 1980 and 2000, to .54. In 30 states and the District of Columbia, the EAPI declined

FIGURE 2

National Trends in Educational Attainment Equity, 1980–2000

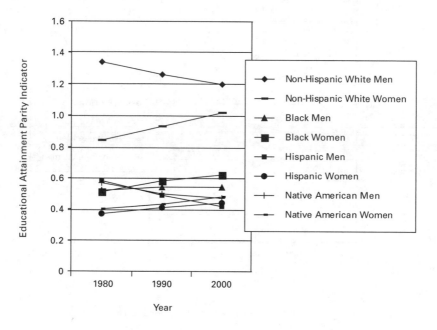

Source: U.S. Census Bureau (1980, 1990, 2000; author calculations).

between 1980 and 2000. In the highly populous states of New York and Pennsylvania, this decline was modest—falling one percentage point. However, in eight states, the EAPI declined between five and ten percentage points, and in eight other states, it declined by more than ten percentage points.

In contrast, the trajectory of EAPI in 17 states was much more promising for black men. At first glance, many of the states that showed a positive change in EAPI since 1980 have very small African American populations (e.g., Montana, Wyoming, Alaska, Maine, and Hawaii). But some states with large African American populations also showed impressive gains in EAPI. For example, the EAPI for black men in Texas and Georgia improved by ten percentage points. These states should seek further data to determine whether or not the changes in EAPI are real or a function of declining population shares. The important point from a national perspective is that educational attainment equity for black men is regressing in the majority of states.

Between 1980 and 2000, the national EAPI trajectory for African American women was positive—nationally, black women gained 11 percentage points on the EAPI, but again, these gains are uneven among the 50 states. In the majority of states and the District of Columbia, the EAPI for black women increased, but these increases varied considerably. One reason that the national EAPI increased is that the EAPI in highly populous states like California and New York increased faster than the nation. In California, the EAPI for black women improved by 14 percentage points to .67, and in New York the EAPI improved by 16 percentage points to .61. In six states, however, the EAPI for black women declined during the past two decades. And, although the EAPI for black women increased by 11 percentage points during the last two decades, it remains far below parity (.62) in 2000.

Hispanics

Between 1980 and 2000, the national EAPI for Hispanic men declined by 16 percentage points, to only .42. This movement away from educational attainment parity could have been worse, but states with large Hispanic populations (e.g., Texas, New York, California, and Arizona) had much smaller declines in the EAPI during this period. At the same time, these states have a vast distance to go before educational attainment parity can be achieved. For example, the EAPI in California is only .29, which is considerably lower than the national EAPI for Hispanic men. The EAPI for Hispanic men in Texas, New York, and Arizona is also very low: .38, .39, and .35, respectively. Put simply, in the four states with very high Hispanic populations, educational attainment of Hispanic men must almost triple in order to achieve equity.

The trend toward educational attainment equity for Hispanic women is not so bleak—but there is a long way to go. Between 1980 and 2000, the EAPI for Hispanic women improved by seven percentage points nationally, to .44. In ten states, the EAPI remained flat or improved modestly at a rate below the national EAPI. For example, the EAPI for Hispanic women in New York improved 14 percentage points, to .44, between 1980 and 2000. The EAPI for Hispanic women in Texas and Arizona also improved faster than the national trend (by 13 and 12 percentage points, respectively). In contrast, the EAPI for Hispanic women in California and Florida grew by only five percentage points between 1980 and 2000. As with African American men and women, however, not all states made improvements during the past two decades. In fact, 16 states and the District of Columbia had decreases in the EAPI for Hispanic women.

Native Americans

The national pattern for Native American men and women between 1980 and 2000 mirrors that of Hispanics—a positive EAPI trend for Native American women and negative trajectory for Native American men. During the last two decades, the EAPI for Native American men declined nationally by 11 percentage points to .47. Although the EAPI declined in 37 states, many of which have a very small proportion of Native American students, several states with large Native American populations had smaller declines or modest increases in the EAPI between 1980 and 2000. For example, the EAPI for Native American men in Arizona and North Dakota declined by only two percentage points. On the other hand, the EAPI for Native American men in Montana, Minnesota, and New Mexico improved by nine percentage points, three percentage points, and one percentage point, respectively.

In contrast, the EAPI for Native American women increased by eight percentage points nationally. In fact, the EAPI for Native American women improved in all but four states and the District of Columbia. These changes do not necessarily indicate large progress toward equality in educational attainment; indeed, the 2000 EAPI of .48 is far below parity. A recent report prepared for the American Indian College Fund emphasizes the importance of tribal colleges for Native Americans as a "nexus for economic development, community education, and Indian languages and culture" (Voorhees, 2003, p. 1). The role of these institutions in providing postsecondary education opportunity for Native Americans could explain why some states with large increases in the EAPI for Native American women are those with tribal colleges. For example, the EAPI in Wisconsin improved by 25 percentage points, to .52. In addition, the EAPI in North Dakota increased by 22 percentage points and the EAPI in Washington and Montana increased by 15 percentage points. Among states with tribal colleges, only in New Mexico and Minnesota did the growth in the EAPI for Native American women increase more slowly than the national trend.

In addition to examining the changes in EAPI to ascertain if an increasing EAPI documents progress toward educational attainment equity, policymakers also need to be aware of the federal and state policy context that affects the pathway to a college degree. From a national perspective, the movement toward educational attainment equity has regressed for black, Hispanic, and Native American men, and, at its best, improved slightly for black, Hispanic, and Native American women. Several state and federal policy trends, especially those related to financing higher education, may be contributing to the nation's paralysis in achieving educational attainment equity.

THE PUBLIC POLICY CONTEXT OF HIGHER EDUCATION

Given the slowed progress toward educational attainment parity since 1980 for blacks, Latinos, and Native Americans, it is reasonable to examine the ways public support for higher education has changed during the last two decades. One of the most important ways federal and state governments provide opportunity for individuals to attend college is through state appropriations that benefit all students regardless of need, and through state and federal financial aid programs that target students who meet specific eligibility criteria (see Heller, this volume, for a detailed discussion of the issue). In these areas, four key trends are clearly visible since 1980:

1. Federal financial aid has shifted significantly away from grants toward loans; in 2004, federal grants made up only about one-fifth of total federal student financial aid.
2. State appropriations continue to grow, though far less rapidly than the cost of college—reaching almost $64 billion in 2003—but the share of state appropriations that cover general and educational expenditures at colleges and universities has declined by 25 percent during the previous two decades.
3. Tuition and fees, as well as the total price for college, are increasing significantly faster than overall inflation—and more importantly are growing faster than family median income.
4. State student financial aid is also growing overall, but this aid is increasingly rewarded based on "merit" rather than need—moreover, three-fourths of the total need-based state grant aid is provided by just ten states.

These trends reflect a shift in public policy away from universal access and equal opportunity toward personal investment and stratified opportunity (Price, 2004a).

The changing demographics of college-eligible students, combined with a federal and state policy environment that increasingly relies on student loans, non-need-based financial aid, and higher tuition, represent the social, political, and economic context of the educational attainment paradox. The significant changes in the federal and state policy context, especially since 1980, should be further explored as a possible explanation for the trajectory of the Educational Attainment Parity Indicator for African American, Hispanic, and Native American men and women.

ACHIEVING EQUITY FOR AFRICAN AMERICANS, HISPANICS, AND NATIVE AMERICANS

If educational attainment parity among different racial and ethnic groups is an important goal, and we believe it is for a multicultural democracy, then policymakers, along with business, civic, and higher education leaders throughout the United States, must face up to the looming demographic challenge facing our higher education system. In this decade, almost two of every five adults between 18 and 54 years of age will be people of color. It is fundamental that public policies and institutional practices reflect the increasingly diverse demographic of postsecondary education.

To help facilitate this, existing and new data must be collected and reported in ways that make the importance of equity in educational attainment clear to a broad section of policymakers and other national, state, and local leaders. More detailed data collection regarding income and educational attainment would contribute significantly to our understanding of student access and success. Also, because a state's EAPI can be greatly affected by state-to-state migration and immigration rates, better data on the relationship between these factors and educational attainment would help states formulate intentional strategies to improve educational attainment.

Second, broad equity indicators such as the EAPI represent only the first stage of inquiry and examination. State and local leaders, including researchers and policy analysts, need to further investigate changes in each state and community in order to craft appropriate policies and practices that improve educational opportunity and attainment. Immigration patterns, economic changes, and population projections are the most obvious areas where additional analyses can help inform the public discourse around higher education. If they have not already done so, states should examine the economic impact (including the tax base) of demographic changes tied to differential educational attainment rates, and disseminate the results to the state's political and business leadership.

Additionally, given that a state's EAPI is affected not just by the attainment rates of traditional-age students but also by the attainment rates of adults, it is important to understand the demographic projections for a state's future college-going pool and workforce. While some states will experience significant growth in the number of high school graduates, other states may experience larger growth among adults already in the workforce. For states in the former category, focusing on academic preparation, awareness, and information for future high school graduates may be the most effective way to reduce gaps in college enrollment and educational attainment. In contrast, states with growing adult populations could increase educational attainment and make real progress on the EAPI by investing in recruitment and retraining for adult students. For example, states could increase funding for adult basic education and other programs, and improve policies and practices that create seamless articulation for adults among two-year and four-year postsecondary education providers.

Furthermore, the federal and state policy context cannot be ignored as a partial contributor to the growing gaps in educational attainment among different racial and ethnic groups. During the last two decades, students and families have experienced escalating prices for higher education and increasingly relied on borrowing to pay for college. A broad body of research suggests that making college more affordable and expanding access for diverse students cannot be accomplished if the current public policy trends summarized in this chapter continue unabated. In short, bold thinking is needed around federal, state, and institutional investments in higher education that focus on 1) containing college costs, 2) keeping tuition levels aligned with families' abilities to pay, 3) increasing need-based grant aid, and 4) reducing the reliance on student loans.

Researchers and analysts are generating innovative ideas to address these four components of more equitable public policy to increase college access and to close educational attainment gaps. For example, scholars from Teachers College at Columbia University propose a National Tuition Endowment (NTE) to provide financial aid scholarships for students to attend college (see Fermin, 2005). In *Borrowing Inequality: Race, Class and Student Loans*, Price (2004a) describes an education trust through which the federal government could originate all loans to students and potentially free up almost $8 billion in subsidized interest payments that could be redirected to increase the Pell Grant maximum. A new, higher Pell Grant could then cover 100 percent of tuition and fees at virtually all public two-year and four-year colleges.

A third innovative idea is to truly "leverage" LEAP (the federal government's Leveraging Educational Assistance Program) to encourage additional investments in need-based aid. LEAP currently matches state investments for need-based aid: in 1999–2000, 1.3 million students received LEAP funds, but the government appropriated only $67 million in 2002–03 for this program (Wolanin, 2003). Why should federal investments in LEAP be limited to matched dollars from other public resources? A renewed federal commitment to LEAP could leverage federal investments with matched resources from both states *and* private organizations.

Put simply, states can no longer afford to be complacent about student educational attainment. The EAPI offers a simple, comparable indicator for states to begin their assessment. When compared over time, the EAPI represents a useful tool to highlight state and national trends toward equity for African Americans, Hispanics, and Native Americans—the very people who must become the next generation of college-educated Americans in order for the future workforce to meet the demands of the 21st century knowledge economy. Data clearly indicate that black, Hispanic, and Native-American populations have not only lower BA attainment rates than non-Hispanic whites and Asians, but also lower high school graduation rates. States need innovative strategies to address the leaks along the pipeline to college, and to expand access points to postsecondary education and training for adults.

In sum, addressing the color line continues to be the challenge for universal access to higher education and for equity in educational attainment. This challenge requires bold ideas and innovative thinking. The solution will require better data and more research focused on racial and economic equity, a national public commitment to higher education for all (especially blacks, Hispanics, and Native Americans, and low-income students from all racial and ethnic groups), and a shared willingness from many stakeholders to invest significantly in the nation's future. We offer the EAPI as a contribution to a new social compact in higher education with a clearly articulated goal of educational attainment equity.

NOTES

1. The U.S. Census changed the way it asks about educational attainment in 1980 to specify the level of degree; before 1980, the question asked about the number of years of college completed.
2. For this chapter, for general use the terms *people* or *students of color* and *minority* are used interchangeably and include African Americans, Asians, and other non-white racial/ethnic groups including Latinos of any race; however, when discussing trends in the Educational Attainment Parity Indicator, the terms *people* or *students of color* refer to blacks, Hispanics, and Native Americans as defined by the U.S. Census.

3. Although mathematically the EAPI represents the ratio of two other ratios, it varies around 1.0, which allows for a simple interpretation of each one-hundredth change in the EAPI as a "percentage point."
4. According to the U.S. Census Bureau (2002b), in 1960, Puerto Ricans, Mexicans, and other people of Latin descent were to be coded as "white" unless, through observation, it was clear that they were "Negro, Indian, or some other race."
5. A report from the National Center for Higher Education Management Systems (in press) adapts the EAPI to reflect international standards of educational attainment, and also documents the growing attainment gaps among different racial and ethnic groups within the 50 states.
6. We exclude Asian men and women from this analysis for two reasons: 1) the data indicate considerable overrepresentation of Asian men and women (i.e., over twice as many Asian men and women have at least a BA than would be estimated based on their share of the total population), and 2) the diversity among Asian groups makes interpretation of the Asian EAPI difficult. Although a similar point can be made about the Hispanic category, in our opinion, the overall size of the Hispanic population necessitates an examination of EAPI. However, the results discussed in the chapter do not account for potential differences of Hispanic groups who might be more accurately categorized as Mexican, Chicano, or Cuban.

REFERENCES

Adelman, C. (1999). *Answers in the tool box: Academic intensity, attendance patterns and bachelor's degree attainment.* Washington, DC: U.S. Department of Education, OERI.

Advisory Committee on Student Financial Assistance. (2002). *Empty promises: The myth of college access in America.* Washington, DC: Author.

American Council on Education. (2002). *Attitudes towards public higher education.* Washington, DC: Author.

Bensimon, E. M. (2003). *Why equity matters: Implications for democracy.* Los Angeles: University of Southern California, Center for Urban Education. Retrieved September 17, 2004, from http://www.usc.edu/dept/education/CUE/documents/viewbook.pdf

Bensimon, E. M. (2004, January/February). The diversity scorecard: A learning approach to institutional change. *Change,* 44–52.

Bensimon, E. M., Hao, L., & Bustillos, L. T. (in press). Measuring the state of higher education equity in public higher education. In P. Gándara, G. Orfield, & C. L. Horn (Eds.), *Leveraging promise: Expanding opportunity in higher education.* Albany: State University of New York Press.

Cabrera, A. F., & La Nasa, S. M. (2000). *Understanding the college choice of disadvantaged students.* San Francisco: Jossey-Bass.

Cofer, J., & Somers, P. (1999). An analytical approach to understanding student debt load response. *Journal of Student Financial Aid, 29*(3), 25–44.

Cofer, J., & Somers, P. (2000). A comparison of the influence of debt load on the persistence of students at public and private colleges. *Journal of Student Financial Aid, 30*(2), 39–58.

College Board. (2002). *Trends in college pricing, 2002.* New York: Author.

Davis, J. S. (1997). *College affordability: A closer look at the crisis.* Reston, VA: Sallie Mae Education Institute.

Feagin, J. R., Vera, H., & Imani, N. (1996). *The agony of education: Black students at white colleges and universities.* New York: Routledge.

Federico Cunningham, A. (2002). *The policy of choice: Expanding student options in higher education.* Washington, DC: Institute for Higher Education Policy.

Fermin, B. J. (2005, January). *Re-directing efficiency: A remedy for cost barriers to postsecondary education.* Paper presented at the EAIR/AIR Joint Seminar on the Quality, Cost, and Access Dilemma in Higher Education, Miami.

Frankenberg, E., & Lee, C. (2002, August). *Race in American public schools: Rapidly resegregating school districts.* Cambridge, MA: Civil Rights Project, Harvard University.

Freeman, K. (1997). Increasing African-Americans' participation in higher education. *Journal of Higher Education, 68,* 523–550.

Gardner, J. N., Siegel, M. J., & Cutright, M. (2001). Focusing on the first-year student. *AGB Priorities, 17,* 1–17.

Heller, D. E. (1997). Student price response in higher education: An update to Leslie and Brinkman. *Journal of Higher Education, 68*(6), 624–659.

Heller, D. E. (Ed.). (2002). *Condition of access: Higher education for lower income students.* Westport, CT: Praeger Publishers, American Council on Education.

Kane, T. J. (1999). *The price of admission: Rethinking how Americans pay for college.* Washington, DC: Brookings Institution Press.

Kipp, S., III, Price, D. V., & Wohlford, J. K. (2002). *Unequal opportunities: Disparities in college access across the fifty states.* Indianapolis: Lumina Foundation for Education.

Lumina Foundation for Education. (2005). *What we know about access and success.* Indianapolis: Author.

McPherson, M., & Schapiro, M. O. (1998). *The student aid game: Meeting need and rewarding talent in higher education.* Princeton, NJ: Princeton University Press.

National Center for Education Statistics. (1998). *Inequalities in public school district revenues.* Washington, DC: Author.

National Center for Education Statistics. (2001). *The condition of education, 2001.* Washington, DC: Author.

National Center for Education Statistics. (2002). *Digest of education statistics, 2001.* Washington, DC: Author.

National Center for Higher Education Management Systems. (in press). *As America becomes more diverse: The impact of state higher education inequality.* Boulder, CO: Author.

National Center for Public Policy and Higher Education. (2002). *Losing ground: A national status report on the affordability of American higher education.* San Jose, CA: Author.

Oakes, J. (2003). *Critical conditions for equity and diversity in college access: Informing policy and monitoring results.* Los Angeles: University of California at Los Angeles, UC/ACCORD. Retrieved September 17, 2004, from http://www.ucaccord.gseis.ucla.edu/indicators/pdfs/criticalconditions.pdf

Price, D. V. (2004a). *Borrowing inequality: Race, class and student loans*. Boulder, CO: Lynne Rienner.

Price, D. V. (2004b). Defining the gaps: Access and success at America's community colleges. In K. Boswell & C. D. Wilson (Eds.), *Keeping America's promise: A report on the future of the community college* (pp. 34–37). Denver: Education Commission of the States.

St. John, E. P. (2003). *Refinancing the college dream: Access, equal opportunity, and justice for taxpayers*. Baltimore: Johns Hopkins University Press.

U.S. Census Bureau. (2002a). *Current Population Survey, March*. Washington, DC: Author.

U.S. Census Bureau. (2002b). *Measuring America: The decennial censuses from 1790 to 2000* (POL/02-MA). Washington, DC: Author.

Voorhees, R. A. (2003). *The status of student information at tribal colleges and universities*. Littleton, CO: Voorhees Group, LLC. Retrieved February 22, 2005, from www.voorheesgroup.org/Status%20of%20TCU%20Student%20Information.pdf

Wathington, H. (2004). *In search of the beloved community: Understanding student interaction across racial and ethnic communities*. Unpublished doctoral dissertation. University of Michigan, Ann Arbor.

Western Interstate Commission on Higher Education. (2003). *Knocking at the college door: Projections of high school graduates by state, income and race/ethnicity, 1998–2018*. Boulder, CO: Author.

Wolanin, T. R. (Ed.) (2003). *HEA: Reauthorizing the Higher Education Act*. Washington, DC: Institute for Higher Education Policy.

Woodard, D. B., Jr., Mallory, S. L., & De Luca, A. M. (2001). Retention and institutional effort: A self-study framework. *NASPA Journal, 39*(1), 53–83.

Thanks to Jerry Davis, Deborah Bonnet, Fred Galloway, Dewayne Matthews, and members of the Financial Aid Research Network for their comments and suggestions. The views and opinions expressed in this paper are exclusively those of the authors and are not necessarily those of Lumina Foundation for Education, Inc.

4

Can Minority Students Afford College in an Era of Skyrocketing Tuition?

DONALD E. HELLER

Much attention has been paid in the media, as well as among policy-makers and researchers, to the large increases in college tuition in recent decades. The College Board, which conducts an annual survey of tuition prices at over 2,000 higher education institutions across the nation, has documented the rise in prices over the last three decades (College Board, 2004a). Average tuition prices at public four-year colleges and universities increased 732 percent between 1976 and 2004, while they increased 634 percent at community colleges and 693 percent at private four-year institutions.[1] The 2004–05 academic year saw prices cross three symbolic thresholds, with average tuition reaching $20,082 at private four-year institutions, $5,132 at public four-year institutions, and $2,076 at community colleges.

In contrast to the rise in tuition prices, the Consumer Price Index increased just 230 percent (Bureau of Labor Statistics, 2004), and median family income in the nation increased only 252 percent (U.S. Census Bureau, 2004a, 2004b).[2] The growth in tuition prices has far outpaced the growth in prices for other goods and services, and the ability of students and families to pay for college.

Because minority students come from families that, on average, have lower incomes, they are most affected by rising tuition prices.[3] For example, data from the 2000 Census indicate that while white families nationally had median incomes of $54,698 in 1999, black, Native American, and Hispanic families all had median incomes below $35,000 (U.S. Census Bureau,

2005a). While at least 17 percent of black, Native American, and Hispanic families in 1999 were living with incomes below the federal poverty level, only 4 percent of white families were (U.S. Census Bureau, 2005b).

Recent trends in college pricing are the culmination of a much longer tradition in this country of requiring that students and their families share in the cost of a postsecondary education.[4] The colonial colleges, beginning with the founding of Harvard College in 1636, charged fees to students—and offered financial assistance to those who could not afford the fees (Holtschneider, 1997). Even though many public institutions were chartered with the requirement that they offer a postsecondary education free of charge—and were assisted in doing so by the Morrill Act of 1862, which created federal land grants to help states support public institutions of higher education—some were already charging tuition and fees to their students.

An early 20th-century study documented annual tuition and fee rates of $12 at the University of Wisconsin (1855), $10 at the University of Tennessee (1866), $5 at the University of Illinois (1868), $15 at Ohio State (1874), and $5 at the University of Missouri (1874; Sears, 1923). Thus, it is clear that the concept of asking students to help share the burden of paying for their postsecondary education—a rationale described by one author as helping to ensure "that the student would appreciate his work more if he paid something for it" (Morey, 1928, p. 186)—is well-rooted in American public higher education.

From the nominal tuition charges first imposed in the 19th century, fees continued to rise in the 20th century, from an average of approximately $50 per year in the 1920s to $80 by 1940 (Holst, 1923; President's Commission on Higher Education, 1947; Sears, 1923). By 1964—at which point the federal Office of Education, and later the Department of Education, began to track prices—the average tuition at a public university had risen to $298.

Tuition prices by themselves, however, do not determine how much each student has to pay for college. Student financial aid—in the form of grants, loans, tax credits, and work study assistance—provides resources to help reduce the cost of attending college or postpone paying for it. And just as tuition prices have risen over the years, so has the availability of financial aid. In 1976, approximately $10.3 billion in aid was available for all students in higher education; by 2003 this had increased more than tenfold, to $122 billion (College Board, 2004b).

Some of the increase in financial aid is offset by increasing enrollments in higher education. Between 1976 and 2003, overall enrollment in the nation (undergraduate and graduate combined) increased 44 percent, from 11 million to 15.8 million (Gerald & Hussar, 2002; National Center for Education Statistics, 2003). Taking these enrollment changes into account, financial aid resources increased almost as fast, from $936 per student in 1976 to $7,723 in 2003, an increase of 725 percent that is still in line with the increase in tuition prices noted earlier. While financial aid has indeed increased, there has been a radical shift in the nature of the aid that is available, a topic I return to later in this chapter.

These trends in tuition prices and financial aid have important implications for college access and affordability, particularly for students from families with the fewest resources available to help pay for college. As described earlier, many of these are minority students, who historically have been underrepresented in American higher education. This chapter opens with an overview of the research on finances and college access, and then provides a summary of recent trends in federal, state, and institutional financial aid policy. I then turn to the details of the prices—both sticker and net of financial aid—that students pay to attend college, as well as what type of financial aid they receive, in order to paint a portrait of the state of college affordability for minority students in the United States. I conclude with what the future is likely to hold if existing trends continue with respect to college affordability for minority students.

RESEARCH ON TUITION PRICES, FINANCIAL AID, AND COLLEGE ACCESS

There is a long and rich history of research that has examined the relationship between college tuition prices, financial aid availability, and the decisions that potential students make about enrolling in college. This research is often referred to as "student price responsiveness," "student demand," or "student price elasticity" studies. Reviews of much of this research have been published over the last three decades by Heller (1997), Jackson and Weathersby (1975), and Leslie and Brinkman (1988).

While these studies have utilized a broad range of research methodologies, have used different samples of students, and have been conducted at different times, there are a number of tenets that are generally accepted by both researchers and higher education policymakers alike. These include:

- Higher education is like most goods and services in our economy—as its price rises, individuals are likely to consume less of it (i.e., be less likely to enroll in college and persist once there), all other things being equal.

- Higher education is what economists refer to as a "normal" good—all other things being equal, as real incomes rise, more students will enroll in college.
- Tuition price changes and financial aid changes have differing effects on students—a $100 increase in price is likely to have a greater impact on college enrollment behavior than is a $100 decrease in financial aid (the "sticker price phenomenon").
- Different types of financial aid have a varying impact on college enrollment behavior. In general, need-based grants tend to have a stronger influence on college access than college loans or work study.
- Students with varying characteristics have different reactions to changes in tuition prices and financial aid offers. In general, African American, Hispanic, and low-income students tend to be more price responsive (i.e., are less likely to enroll in college or change the type of institution in which they enroll in the face of tuition increases) than are white and middle- and upper-income students.
- Enrollments in community colleges tend to be more price responsive than enrollments in four-year institutions, though much of this effect appears to be because of the disproportionate share of lower-income students who enroll in community colleges.
- Tuition and financial aid policies in one college sector can influence enrollments in a different sector ("cross-sector price elasticities"), though these effects are generally not as large as the reaction to same-sector price changes.

There are a number of important caveats to be aware of when considering these findings. First, the reader should remember that these effects are generally consistent when you are examining the behavior of large populations of students. You cannot use these to predict with certainty how a particular policy change may affect the behavior of any single student, or the aggregate behavior of a relatively small group of students, or even enrollment in a single state.

Second, it is also important for policymakers and other observers to keep in mind that the research shows that financial issues—such as tuition prices and financial aid—are only one factor in the decisions made by most students about enrolling in college. Other factors, when taken together, also play an important role in influencing college enrollment behavior. These factors include the student's academic aptitude and achievement; course-taking patterns in high school and earlier grades; the role of parents, siblings, peers, and others in promoting college as a post-high school option; the proximity of postsecondary education institutions; and economic conditions such as the status of the local economy and labor markets. Nevertheless, college pricing and financial aid policies are important levers in influencing college-going behavior for one critical reason: They are among the only factors that are under the direct control of postsecondary education policymakers in state governments, the federal government, and in public and private colleges and universities. In addition, the financial factors play an overarching role for students from low-income families because of the lack of resources of their own for paying for college.

Third, researchers do not know whether the effects of price changes on enrollment are exactly symmetrical, that is, whether the findings outlined above regarding the effects of price increases would be the same size in the opposite direction in the case of a price decrease. Some research has been conducted on public sector tuition price cuts enacted in the mid-1990s, when some states (including Arkansas, California, Massachusetts, and Virginia) experimented by cutting the tuition price at public institutions. There is some evidence that these price cuts helped spur overall enrollment growth, when compared to states that continued to increase tuition prices (Swail & Heller, 2004). But this research has not examined whether the tuition cuts benefited lower-income and minority students.

Fourth, and perhaps most important, all other things are *not* equal. When economists and other researchers analyze the effects of a particular policy change, it is generally done with the assumption that all other factors are held constant or unchanged, or what economists refer to as *ceteris paribus* (Latin for "other things being equal"). However, in real life it is rare for the researcher to be assured that all other things are truly equal, especially when examining changes over time.

For example, as described earlier, tuition prices in both public and private colleges have experienced unprecedented increases since the 1970s, increases that far outpace the change in the ability of students and their families to pay for them. In addition, the 1980s and early 1990s were the "baby-bust era," when many observers expected college enrollments to decline due to the shrinking pool of high school graduates. Yet even in the face of escalating prices and declining demographics, college enrollments continued to rise during this era. The reason? Most analysts point to changes in the labor market and, specifically, the increase in the college wage premium (the higher wages earned by college graduates relative to those without a college degree) over the last 20 years. Most youth understand that to earn a decent wage in today's global and information economy, a salary that used to be described as one with which you could support a family in a middle-class lifestyle, you have to go to college. Thus, today's students are more willing to endure higher relative prices to go to college (and earn the requisite rewards in the labor markets) than were students a generation earlier.

The lesson to remember from this caveat is that the predictions about how a particular policy change may impact college participation are made with the assumption of *ceteris paribus*. If other factors that affect college participation change simultaneously with the targeted policy change, the overall impact on college-going behavior may be quite different from what one would expect. However, in the absence of other changes, the research is quite clear in determining that rising tuition prices will restrict access for low-income and minority students, and that need-based grants can help protect these students from rising prices.

RECENT TRENDS IN FINANCIAL AID POLICY

Trends in Federal Aid

Over $122 billion in student financial aid was available from all sources and for all students (undergraduate and graduate) in the 2003–04 academic year (College Board, 2004b).[5] The distribution by type of aid was:

- loans: $68.1 billion (56%)
- grants: $46.5 billion (38%)
- federal tax credits: $6.3 billion (5%)
- federal work study assistance: $1.2 billion (1%)

The federal government is the largest single source of aid, providing $81.5 billion, or 67 percent of the total available aid. The bulk of this support, $56.8 billion, or 70 percent of the total provided by the federal government, was in the form of loans. Over the last three decades, loans have grown to supplant grants as the primary form of federal student aid. In 1974, the first full year of operation of the Basic Educational Opportunity Grant program (later renamed Pell Grants after Senator Claiborne Pell), 70 percent of federal aid was provided in the form of grants and 25 percent in the form of loans (with the remainder in work study).

The passage of the Middle Income Student Assistance Act (MISAA) in 1978 was a turning point in the history of federal student aid. This act removed the means testing from the federal subsidized loan programs, thus opening them up to all students. Within two years, federal loan volume outpaced grants for the first time, and even though means-testing was restored to the federal loan programs three years later, the growth of these programs has far outpaced that of grants and other forms of aid. Since 1974, spending on federal grants has increased from $5.0 billion to $17.2 billion, or 244 percent. During the same period, federal loan volume has increased from $1.8 billion to $56.8 billion, or 3,055 percent.

Loans, unlike grants, do not lower the price of attending college. Rather, they allow students to postpone when they pay for college and to go to college when they could not otherwise pay the bill. There are also important differences between various types of loans. For example, federal subsidized college loans offer an interest rate subsidized below market levels, and the government pays the interest on the loans as long as the student is enrolled in college. In contrast, private loans offer neither of these advantages to the borrower.

The emphasis on loans in the federal aid programs is at least in part due to increasing political support for assistance for middle-income families. This focus has helped to erode the support for Pell Grants, which predominantly serve students from families earning below the national median income. In 1976, the maximum Pell Grant award of $1,400 was approximately 72 percent of the tuition and fees, room and board at the average public four-year institution, and 35 percent at a four-year private college (College Board, 2004a, 2004b).[6] In 2003, the maximum Pell Grant of $4,050 covered only 38 percent of the total costs at a public four-year college or university and 16 percent at a private four-year institution.

Another major change in funding was the introduction of the Hope and Lifetime Learning tax credits in the Taxpayer Relief Act of 1997. These credits allow taxpayers to deduct a portion of college tuition costs from their federal income taxes. The value of these credits grew to over $6 billion by 2003, or one-half of what the federal government spent on the Pell Grant program that year. Research on the impact of the educational tax credits has found that they benefit primarily middle-class and wealthier taxpayers, and have had little or no impact on improving college access. A recent study concluded that "insufficient tax liability due to low income levels, competing tax credits and deductions, and the interaction with other aid programs prevents many low-income individuals from qualifying for the aid. This study found no evidence of increased postsecondary enrollment among eligible students" (Long, 2003, p. 44).

The Growth of Merit Aid in the States

Historically, most financial aid was awarded to help increase access to higher education. Title IV of the Higher Education Act of 1965, which authorizes the federal student financial assistance programs, opens with this statement:

> It is the purpose of this part to provide, through institutions of higher education, educational opportunity grants to assist in making available benefits of higher education to qualified high school graduates of exceptional financial need, who for lack of financial means of their own or of their families would be unable to obtain such benefits without such aid. (Higher Education Act of 1965, 1965, §401)

In order to meet the dictates of this statute, federal grants—particularly Pell Grants—have been awarded for the last four decades using the financial need of the student and their family as the primary criterion.[7]

From the 1970s to the early 1990s, states also committed to the awarding of need-based aid. The total dollars awarded by states to undergraduates grew from $626 million in 1976 to $2.4 billion in 1993. During this same period, the percentage of dollars awarded by the states without using financial need as a measure fluctuated between 8.9 percent and 11.1 percent of the total (National Association of State Scholarship and Grant Programs, 1994; National Association of State Student Grant and Aid Programs, 2004).

The 1990s, however, saw major changes in state financial aid policy, with some states moving away from financial need as the primary criterion used for awarding grants. Much of the political influence behind this movement was an interest in providing more financial assistance for college to middle- and upper-income families, most of whom did not qualify for need-based grants (Mumper, 1999). With the development of the Helping Outstanding Students Educationally (HOPE) program in 1993, Georgia became the first state to develop a broad-based merit grant program that functioned as an entitlement (i.e., every student who met the award criteria was guaranteed a grant) and did not use financial need as a criterion for the award.[8] All students in the state who graduated from high school with a B average were awarded a full tuition scholarship at any public institution in the state, or $500 to attend a private institution in Georgia.[9]

From this start, merit scholarship programs—those that award their grants without consideration of financial need—have become the fastest-growing category of financial aid in the U.S. In 1992, the year before the development of Georgia HOPE, 9 percent of state aid to undergraduate students was awarded without consideration of financial need. This increased to 27 percent in 2002, the most recent year for which data are available (National Association of State Student Grant and Aid Programs, 2004). During this period, the total dollars awarded by the states without consideration of financial need rose 629 percent, while the volume of need-based grant dollars increased 108 percent. Over a dozen states now have programs similar to HOPE; while the merit criteria used to award the grants vary, the programs are similar in that they are structured largely as entitlements and they award the grants without means testing (Heller, 2002b).

In contrast to the research on need-based grants cited above, which has found them to be instrumental in promoting access for lower-income students, merit grants have a quite different impact. Because of the strong correlation between socioeconomic status and the academic criteria used for awarding the grants—which generally include high school grades, standardized test scores, or some combination of the two—the benefits flow disproportionately to students from more well-off families. A 2002 report that analyzed four of the largest state merit aid programs concluded that

> overall, the studies in this report make it clear that the students least likely to be awarded a merit scholarship come from populations that have traditionally been underrepresented in higher education. This hinders the potential to increase college access among minority and low-income students, especially if these scholarship programs continue to overshadow need-based programs. (Marin, 2002, p. 114)

Thus, the research evidence shows that merit scholarships are likely to have little effect on college participation. While some lower-income students do qualify for merit scholarships, they are relatively small in number compared to the much greater proportion of higher-income students who are qualifying for these scholarships. One study of the Georgia HOPE scholarship program concluded that over 90 percent of state expenditures on HOPE went to subsidize students who would have attended college anyway (Cornwell & Mustard, 2002). Another study concluded that the HOPE program actually led to an increase in the gap in college participation between white and black students in Georgia (Dynarski, 2002).

Institutional Grants

Through most of the history of American higher education, financial aid was largely the province of private institutions. In recent years, however, public institutions have entered the institutional financial aid field, expanding their awarding of grants from their own resources. These grants have been used for two purposes: to promote access for underserved populations, and for enrollment management purposes. While these efforts are modest in comparison to most private institutions, they are increasing.

Like the federal government and states, some public colleges and universities have recognized the importance of financial aid in ensuring that poorer students will be able to enroll in college. As tuition prices have risen faster than the ability of lower-income students and their families to pay them—even with the assistance of state and federal grants—public institutions began to offer their own need-based grants.

Public institutions have also felt the pressure to use financial aid for enrollment management purposes. The tactic of tuition discounting, or offering institutional grants to attractive students—those with high measures on academic criteria such as high school grades or standardized test scores who are often perceived to benefit the institution in national college guides and rankings such as those produced by *U.S. News & World Report*—has also spread from private colleges into public institutions. While the rankings reward institutions for becoming more exclusive, the institutions do not benefit in the rankings by making a commitment to increasing access for underrepresented students.

Table 1 shows the changes in institutional need-based and non-need or merit grants in public colleges between 1992–93 and 1999–2000. The analysis uses data from the National Postsecondary Student Aid Study (NPSAS), a nationally representative survey of how college students finance their educations.

Between 1992–93 and 1999–2000, overall spending on institutional grants to dependent undergraduates nationally increased 78 percent, with spending on merit grants outpacing that on need-based grants. The increase in grant spending was the result both of an increase in the number of grants awarded, as well as an increase in the average amount of each grant, 44 percent and 23 percent increases, respectively.

The increase in grant spending is less impressive, however, when taken in the context of the change in tuition prices. Tuition prices increased 44 percent at four-year public institutions and 48 percent in community colleges over the seven years (College Board, 2004a). Thus, while more students received both need-based and merit grants (and enrollment was stable during this period), the increase in the average award, 23 percent, was for less than the tuition price increases.

Another important trend in institutional grant awards—one that mirrors what was happening in state financial aid during this period—was that merit awards increased both in size and in number at a faster pace than

TABLE 1
Institutional Grant Awards to Dependent Undergraduates
in Public Institutions

	1992–93	*1999–2000*	*% Increase*
Total Dollars (millions)			
Need-Based	$423	$678	60
Merit	677	1,283	89
Total	1,100	1,961	78
Number of Grants			
Need-Based	317,000	448,000	41
Merit	334,000	490,000	47
Total*	621,000	896,000	44
*Average per Student** *			
Need-Based	$1,336	$1,515	13
Merit	2,024	2,618	29
Total	1,773	2,189	23

Source: Author's calculations from National Center for Education Statistics (2004a, 2004b).

*Total does not equal sum of need-based and merit grants, as some students received both types of award.

**For students who received a grant.

need-based awards. Merit awards, which are used primarily for enrollment management purposes, became a more prominent tactic of financial aid policy in public institutions.

In an earlier study I examined changes in institutional grant awards to traditional college students in both public and private four-year institutions, using data from the 1989 and 1995 NPSAS surveys. While merit aid spending grew 99 percent over the six years, I found that the growth in awards to black (66%) and Hispanic (68%) students lagged far behind the growth for white (128%) and Asian (112%) students (Heller, 2001). This is evidence that, at least during this time period, institutions were allocating fewer merit award dollars to underrepresented minority students than to others.

RACE, COLLEGE COSTS, AND AFFORDABILITY

To understand how affordable college is for students, you need to examine the prices students pay in relation to the resources available from the students and their families. The gap between college prices and available resources—which can come from student and family incomes and assets, as well as from financial aid—has been labeled "unmet need." The impact of unmet need on college participation was well documented in a 2002 report from the federal Advisory Committee on Student Financial Assistance. In order to separate the impact of financial factors from the academic barriers to college attendance faced by poor and minority students, the report focused in on those students "having adequate academic course preparation, grades, and aptitude test scores to meet the minimal entrance requirements of most four-year colleges" (p. 16). The study used data from the U.S. Department of Education to analyze the impact of unmet need on a cohort of students who graduated from high school in 1992.

The Advisory Committee found that among students with low unmet need—those who, with their own and family resources and financial aid, were able to meet the cost of college, except for an average of about $400—96 percent enrolled in some form of postsecondary education within two years of graduating from high school in 1992. In contrast, only 78 percent of students with high unmet need (averaging $3,800) attended college within the same time frame. There were also differences between the two groups in the type of institution attended. Eighty-three percent of students with low unmet need attended a four-year college, while just over half of students with high unmet need were able to enroll in a four-year institution.

The impact of unmet need is magnified when students have to overcome this barrier for more than just one year. While the difference in the rates at which students entered a four-year college was 31 percentage points (83% for students with low unmet need and 52% for those with high unmet need), the Advisory Committee found that the gap increased to over 40 percentage points when it examined BA attainment rates (62% and 21%, respectively). In other words, equally qualified students with high unmet need were only one-third as likely to finish college as students with low unmet need.

The Advisory Committee did not examine the unmet need of students from different racial and ethnic groups, but the National Postsecondary Student Aid Study, described earlier in this chapter, can be used to estimate college prices, financial aid, and unmet need for these students who were enrolled in college in the 1999–2000 academic year (National Center for Education Statistics, 2004b). There is another important limitation of these data that must be acknowledged: All the data discussed here are based on students who were able to enroll in college. What these figures do not measure are the price barriers faced by students *who were never able to enroll in*

TABLE 2
Percentage of Dependent Students* Receiving Grants,
by Racial and Ethnic Category

Racial/Ethnic Category**	Federal Pell Grant	State Merit Grant	State Need-Based Grant	Institutional Merit Grant	Institutional Need-Based Grant
White, non-Hispanic	22	4	17	19	17
Black, non-Hispanic	55	7	22	13	15
Hispanic or Latino	53	2	24	9	21
Asian	32	3	21	10	24
American Indian/ Alaska Native	54	5	20	10	22
Native Hawaiian/ Other Pacific Islander	32	1	16	17	20
All Races	30	4	18	16	18

Source: Author's calculations from National Center for Education Statistics (2004b).

* Students attending a single institution full-time for at least nine months.

** Discrete categories as designated by NPSAS; students in these categories are U.S. citizens or permanent residents.

college because the barriers were too large to overcome. The implications of this are discussed below.

Table 2 shows the proportion of students in each racial and ethnic group receiving grant aid from each of the major sources. It includes all dependent undergraduates who attended college full-time for the entire academic year.[11] Among students of all races, 30 percent received a federal Pell Grant. There were large differences in the rates at which students from different groups received Pell Grants, primarily because of large differences in family income among these groups. Data from the U.S. Census Bureau (2004a) show that while the median income of white families in 1998 was $51,607, of Asian/Pacific Islander families, $52,826, black families had median incomes of $29,404, Hispanics, $29,608.[12] Since Pell Grant eligibility is determined largely by two factors, the income of the student and their family, as well as the cost of attending college, the lower family incomes of black and Hispanic students increase their eligibility for Pell Grants.

Black students were also more likely to receive a state merit grant, with 7 percent of students receiving them, compared to 4 percent of all students. Geography, however, needs to be taken into account when interpreting this finding. Of the nine states with broad-based merit scholarship programs in 1999, six were southern states with disproportionately larger black populations than the rest of the nation. Thus, the fact that larger proportions of black students were residing in states with merit scholarship programs helped to increase the proportion receiving these grants compared to students of other racial groups. Black and Hispanic students were also more likely than whites to receive state need-based grants, as were Asian American students.

White students were more likely to receive an institutional merit grant than were students from other racial or ethnic groups. The distribution of institutional need-based grants displays a different pattern than either Pell Grants or state need-based grants. Among the full-time students, black students were least likely to receive a need-based grant from institutional funds than were students in the other groups. Part of this difference may be attributable to the sector in which black students enroll. Of all six racial and ethnic groups, black students who attended college full-time were least likely to be enrolled in a private, four-year college or university (21% of black students enrolled in this sector, compared to 27% of all students). This sector provides the largest proportion of grants to students overall. And many of the black students who are enrolled in private institutions attend historically black colleges and universities, which traditionally have offered little institutional financial aid.

Table 3 presents data on the income of students, the cost of attendance, and the amount of unmet need they faced in the 1999–2000 school year. Estimates are provided for all postsecondary students, and for students attending community colleges, public four-year institutions, and private four-year institutions.[13] Cost of attendance is determined by the institution, and includes tuition and fees, books and supplies, room and board (or an allowance for housing and food expenses for students living off campus), transportation, and personal expenses. As described earlier, unmet need is determined by the formula:

unmet need = cost of attendance – expected family contribution – all financial aid

Overall, the average parental income of all full-time dependent undergraduates was $65,752. White students had an average parental income of $71,732, while black, Hispanic, and Asian students had parental income averages of $46,283, $44,102, and $57,587, respectively.[14] For white students, the average parental income was 139 percent of the median family income reported by the Census Bureau. For black and Hispanic students,

TABLE 3
Parental Income, Cost of Attendance, and Unmet Need of Dependent
Students,* by Race and Institution Type

Racial/Ethnic Category	Average Parental Income	Average Cost of Attendance	Average Unmet Need	Cost of Attendance as % of Income	Unmet Need as % of Income
All Sectors					
White, non-Hispanic	$71,732	$15,494	$5,547	22	8
Black, non-Hispanic	46,283	13,786	4,462	30	10
Hispanic or Latino	44,102	12,495	4,976	28	11
Asian	57,587	16,320	6,677	28	12
American Indian/ Alaska Native**	56,524	14,283	4,861	25	9
Native Hawaiian/ Other Pacific Islander**	64,302	14,049	5,855	22	9
All Races	65,752	15,107	5,477	23	8
Community Colleges					
White, non-Hispanic	59,184	8,698	3,794	15	6
Black, non-Hispanic	39,971	7,928	3,683	20	9
Hispanic or Latino	45,019	8,209	4,252	18	9
Asian	52,389	8,990	4,459	17	9
All Races	55,093	8,592	3,935	16	7
Public Four-Year					
White, non-Hispanic	72,582	12,641	4,381	17	6
Black, non-Hispanic	47,388	12,069	3,580	25	8
Hispanic or Latino	48,329	10,829	4,249	22	9
Asian	56,663	13,581	5,246	24	9
All Races	66,936	12,495	4,380	19	7
Private Four-Year					
White, non-Hispanic	79,889	25,222	8,187	32	10
Black, non-Hispanic	52,025	23,161	6,562	45	13
Hispanic or Latino	39,939	17,797	5,763	45	14
Asian	66,314	29,229	11,156	44	17
All Races	73,142	24,595	7,990	34	11

Source: Author's calculations from National Center for Education Statistics (2004b).

* Students attending a single institution full-time for at least nine months.

** The sample sizes in NPSAS are not large enough to estimate reliably the figures in each sector for American Indian/Alaska Native and Native Hawaiian/Other Pacific Islander students.

these ratios were 157 percent and 149 percent, respectively. Asian students had incomes that were closest to the Census Bureau estimates, with the parental income of students in NPSAS 109 percent of the Census median family income.

Across all sectors, students faced an average cost of attendance of $15,107. White and Asian students attended colleges with a mean cost of attendance higher than this figure, with the rest of the groups attending institutions with costs below $15,000. The cost of attendance as a percentage of parental income ranged from a low of 22 percent for white students to a high of 30 percent for black students.[15]

Unmet need for all students in all college sectors averaged $5,477, or approximately 8 percent of the average student's parental income. There was a difference of approximately $2,200 between the unmet need of Asian students ($6,677) and black students ($4,462), who had the lowest level of unmet need. Unmet need as a percentage of parental income ranged from a low of 8 percent for white students to a high of 12 percent for Asian students.

When examining students in community colleges, there is an important caveat. Relative to the four-year public and private college sectors, few community college students enroll in the traditional pattern of full-time, for an entire year, attending just one institution. Only 33 percent of community college students had this attendance pattern, while 68 percent of students in public four-year institutions and 79 percent in private four-year institutions did (author's calculations from NCES, 2004b). Thus, the estimates provided here are for a much smaller proportion of the overall population of students attending community colleges than the other two sectors.

Students who did fit this traditional enrollment pattern in community colleges came from families with average incomes lower than those of all postsecondary students. This finding is consistent with other research that has documented that community colleges have larger proportions of poorer students (Horn, Peter, & Rooney, 2002; McPherson & Schapiro, 1998; Pell Institute for the Study of Opportunity in Higher Education, 2004). Cost of attendance at community colleges is lower, due to the lower tuition levels charged in these institutions. The differences in the mean cost of attendance among the racial groups were small, as were the differences in levels of average unmet need. The cost of attendance as a proportion of parental income ranged from a low of 15 percent for white students to 20 percent for black students. Unmet need as a proportion of parental income ranged from 6 percent for white students to 9 percent for black, Hispanic, and Asian students.

The income profile of students in public four-year institutions closely matched that of all postsecondary students. While the cost of attendance in these institutions was approximately 50 percent higher than in the community college sector, unmet need was very close to the averages in the community college sector. This is indicative of the higher levels of financial aid available to students in the public four-year institutions. Black, Hispanic, and Asian students all faced a higher cost of attendance as a proportion of parental income than white students, and even taking into account the family contribution and financial aid, these groups all faced unmet need that was a higher proportion of parental income than white students.

In private four-year colleges and universities, the parental income of all racial groups other than Hispanics was the highest of all three sectors. White students, for example, had parental income of almost $80,000, or one-third higher than white students in community colleges and 10 percent higher than those in public four-year institutions. The average cost of attendance of all students enrolled in this sector was approximately $24,600, and both white and black students had average costs close to this figure. For Hispanic students, the cost of attendance was 27 percent less than this average, and for Asian students, the cost was 19 percent higher. There is little in the NPSAS database to tell us why there is such a wide differential between costs of the institutions attended by Hispanic as compared to Asian students.

The average cost of attendance as a proportion of the mean parental income was 32 percent for white students; for the other three races, the cost was 44 or 45 percent of parental income. Unmet need ranged from a low of $5,763 for Hispanic students (14% of parental income) to a high of $11,156 (17% of parental income) for Asian students. White students had the lowest average unmet need as a proportion of parental income, at 10 percent.

Across all college sectors, black and Hispanic students faced an unmet need burden (measured as a proportion of parental income) that was greater than that for white students. This is an indication that the financial aid system is not meeting the needs of minority students.

THE FUTURE OF COLLEGE AFFORDABILITY
FOR MINORITY STUDENTS

The data presented in the previous section demonstrate that, in general, the price of college is less affordable for minority students than it is for white students. This is true whether one examines the sticker price of college— what it costs to attend before taking into account financial aid—or the unmet need students and their families face after taking into account their own resources and financial aid.

One limitation of this analysis is that there have been important changes in college affordability since the 1999–2000 academic year, the source of the data on college affordability in the previous section of this chapter.[16] The recession in the early part of this decade, which caused constraints on the revenues available to most states and private colleges and universities, has helped create great upward pressure on tuition prices. Between 1999 and 2004, average tuition prices increased 29 percent at private four-year colleges, 53 percent at public four-year institutions, and 26 percent at community colleges (College Board, 2004a).

The ability of students and their families to pay for tuition has not risen commensurate with the price increases. Between 1999 and 2003 (the most recent year for which data are available), median family income for white and Asian families increased 11 and 12 percent, respectively, while the median income of black and Hispanic families each grew only 8 percent (U.S. Census Bureau, 2004a, 2004b). Thus, college prices—particularly in public four-year colleges and universities, the sector that enrolls more than half of all full-time students—grew at rates that far outpaced growth in income.

Students, particularly those from black and Hispanic families, have received little additional financial aid assistance in the form of grants during this period. Between 1999 and 2004, the maximum Pell Grant increased $925, well below the tuition price increases in both public ($1,770) and private ($4,564) four-year institutions. When one examines a measure of college costs that includes room and board in addition to tuition and fees, the increase in the maximum Pell Grant falls even further below the increase in costs at four-year public ($3,274) and private ($6,041) institutions (College Board, 2004a, 2004b).

State grant programs have also done little to help protect lower-income and minority students from rising tuition prices in recent years. In the most recent recession, many state need-based grant programs have seen little or no expenditure growth, and what growth has been enacted has largely gone to meet the demands of increasing numbers of eligible students, rather than for increasing awards to keep pace with tuition increases (Heller, 2002a). Since 1999, spending by the states on merit aid programs has continued to grow faster than spending on need-based grant programs. As described earlier in this chapter, merit aid programs have had little impact on college participation for poor and minority students.

Merit aid is also the fastest growing type of grant awarded by institutions. As merit grants continue to outpace need-based grants in institutions, poor and minority students will continue to lose ground in their ability to be able to afford and enroll in college. The high levels of unmet financial need faced by minority students (described in the previous section of this chapter) will only grow as states and institutions emphasize merit criteria over financial need in the awarding of grants. And as unmet need grows, fewer and fewer students will be able to enroll in college, or to persist through to a degree even if they are able to enroll initially.

As discussed earlier, most of the data we have on financial barriers are based on students who were able to overcome the barriers and enroll in college. The Advisory Committee on Student Financial Assistance (2002), in its report *Empty Promises*, examined the impact of these price barriers nationally. The Advisory Committee estimated that in 2002, over 400,000 high school graduates from low- and moderate-income families (those with incomes below $49,000) who were qualified for college were unable to enroll in a four-year institution because of price barriers. And almost 170,000 of these students were unable to enroll in *any* postsecondary institution. While the Advisory Committee did not estimate the impact of these barriers on students from different racial groups, the fact that black and Hispanic students come from families with incomes that are on average well below those of other families indicates that they likely are disproportionately affected by these barriers.

There are a number of important steps that policymakers and institutional leaders can take to ensure that financial obstacles do not keep qualified minority students from attending the college of their choice. First, all parties must commit to using financial need as the criterion for awarding assistance for paying for college. We must return to the ideals expressed in the Higher Education Act, which state that the purpose of federal aid is to assist financially needy students in paying for college. Both states and institutions have drifted away from this ideal, as more and more financial aid is being awarded to influence where students attend college, not to enable financially needy students to enroll. As financial need becomes less important in awarding aid, fewer minority students will receive financial aid, thus further hampering their ability to afford college.

Second, need-based grant programs must be funded at levels commensurate with the demand of the population of students who depend upon them. While the federal government has maintained this commitment in the *structure* of the Pell Grant program, it has not maintained the commitment in the *funding* for the program. State merit scholarships and federal loan programs, which over the years have become an important college finance mechanism for middle- and upper-income students, are structured as entitlements, meaning that the funding for these programs is driven by the demand for them. The federal and state need-based grant programs, in contrast, are not entitlements. Annual appropriations for these programs are established by Congress and state legislatures, and the number and size of the awards have to fit within the appropriated levels, no matter what the level of demand. This means that in bad fiscal times in particular—which generally coincide with when tuition prices increase the fastest—there is a shortfall of funds to help minority and other financially needy students pay for college.

Third, colleges and universities have an obligation to do all they can to ensure that they are offering the highest-quality education at the lowest-possible price. Institutional leaders must make certain that both public and private resources are used efficiently and effectively so as to help hold down the level of tuition increases faced by students.

As tuition prices continue to increase—a trend that shows no sign of abating in either the near or long-term future—and financial aid policy shifts more toward the use of loans and merit criteria than financial need in awarding grants, the racial and ethnic gaps in college participation and attainment documented throughout this book are certain to grow. Following the recommendations outlined here can help recommit the nation to the college access needs of minority and lower-income students.

NOTES

1. Unless otherwise stated, all prices and price changes are expressed in current dollars. Prices are for undergraduate students and in-state students at public institutions.
2. The change in family income is for the period 1976 to 2003.
3. Unless otherwise indicated, "minority" as used in this paper refers to black, Hispanic, and Native American students. These are the groups that have historically been underrepresented in American higher education.
4. Until very recent years, most other countries around the world charged few, if any, fees for students attending higher education. This trend has been changing, however, particularly in the European nations, as tuition fees have been introduced in recent years (Teixeira, Jongbloed, & Vossensteyn, in press).
5. The College Board notes that it is "unable to include all of the forms of grant aid available to students, but the omissions are relatively small. Our measure does not

include tuition assistance that students receive from their employers or scholarships from a variety of private sources" (2004b, p. 3). Unless otherwise noted, the College Board report is the source of data on financial aid expenditures in this section.

6. At the time, the Pell Grant capped a student's award at no more than 50 percent of the cost of tuition and fees, room, and board. The cap was increased to 60 percent in 1985, and removed in 1993.

7. Pell Grants, and all federal aid, do have a merit component. In order to be awarded federal aid, a student has to be a high school graduate (or GED recipient), be accepted into an accredited institution of higher education, and once enrolled, maintain satisfactory progress toward a degree or certificate as determined by the institution.

8. When first implemented in 1993, a family income eligibility cap of $66,000, or approximately twice the median family income in the state, was imposed. This was increased to $100,000 the following year, and the cap was eliminated entirely in 1995.

9. See Cornwell and Mustard (2002, 2004), Dynarski (2002), and Mumper (1999) for history and analyses of the Georgia HOPE scholarship program.

10. A follow-up report examined more of these state scholarship programs (Heller & Marin, 2004).

11. All of the analyses shown here from NPSAS are for dependent undergraduate students only. These students, often called "traditional college-aged students," are by federal definition under the age of 24, unmarried, without dependents of their own, and not veterans of the armed forces. While 49 percent of all undergraduates in 1999–2000 were dependent students, 74 percent of those who attended college full-time for the entire year were dependents (Berkner, Berker, Rooney, & Peter, 2002). The analyses shown here focus exclusively on dependent students because many state and institutional financial aid programs target their awards to these traditional college students.

12. The Census Bureau does not provide estimates for American Indian families. Income data from 1998 are shown here because eligibility for need-based grants of students attending college in the 1999–2000 school year was determined based on incomes in the 1998 calendar year.

13. It is difficult to compare directly the median family income figures from the Census Bureau with the parental income amounts reported in NPSAS. First, the former are median income estimates; the latter are mean income estimates. One would expect mean incomes to be larger due to the influence of those incomes at the highest end. Second, the Census Bureau estimates of family income include the income of all members of the family, which can include the earnings of dependent children. The NPSAS measure of parental income includes only the income of the parents. However, one can calculate the ratio of parental income reported in NPSAS to the family incomes reported by the Census Bureau, and compare these ratios among different racial groups.

14. Note that the Census Bureau and NPSAS definitions of the Asian category are slightly different.

15. Note that these percentages are calculated as the average cost of attendance divided by the average income; they are *not* the mean of each student's cost of attendance divided by each student's parental income.

16. The National Center for Education Statistics conducted an update of the National Postsecondary Student Aid Study in the 2003–04 school year, but the data from that study were not yet available to researchers at the time this chapter was written.

REFERENCES

Advisory Committee on Student Financial Assistance. (2002). *Empty promises: The myth of college access in America*. Washington, DC: U.S. Department of Education.

Berkner, L., Berker, A., Rooney, K., & Peter, K. (2002). *Student financing of undergraduate education: 1999–2000* (NCES 2002-167). Washington, DC: U.S. Department of Education, National Center for Education Statistics.

Bureau of Labor Statistics. (2004). *Consumer price index: All urban consumers* [On-line data file]. U.S. Department of Commerce. Retrieved December 15, 2004, from http://www.bls.gov/cpi/home.htm

College Board. (2004a). *Trends in college pricing, 2004*. Washington, DC: Author.

College Board. (2004b). *Trends in student aid, 2004*. Washington, DC: Author.

Cornwell, C., & Mustard, D. (2002). Race and the effects of Georgia's HOPE scholarship. In D. E. Heller & P. Marin (Eds.), *Who should we help? The negative social consequences of merit scholarships* (pp. 57–72). Cambridge, MA: Civil Rights Project at Harvard University.

Cornwell, C., & Mustard, D. B. (2004). Georgia's HOPE scholarship and minority and low-income students: Program effects and proposed reforms. In D. E. Heller & P. Marin (Eds.), *State merit scholarship programs and racial inequality* (pp. 77–100). Cambridge, MA: Civil Rights Project at Harvard University.

Dynarski, S. (2002). Race, income, and the impact of merit aid. In D. E. Heller & P. Marin (Eds.), *Who should we help? The negative social consequences of merit scholarships* (pp. 73–91). Cambridge, MA: Civil Rights Project at Harvard University.

Gerald, D. E., & Hussar, W. J. (2002). *Projections of education statistics to 2012: Thirty-first edition* (NCES 2002-030). Washington, DC: U.S. Department of Education.

Heller, D. E. (1997). Student price response in higher education: An update to Leslie and Brinkman. *Journal of Higher Education, 68*, 624–659.

Heller, D. E. (2001). Race, gender, and institutional financial aid awards. *Journal of Student Financial Aid, 31*(1), 7–24.

Heller, D. E. (2002a, September). *Lean times: Policy choices and challenges for higher education*. Keynote address at the Annual Policy Conference of the Colorado Student Loan Program, Estes Park, CO.

Heller, D. E. (2002b). State merit scholarship programs: An introduction. In D. E. Heller & P. Marin (Eds.), *Who should we help? The negative social consequences of merit scholarships* (pp. 15–23). Cambridge, MA: Civil Rights Project at Harvard University.

Heller, D. E., & Marin, P. (Eds.). (2004). *State merit scholarship programs and racial inequality*. Cambridge, MA: Civil Rights Project at Harvard University.

Higher Education Act of 1965, Pub. L. No. 89-329 (1965).

Holst, J. H. (1923). The imposition of fees in state-supported institutions. *Educational Review, 65*(January), 35–39.

Holtschneider, D. H. (1997). *Institutional aid to New England college students: 1740–1800.* Unpublished doctoral dissertation, Harvard University, Cambridge, MA.

Horn, L. J., Peter, K., & Rooney, K. (2002). *Profile of undergraduates in U.S. postsecondary education institutions: 1999–2000* (NCES 2002-168). Washington, DC: U.S. Department of Education, National Center for Education Statistics.

Jackson, G. A., & Weathersby, G. B. (1975). Individual demand for higher education. *Journal of Higher Education, 46,* 623–652.

Leslie, L. L., & Brinkman, P. T. (1988). *The economic value of higher education.* New York: American Council on Education, Macmillan.

Long, B. T. (2003). *The impact of federal tax credits for higher education expenses* (Working Paper No. 9553). Cambridge, MA: National Bureau of Economic Research.

Marin, P. (2002). Merit scholarships and the outlook for equal opportunity in higher education. In D. E. Heller & P. Marin (Eds.), *Who should we help? The negative social consequences of merit scholarships* (pp. 109–114). Cambridge, MA: Civil Rights Project at Harvard University.

McPherson, M. S., & Schapiro, M. O. (1998). *The student aid game: Meeting need and rewarding talent in American higher education.* Princeton, NJ: Princeton University Press.

Morey, L. (1928). Student fees in state universities and colleges. *School and Society, 28,* 185–192.

Mumper, M. (1999, November). *HOPE and its critics: Sorting out the competing claims about Georgia's HOPE scholarship.* Paper presented at the annual meeting of the Association for the Study of Higher Education, San Antonio, TX.

National Association of State Scholarship and Grant Programs. (1994). *NASSGP annual survey report.* Harrisburg: Pennsylvania Higher Education Assistance Agency.

National Association of State Student Grant and Aid Programs. (2004). *NASSGAP 34th annual survey report on state-sponsored student financial aid 2002–2003 academic year.* Springfield: Illinois Student Assistance Commission.

National Center for Education Statistics. (2003). *Digest of education statistics, 2002* (NCES 2003-060). Washington, DC: U.S. Department of Education.

National Center for Education Statistics. (2004a). *National Postsecondary Student Aid Study 1992–1993 data analysis system.* Washington, DC: U.S. Department of Education. Retrieved December 15, 2004, from http://nces.ed.gov/das/

National Center for Education Statistics. (2004b). *National Postsecondary Student Aid Study 1999–2000 data analysis system.* U.S. Department of Education. Retrieved December 15, 2004, from http://nces.ed.gov/das/

Pell Institute for the Study of Opportunity in Higher Education. (2004). *Indicators of opportunity in higher education.* Washington, DC: Author.

President's Commission on Higher Education. (1947). *Higher education for American democracy.* New York: Harper & Brothers.

Sears, J. B. (1923). Our theory of free higher education. *Educational Review, 65*(January), 27–34.

Swail, W. S., & Heller, D. E. (2004). *Changes in tuition policy: Natural policy experiments in five countries.* Montreal, Canada: Canada Millennium Scholarship Foundation.

Teixeira, P., Jongbloed, B., & Vossensteyn, H. (Eds.). (in press). *Cost-sharing and accessibility in higher education*. Berlin: Springer.

U.S. Census Bureau. (2004a). *Race and Hispanic origin of householder—Families by median and mean income: 1947 to 2001* [On-line data file]. Washington, DC: Author. Retrieved December 15, 2004, from http://www.census.gov/hhes/income/histinc/f05.html

U.S. Census Bureau. (2004b). *Selected characteristics of families by total money income in 2003*. Washington, DC: Author. Retrieved December 15, 2004, from http://ferret.bls.census.gov/macro/032004/faminc/new01_000.htm

U.S. Census Bureau. (2005a). *P155 Median family income in 1999 (dollars)*. Washington, DC: Author. Retrieved February 16, 2005, from http://www.census.gov/Press-Release/www/2002/sumfile3.html

U.S. Census Bureau. (2005b). *P160 Poverty status in 1999 of families by family type by presence of related children under 18 years by age of related children by race and Hispanic/Latino origin*. Washington, DC: Author. Retrieved February 16, 2005, from http://www.census.gov/Press-Release/www/2002/sumfile3.html

5

Illusions of Opportunity?

From College Access to Job Access at Two-Year Colleges

REGINA DEIL-AMEN
JAMES E. ROSENBAUM
ANN E. PERSON

In the last several decades, many of our nation's urban centers have experienced fundamental transformations that have seriously altered the structure of opportunity for many African Americans and Latinos.[1] The decline of manufacturing coupled with the movement of business activity and more affluent whites to the suburbs has resulted in a shrinking urban core in which blacks and Latinos are concentrated (Wilson, 1987). Chicago provides a vivid example of this transformation and its consequences for African Americans and Hispanics: "By a variety of measures, metropolitan Chicago is among the nation's leaders in segregation and inequality for Blacks and Hispanics" (Orfield, 1990, p. 129). Chicago's inferior schools serve the vast majority of all the black and Hispanic students in the state "and prepare them for neither college nor a decent job" (p. 131). As access to well-paying, low-skill, blue-collar industrial jobs dwindled, sectors such as business services, information processing, communications, and finance, which required higher-level skills, grew. This resulted in a mismatch between employers' skill needs and the skill levels of the city's majority nonwhite labor force in a changing postindustrial, knowledge-based economy (Joseph & Lynn, 1990).

Unlike the industry-based economy of the past, access to jobs in the postindustrial, rapid-growth sectors requires a postsecondary credential of some kind. A one-year certificate or a two-year associate's degree has now become the minimum criterion for such access. In light of these trends, any discussion of the "color line" in higher education must consider subbaccalaureate colleges that provide the education to prepare African Americans and Latinos to participate effectively in this new economy. Across the United States, nearly half of all black undergraduates and over half of all Latino undergraduates are enrolled in community colleges and two-year private career and technical colleges (U.S. Department of Education, 2002). These numbers are even higher in the Chicago metropolitan area, where more than 80 percent of the blacks and 66 percent of the Latinos in Cook County reside (Joseph & Lynn, 1990).

Despite decades of legal desegregation, the color line in higher education persists, due in part to the perpetuation of rarely noticed practices. It is often difficult to see where social inequalities are created in institutions. This chapter addresses two main questions: What social mechanisms influence opportunities and contribute to the color line in higher education? What policies can improve opportunities for African American and Latino students?

In this chapter we report on a series of studies of social mechanisms that affect opportunities and describe social policies relevant to improving opportunities for black, Latino, and low-socioeconomic-status (SES) and first-generation students in general. We find that, instead of discouraging students' plans (as they formerly did), high schools and colleges are now more likely to *encourage* college dreams. However, they fail to provide students with realistic strategies for attaining these goals. We recommend policies that may help students get into real college courses (not noncredit remedial courses), stay in college, and get good jobs after college through institutional contacts.

DATA

We report on two kinds of studies. The first involves quantitative analyses of national survey data. The second includes case studies of 14 two-year colleges—seven public community colleges and seven private for-profit and nonprofit occupational colleges in Chicago's metropolitan area.

While most two-year college students nationally are at public community colleges, about 4 percent attend private colleges. Like community colleges, the private occupational colleges we studied offer accredited two-year degrees and similar applied programs, such as business, accounting, office technology, computer information systems, electronics, various health assistance fields, and computer-aided drafting. Each college offers degrees in three or more of these program areas, which are intended to lead directly to related jobs.

Our research selected occupational colleges (for-profit and nonprofit) that passed the same accreditation standards as community colleges and offer associate's degrees of similar quality to community colleges. As such they are comparable to community colleges, but dissimilar to 94 percent of other business and technical schools, which offer no degree above a certificate (Apling, 1993). These private colleges should not be considered a random sample or a representation of average occupational colleges. They should be viewed as potentially representing some of the best programs in these fields, and may be considered an institutional model or ideal type, identified to provide a contrast to the community colleges in our study.

Three of the seven community colleges are urban, two of which have black student enrollments of 47 percent and 76 percent, with combined black/Latino enrollments of up to 91 percent. In the third college, blacks and Latinos together constitute about 40 percent of enrollments. In the four suburban community colleges, blacks and Latinos collectively constitute 15 percent to 35 percent of enrollments. In the four urban occupational colleges, blacks and Latinos collectively constitute between 60 percent and 90 percent of total enrollments. The three suburban occupational colleges have black/Latino enrollments ranging from 20 percent to 40 percent.

These institutions are precisely the kinds of colleges that Chicago's urban and inner-suburban black and Latino students depend on to gain a foothold in today's postindustrial economy, where technically oriented health, business, and computer fields are among the fastest growing sectors. In a labor market in which 70 percent of job openings will *not* require any college degree and only 21 percent will require a BA or higher, the most feasible window of opportunity for lower-income students will come from the probable growth in demand for jobs that will require an associate's degree or certificate (Hecker, 2001; Rothstein, 2002). As Rothstein (2002) notes,

> employers are increasingly turning to community colleges for work-specific training. . . . So it is possible, perhaps even likely, that the number of jobs requiring a full four-year college degree could fall as they evolve into jobs requiring two-year certificate programs. . . . For example, employers may come to prefer graduates of skills-specific community college programs to liberal arts baccalaureate degree holders in

filling some technical, administrative, and lower-level managerial jobs. (p. 6)

The qualitative component of the case studies involves semistructured, open-ended interviews conducted with over 130 students and nearly 100 faculty, staff, and administrators. The survey component includes surveys of almost 4,400 students in occupational classes who were selected to target a cross-section of credit-level students in comparable occupationally focused programs across the various colleges. The surveys reveal that students' families are generally of lower and middle income; 41 percent of community college students and 45 percent of occupational college students report parental income under $30,000 (and nearly one-quarter under $19,000). Nearly 90 percent of the students have parents with less than a bachelor's degree.

WHAT SOCIAL MECHANISMS INFLUENCE OPPORTUNITIES AND CONTRIBUTE TO THE COLOR LINE?

Access to College, but Not to College Credits or Degrees

In the past few decades, college enrollment rates have soared. About 85 percent of high school graduates now plan on obtaining a college degree, an increase of almost two-thirds since the 1970s (Schneider & Stevenson, 1999; U.S. Department of Education, 2002). Community college students constitute about 40 percent of all undergraduates, 42 percent of black undergraduates, and over 56 percent of Latino undergraduates. Unfortunately, a recent national survey found that, of students who began in public two-year colleges, only 26 percent had completed any degree six years after entrance, and the rate for blacks was less than 11 percent (Bailey, Badway, & Gumport, 2002; U.S. Department of Education, 2002). Nearly half (46%) of high school students who go to college and nearly two-thirds (64%) of the students who enroll in community colleges end up in remedial classes—high school-level courses that carry no college credit (Adelman, 1995).

Thirty years ago, high school seniors' plans strongly predicted college attainment (Sewell & Shah, 1968), and reformers tried to increase the number of college graduates by raising students' sights, especially African Americans'. Although blacks today have much higher aspirations, often as high as whites, plans are now weak predictors of college attainment for all students, but especially for blacks (Wong & Rosenbaum, 2002). Emphasizing plans is useful but not sufficient.

Large numbers of students plan to get college degrees, yet most do not, especially those with low grades in high school (Rosenbaum, 2001). While 84 percent of seniors plan to get college degrees, only 38 percent of this group actually complete any degree in the next ten years (Rosenbaum, 2001). One-quarter of those seniors planning on college who had grades of C or lower almost always failed to earn a degree (86% got no degree), and 50 percent got no college credit, and thus no measurable benefit from their college plans.

High School Counselors Encourage Dreams, but Not Implementation Strategies

High school counselors were formerly gatekeepers who selected which students could apply to college, often in arbitrary and biased ways, and they often steered low-income and black and Latino students away from college (Cicourel & Kitsuse, 1964; Oakes, 1985; Rosenbaum, 1976). However, recent studies indicate that counselors now believe that open admissions means they don't have to discourage any student's college plans, and thus they don't deter students with poor chances of success in college, even those with an 86 percent chance of failing to earn a degree. Many guidance counselors practice a college-for-all philosophy, especially with the pressure they get from parents and principals, and advise nearly all students to try out college, saying, "Who am I to burst their bubble?" (Rosenbaum, Miller, & Krci, 1996, p. 267; 1997). Counselors may be well-intentioned, but their emphasis on college access regardless of college readiness prevents them from helping students understand their options, make informed choices, and formulate realistic strategies for attaining their goals.

Community Colleges Encourage Dreams, but Not Strategies for Attaining Various Options

Community colleges have been criticized for their "cooling out" function that lowers the BA aspirations of low-performing students through counseling, testing, and other academic policies (Clark, 1973). Subsequent quantitative analyses have shown that community college attendance does reduce the likelihood of completing a bachelor's degree (Dougherty, 1994).

Unlike those in past research, the community college staff and faculty in our study avoid cooling out students' aspirations and actively encourage bachelor's degree aspirations. They avoid channeling students toward more realistic goals, even low-performing remedial students. Consequently, remedial education may have replaced counseling strategies as a primary cooling-out mechanism in community colleges like the ones we studied (Deil-Amen & Rosenbaum, 2002).

Unfortunately, this combination of high aspirations, optimistic counseling, and low academic performance may constitute a more covert and gradual cooling-out process that begins in high school and extends into community college. In contrast to the overt strategies described by Clark (1973) to guide students away from the pursuit of a BA, students today may be led into retaining unrealistic goals and be uninformed about what it takes to achieve a degree.

When community colleges avoid cooling out students' plans by withholding discouraging information about their remedial status, many students don't realize that remedial courses do not earn college credits and that their two-year degree may take three or four years to complete (Deil-Amen & Rosenbaum, 2002). Community college counselors in our study also often fail to emphasize applied degree options that can lead to good jobs and reduce the need for remedial courses.

Occupational Programs Provide Job Skills, but Do Not Improve Job Access

Research indicates that high school vocational programs often lead to higher earnings, but only if students get skill-relevant jobs, which many do not (Bishop, 1988). Similarly, two-year college degrees often lead to higher earnings, but only for some majors (Grubb, 1996). While reformers focus on curriculum changes, few reforms aim to improve student placement in relevant jobs. With the exception of contract education, which tends to serve individuals who are already employed, job contacts and links to the labor market are not emphasized at the community colleges we studied.

Research shows that black, Latino, and lower-income job applicants tend to have less access to good jobs through personal contacts (Granovetter, 1995; Lin, Ensel, & Vaughn, 1981; Peterson, Spaorta, & Seidel, 2000; Wegener, 1991). However, if colleges had employer contacts that helped students get relevant jobs, they might be able to reduce the racial gap in employment.

College-employer contacts may also improve degree completion. Our surveys indicate that students who think their college's employer contacts will help them get a good job are less likely to consider dropping out. The disproportionate concentration of blacks and Latinos in these colleges suggests that such links may provide additional "glue" to help them complete degrees.

Advisory Boards

Unfortunately, the community colleges studied rarely use employer contacts for job placement. The state of Illinois requires community colleges to convene advisory boards before starting new occupational programs, and then to follow up with annual meetings. However, in these meetings, occupational program chairs tend to focus on curriculum and rarely initiate discussions about job placement, believing that employers automatically recognize their graduates' degrees. As in prior studies, we find that these community colleges have infrequent, short, sometimes nonpurposeful advisory meetings (Brewer & Gray, 1999), and they delegate employment advisory duties to already overburdened program chairs, for whom they are a low priority. Most program chairs see little purpose in these boards and were not interested in learning from them. In one program, a business department chair, who taught there for 25 years, was asked, "How would you define what the employer market looks like for your students?" He replied, "I'll be very candid with you and say I don't know." His program had not met with an advisory board in years, and he was not sure what jobs his graduates got. Some community college program chairs reported having advisory boards only on paper. For example, the chair of one computer information systems department said that "anecdotal" information was sufficient, adding, "An advisory council . . . would just be five of my best friends . . . and we'll have a lunch somewhere."

When creating advisory boards, these community college program chairs do not necessarily select employers who are likely to hire their graduates. They instead select executives from large, prominent firms, regardless of whether they are potential employers for their students. Many faculty and administrators fear that employers want a curriculum tailored to meet their company's specific needs, which contradicts the community college's mission to provide a broader set of skills.

Career Services Offices

All seven community colleges have career services offices that provide general information (resume formatting, job search tips, interviewing etiquette) and administer career interest and aptitude tests. However, at all seven colleges, career services officers do not recommend specific employers to visit or explain what specific skills employers value. These offices post job openings on bulletin boards or computers, and staff are not responsible for supervising students' job application process.

At all seven community colleges, career services administrators stress that their offices are understaffed and able to serve less than one-fifth of the students, in addition to local community members. Given the recent federal policy emphasis on serving clients receiving Temporary Aid for Needy Families (TANF) and the public community college mission to serve local taxpayers, career services focus on local community members and jobs that don't require degrees (Jacobs & Winslow, 2003; Shaw & Rab, 2003). One career services manager reported a 1:4 "ratio between students . . . and community residents using the career counselors." Meager resources also prevent career services offices from collecting adequate labor market information.

Career services offices seem designed to be peripheral, and since seeking services is initiated by the student, they only serve the few students who realize they would benefit from such services. In fact, many students may not know about this service, since it is not widely promoted and tends to be located in a hard-to-find part of the campus. At one college the career services office is on a third floor, around the bend of a long, dark hall. As one career counselor notes,

> We are really tucked away here. The action . . . is all at the other end of campus. . . . We're just not in a high traffic area. . . . If we were located somewhere else, . . . we'd never be able to handle the flow.

Even faculty members don't always understand what the office does. When we asked program chairs at several community colleges about labor market information, they told us "the career office must do that," and said they referred students there. However, on visiting these career offices, we learned that they lacked any information about the local labor market and assumed no responsibility for job information or placement.

Job Placement

In fact, these seven community colleges devote little effort to job placement. No centralized, full-time job placement function exists for graduates, although some services focus on part-time work for current students. Some schools' program chairs report actively helping students get jobs or responding to employers' phone calls, but such efforts are often haphazard. Most admit that they do not see this as valuable use of their time, some emphatically deny that this is part of their duties, and several express resentment at employers' inquiries, saying such inquiries interfere with their primary responsibilities. As one program chair reported, "Sometimes I'll just . . . give the employer a list of students . . . and let them deal with it. Other times I may not [even] respond."

During our study, none of these community colleges had anyone specifically in charge of deciding where students will land in the labor market or collecting systematic information on what jobs graduates get, or whether they even get jobs. The college's main responsibility was understood to be to confer credits, degrees, and their accompanying skills. The transition into the labor market was considered a separate task handled by each individual student.

WHAT POLICIES CAN IMPROVE OPPORTUNITIES FOR AFRICAN AMERICANS AND LATINOS?

Realistic Advice and College Readiness Exams

Many high school students do not begin college in "real" college courses but in noncredit remedial courses. Our research suggests that in high school, many students do not understand the impact their performance and learning will have on their future education and career. Our interviews with these community college students found that many were unaware of their achievement deficiencies in high school, and they had not anticipated a remedial placement in college. They were uninformed about placement testing procedures and content, and unaware that the skills they had acquired and/or the courses they had taken in high school were insufficient for them to get into college-level classes. Many had high school counselors who encouraged them to pursue college without warning them that they might be placed in remedial courses. Because students were unaware that they lacked the skills necessary for college, they could not take steps to improve their skills while still in high school.

In Chicago, large numbers of students with As and Bs in their high school math and English classes place below tenth grade on the City College of Chicago's placement exam. Many students in our study who had good or average grades in high school took courses that had low standards and required little effort. Some reported that they got good grades in high school without ever having to do homework or take their books home, and one said that his math teacher passed everybody in the class. They did not realize what the consequences would be once they got to college. One class valedictorian was placed in remedial English. These students thought their grades reflected skills that were adequate for college, and they were surprised to discover how different the standards were in college: "All you had to have was a D in high school to pass, so who couldn't get a D?" None of these students recalled a teacher or guidance counselor who warned them about what they might encounter once they entered college, yet all were encouraged to go. These students from Chicago high schools, who are largely black and Latino, do not appear to be getting critical information about college-level academic skills and standards, and this could be robbing them of the opportunity to play an informed and active role in their own life trajectories.

While state exit exams are the current fad for raising students' achievement, exit exams often mislead students because they are poorly aligned with college-level placement exams and standards. For instance, many students pass the New Jersey state exit exam and then fail the state exam required for college credit courses (Rosenbaum, 2001). When New York State initially required all students to pass the difficult Regents exam to graduate, a majority failed. The state found it politically impossible to withhold diplomas from so many students. Exit exams may be useful for raising minimum scores, but they are usually too rudimentary and not intended to indicate college requirements or college readiness.

Instead of exit exams, high schools should provide a college readiness exam to inform students whether they are likely to be consigned to noncredit remedial courses. Unlike the SAT, this exam would measure academic skills required in college credit courses. Unlike exit exams, this test would not limit diplomas, but it could help students make informed choices about their high school efforts and course selections. Without such exams, too many students will only learn about their poor skills *after* they enter college, when it is costly and sometimes too late.

Explicit Structures, Not Implicit Rules

College policies often ignore the many economic, social, and cultural pressures that cause students to drop out of college, especially low-income African American students. The private occupational colleges in our study provide an informative contrast to the community colleges, and are a model for our suggestions about how to help students persist in college. Our findings reveal that these occupational colleges have devised innovative procedures to help students overcome the customary economic and social obstacles to college completion. They use financial aid practices to improve access to grants and loans, which were recommended by Orfield and Paul (1994). Other practices go beyond anything in the academic literature and include innovative uses of peer groups, dropout-prevention strategies, and procedures for early detection of problems and for handling unsupportive families and work pressures (Deil-Amen & Rosenbaum, 2002).

Given students' many problems in community colleges, it is instructive to examine alternatives. We discovered that the occupational colleges we studied "structure out" the need for much of the socio-organizational know-how that the community colleges require. They have developed original structures and processes that seem to reduce barriers to disadvantaged students with limited know-how by helping them navigate administrative obstacles in college.

The occupational colleges studied have found ways to transform implicit rules into explicit organizational structures and policies. They create programs that students can easily understand, master, and negotiate, even if they know little about how college works. In fact, many of these occupational colleges have found that they can improve student success by making their curriculum *more* structured, not less. These colleges have discovered that degree completion and work entry, particularly for students from disadvantaged backgrounds, can be improved by structuring students' choices through several procedures.

Minimal Bureaucratic Hurdles

At the occupational colleges studied, enrolling is a simple process handled mainly by a single staff person who makes all the arrangements for a student. Every student is then assigned to a single advisor, who helps select courses. Information is available in one place, and students do not have to run around the college getting information and dealing with a bureaucratic tangle of offices. Furthermore, registration each term is a simple matter; course choices are simple and offered in the same time slots over the year, avoiding work and family schedule conflicts. Students choose a package of coordinated courses, rather than selecting from a long menu of individual course choices with fluctuating and overlapping time slots.

These occupational colleges also reduce bureaucratic hurdles to financial aid, whereas obtaining financial aid at these community colleges is largely up to students and little help is provided. Heckman (1999) noted the low take-up rate on federal and state financial aid programs, speculating (based on no empirical data) that it was due to students' decision not to seek aid. Our interviews with community college staff and students indicate that students do not apply because they don't know about it, can't figure out the complex forms, are skeptical of loans, or have parents who are hesitant to reveal tax and income information. In contrast, these occupational colleges treat financial aid as an integral part of the admissions process. They help students get the best aid package possible by physically walking applicants to the financial aid office, where a staff person explains the process, answers all questions, and fills out the financial aid application with each student (and their parents, if desired). This is rarely done by the community colleges we studied or by those others have studied (Orfield & Paul, 1994).

Structured Programs

While the community college students we interviewed face a confusing array of difficult-to-understand course and program choices with unclear connections to future career trajectories, the occupational colleges studied offer a clear set of course sequences geared toward specific career goals. When students first arrive at these community colleges, they are often uncertain about what degree or program to pursue and are encouraged to explore, yet the model for exploration is based on that of four-year colleges—sample from a wide variety of unrelated courses that are highly general, do not specify clear outcomes, and may count for some programs but not others. Much like a cafeteria, students can sample from five or more academic disciplines without much regard for future career goals.

This nondirective approach may work well for middle-class students who can count on four years of college, but this approach is problematic for many nontraditional students with limited resources who must obtain a marketable degree with a minimum of missed wages or tuition dollars (Wilms, 1974). Many disadvantaged students misunderstand college offerings, face strong pressures to get through school quickly, and seek an efficient way to improve their qualifications and get better jobs. The bulk of the exploratory options involve liberal arts courses, in which many community college students have done poorly in the past. Confusion also arises from the lack of clarity about the relevance of specific choices to future careers.

These occupational colleges present an interesting contrast by helping students determine from the outset what degree program best coincides with their abilities, interests, and needs. At enrollment, every student is required to sit down with an admissions counselor who goes through all the degree programs and the courses they entail, with an explanation of implications, sequences, requirements, and job outcomes. Students' achievements and goals are assessed. For students unsure of their future goals, this personal attention from a counselor who is familiar with all the degree possibilities can be very helpful.

While this approach lacks the breadth of exploration in community colleges, it does entail directed exploration with the possibility of changing career trajectory after the first semester or first year. Obviously, for these nontraditional students, many of whom did poorly in high school, the very effort to try out college is a daring, risky exploration, and each college course provides a challenge that could threaten this effort. Moreover, at these occupational colleges, students who do well in the associate's program are encouraged to transfer to a BA program in a related field.

Mandatory Regular Advising

In contrast to the burden of student-initiated guidance, the occupational colleges we studied have actually "structured out" the need for students to take the initiative to see a counselor or advisor when they need assistance.[2] Instead, the colleges take the initiative by developing systems that provide guidance without students having to ask for it. They automatically assign each student to a specific advisor who monitors their academic progress. Students must meet with their advisor each term before registering for courses, and the advisors provide assistance specific to each student's needs.

Additionally, registration guides detail exactly what courses to take each term to complete each degree. Although this limits course flexibility, most students report that they appreciate the system because it helps them to complete a degree quickly and prevents them from making mistakes. In our student survey we asked, "Have you ever taken any course which you later discovered would not count toward your degree?" Forty-five percent of the community college students responded "yes," compared to only 16 percent of the private occupational college students.

Abundant Advisors

While the community colleges studied offer few counselors, these occupational colleges have invested in advising services and job-placement staff. For example, one of the occupational colleges has four academic advisors and one dean devoted exclusively to counseling 1,300 first-year students, a ratio of 260 students to each staff person. Moreover, this college has five additional advisors for assisting with job placement. This provides a sharp contrast to community colleges, where counselors perform many counseling tasks, including personal, academic, and career counseling, and typically have 800:1 student-counselor ratios for all these services.

Unlike the community colleges in our study, all seven occupational colleges devote substantial resources to job placement, separate from the other counseling and advising functions. Job-placement offices are well staffed, with low student-staff ratios, ranging from 90:1 to 122:1. In contrast, none of these community colleges has any full-time staff devoted to job placement, and other research suggests this may be typical (Brewer & Gray, 1999; Grubb, 1996).

Informed Advisors

These occupational college instructors communicate with advisors to exchange information about students' progress. Advisors are regularly informed about departmental requirements, and faculty members talk with advisors about particular students—a simple process, given the highly explicit organization of programs. This does not take place at these community colleges.

Information Systems

The required meetings at these occupational colleges improve advisors' information about students' progress or difficulties, unlike the difficulty they have detecting student mistakes at the community colleges. Several of these schools take attendance regularly. Advisors are quickly informed of absences, and students who are frequently absent are contacted by their advisor before the problem gets serious. After midterms, instructors notify advisors about students who are performing poorly, and the advisor is responsible for mediating problems between student and teacher and making sure the student receives academic support. Through scheduled interactions, students get to know their advisors and are therefore more likely to approach them for help even when not required to do so. This is a stark contrast to the more anonymous community college system of advising.

Shorter Academic Terms

These occupational colleges make an effort to alleviate external pressures that increase students' chances of dropping out. Several of these schools have adapted to students' needs by compacting the school year. Instead of offering semester-long classes, one college has altered the academic year so it now consists of five ten-week terms, with only two one-week vacations, in December and July. Several others have short terms and year-round scheduling. In one college, students can obtain a 15-month associate's degree.

Disadvantaged students face pressures and crises that cause them to temporarily stop attending college. These occupational colleges have reduced the cost of such pauses by shortening the length of the school term. If outside pressures force students to suspend their studies and lose one term, it is a relatively short term, and they can often resume their studies in a short time. Moreover, prospective students don't have to wait long before a new term begins. Wilms (1974) estimated that for-profit occupational colleges have competitive cost-benefit ratios, despite much higher tuitions, because of their speed at getting students to a degree, which raises their earnings sooner. While the topic has not been studied recently, getting a degree nine months earlier is likely to increase earnings by increasing students' wages and work hours sooner. In addition, completing schooling quickly reduces the pressures from parents, spouses, children, and jobs.

Reduced Commuting

Unlike these community colleges, which have complex class schedules in noncontinuous time slots, these occupational colleges schedule back-to-back those courses that would typically be taken in a program. This blocking of courses decreases commuting time and makes it easier for students to attend school while they continue to work. Also, whereas the class schedules at these community colleges change from term to term, the occupational colleges offer the same time schedules from one term to the next. As a result, work and child-care arrangements made for one term will continue to work out in the following term.

Dependable Course Sequences

While these community colleges offer so many courses that they cannot promise to offer needed courses each term, the occupational colleges pre-plan sequences of courses for each program, and they ensure that every program offers the courses necessary to make progress every term. Obviously, all students in a program taking the same courses is relatively easy and economically efficient, but the commitment of these colleges goes beyond that. In several cases, a few students fell out of their cohort's sequence in taking courses, and the colleges offered classes with only three students just so the few could finish their degree within the promised time frame. This is very expensive, but these colleges stood behind their promise that students can complete the degree in the customary time. In the community colleges studied, classes below a minimum enrollment were routinely cancelled.

Prescribed Solutions to Common Problems

In contrast to what we heard in the reports of the community college staff and faculty—namely, a lament that students work too much and do not resemble "traditional" students—these occupational colleges turn a potential negative into something that can advance students' career goals. Students receive detailed guidance on how to combine their need to work with their educational goals. These occupational colleges consider work a valuable experience related to their degrees, and they help students find relevant jobs, even if they may pay less. Advisors try to guide students to use their work to advance their career goals.

Institutional Job Contacts

While contacts are the best way to get jobs, blacks are less likely than whites to have relatives with contacts to good jobs (Rosenbaum, 2001). However, American social policy has largely ignored institutional contacts, which are common in other nations (Hamilton, 1989; Rosenbaum & Kariya, 1989). High schools provide vocational courses, but most do not help students get access to jobs. Although most high school seniors plan college, many never attend and many others drop out, often without college credits. Blacks are highly represented in both categories (Rosenbaum, 2001). Social policies need to address the needs of non-college-bound students, those who leave college, and those who attain a subbaccalaureate degree as they look for promising jobs (Orfield, 1997).

Research indicates that some American high schools and colleges create institutional contacts to employers, sometimes through formal job-placement offices and sometimes through the informal personal contacts of individual teachers. These contacts provide access to jobs with good career advancement, and they are not correlated with social class. Surprisingly, females, blacks, and Latinos are more likely to get contact help from their schools than white males, and they experience substantially higher earnings trajectories than they would otherwise (Rosenbaum, 2001).

There are various ways that educational institutions can create and maintain school-employer contacts and help disadvantaged students get good jobs relevant to their training (Person & Rosenbaum, in press). While both community and occupational colleges provide similar activities regarding employer links (employer advisory boards, career services, job placement, and labor market monitoring), their approach is quite different. In contrast to staff at these community colleges, the staff at the occupational colleges use employer interactions to develop trusted relationships and information exchange and to convince employers of their graduates' competence (Deil-Amen & Rosenbaum, 2004). Creating such an institutional bridge can be crucial for black and Latino students. Past research suggests that when left without the benefit of such institutional advocates, entry-level black and Latino job applicants suffer from employers' negative evaluations, often based on subjective, noncognitive attributes (Heckman &

Lochner, 2000; Holzer, 1996; Moss & Tilly, 2000; Neckerman & Kirschen-man, 1991). As our surveys and interviews indicate, when students realize that their college will actively help them find good jobs after they complete their degree, they are less likely to consider dropping out (Person & Rosenbaum, in press).

At all seven occupational colleges, staff report an interest in both information exchange and convincing employers that their program serves employers' specific needs. They use employer advisory boards to facilitate a systematic flow of trustworthy information from employers about their hiring needs and to employers regarding the appropriate qualities their graduates possess to fulfill employers' needs, thereby increasing the likelihood that graduates will be perceived as preferred job candidates.

In all seven occupational colleges, administrators report soliciting employers' reactions to how prior graduates met employers' needs and advanced over time. These administrators use employer advisory committees to learn employers' expectations of job candidates and to convince employers that the school strives to meet their needs and values their relationship. Since labor market needs and school staff change over time, the occupational colleges try to build enduring institutional relationships with specific employers.

While these community colleges pile advisory committee tasks onto already overcommitted program chairs for whom other tasks are a higher priority, all seven occupational colleges make advisory committees the top priority for certain staff. These job-placement staff select employers who offer jobs with good pay and advancement opportunities.

Job Placement Services

All seven occupational colleges studied devote substantial energy and resources to job placement, which is a central and highly visible function of career services. This aspect is so prominent that some of the career services offices are labeled "Job Placement Office" and are located in high-traffic areas. At all but one occupational college, the career services office is visible from the main entrance, and students are required to use it. While the community colleges generally have 800 students per counselor and no job placement staff, every one of these occupational colleges has full-time professional staff and clerical support solely responsible for job placement, with ratios ranging from 60–122 students per staff member. Consequently, the same kinds of employer requests that are sometimes resented by community college program chairs are encouraged at the occupational colleges.

The staff help every student craft a resume, since they know employers' specific needs and what skills and experiences each occupational program provides to meet those needs. While these community colleges provide a few students with general advice on resume preparation (some boast software creating an attractive layout), the occupational colleges require students to meet with staff who tell them what local employers in their field want to see in a resume, which of their courses and skills meet employers' needs, and how to present them in a resume and interview. They also supervise the job application process for every student and help match students to employers looking for candidates with compatible qualities. If a student fails to get a job offer, staff will sometimes ask employers how the student did in an interview to gauge the student's interviewing skills and better understand the employer's needs.

Relationships with Employers

This assistance is beneficial to students (especially those who wouldn't otherwise seek such help), employers, and the college's reputation more generally. Administrators report that a student's poor presentation might harm not only the student's employment opportunities, but also the college's reputation. Maintaining trusted, dependable relationships with employers improves occupational college students' future access to these and similar employers. Knowing students well facilitates their ability to benefit individual students and sustain employer trust.

In all the occupational colleges, job-placement staff develop trusted personal relationships with recruiters in several ways. First, they initiate contacts by attending chamber of commerce meetings, phoning employers, visiting workplaces, and making contacts at job fairs. Second, job placement staff at all seven occupational colleges stress systematic responsiveness. They respond quickly to employers' requests and tailor their recommendations to employers' specific needs, sometimes faxing ten appropriate resumes from their files in the ten minutes after a job request comes through. Employers realize these colleges are a free employment service that provides appropriate candidates. Third, while none of these community colleges oversees the job application process, job placement staff at all of these occupational colleges channel appropriate information to employers. They send only relevant resumes that meet the specific job qualifications, rather than relying on students' response to bulletin-board postings. Finally, job placement staff develop personal relationships with job recruiters. While the community college staff give low priority to employers' requests, the occupational college job-placement staff at all seven colleges meet recruiters in both collegewide and program-level advisory board meetings, learn their specific needs, and continue to work on a one-on-one basis with them. They talk with companies about their specific needs so that they can coach their students. They initiate calls to ask employers how satisfied they are with graduates' performance to show the school's commitment to serving employers' needs and sustaining the relationship. Of course, these practices also help them learn about further openings.

These personal relationships are based on mutual benefit between schools and recruiters, the kind of mutual obligation that creates social capital (Coleman, 1988). When they know an employer's particular needs, placement staff can select students who are a good fit for this employer and inform the employer of desirable personal attributes that are hard to assess in job interviews. They make it clear that their job is to satisfy employers, so employers can trust that job-placement staff seek to make dependable, long-lasting relationships.

These occupational colleges also work hard to "create" labor market demand for their associate's degree. All seven occupational colleges collect graduate follow-up information and record job-placement rates. Staff identify and contact local employers in relevant fields, attempt to convince them to try their students and explain that their students have the necessary qualifications, often carefully selecting especially good students to confirm their promises to new employers so that they will return with future job offers. Staff report that sometimes they are even able to convince employers to give preferential consideration to their graduates.

CONCLUSION

Community colleges represent a brave experiment in providing second chances for higher education at a time when higher education is increasingly important. This is inevitably a high-risk endeavor. Just as hospital ICUs have higher mortality rates than other wards, second-chance colleges will have higher attrition than selective colleges. While cost-effectiveness can be improved by abolishing hospital ICUs and second-chance colleges, society has rightly chosen to pursue these goals in spite of their cost.

While community colleges are understandably reluctant to curtail options, our findings raise questions about whether they are spreading their limited resources too thin by trying to be everything to everybody. Amid the complexity of the community colleges' multiple missions, their most vulnerable students may be falling through the cracks. We urge individual comprehensive community colleges to push for the autonomy to prioritize their missions and possibly pare back lower-priority college functions that may be limiting the ability of a community college to fully and effectively sustain their higher-priority programs.

Clearly, many of the students in our study found these occupational colleges preferable to the more general-purpose community colleges, and much of this had to do with the ways students experience the explicit structuring or "packaging" of their education and related assistance in navigating the college and job-search processes. Although it may not be politically feasible for community colleges to simply drop some of their missions, it may be beneficial for them to think more carefully about how their numerous options are presented and experienced by disadvantaged and first-generation students who wish to benefit from only one or two of their missions.

We urge community colleges to make their programs more focused and better structured to accomplish their goals. Our studies of the mechanisms used in private occupational colleges indicate that degree completion rates may be improved by providing students with better information about process and outcomes, and providing clear options and good advice about these options. This chapter suggests that improved information and social structures may help disadvantaged students get into real college courses (not noncredit remedial courses), stay in college, and get good jobs after college.

Obviously, the occupational colleges in our study function within a resource and funding environment that is very different from the community colleges' environment. However, our recommendation to community colleges is to isolate those aspects of students' experience that we found problematic and consider how the organizational structure of community colleges can be altered to accommodate their needs. For example, can the presentation of information regarding various programs, classes, and degree options be simplified and made more understandable? Should what happens outside the classroom in the realm of student services and career services be given higher priority and take a more proactive approach to assisting students? Can assistance in encouraging and completing financial aid forms be improved? Should community colleges think more along the lines of large high schools that have attempted to develop community by creating smaller schools within very large schools? Additionally, could communication between community colleges and feeder high schools clarify the details of the gap between high school graduation requirements and college readiness so that students are not wrongly assuming that their competence in high school will translate directly into college-level classes?

Community colleges should look specifically to the example of other community colleges that have successfully minimized the problems highlighted by our research. Future research should identify and study community colleges that are improving in the areas we have discovered so that an organizationally relevant and realistic picture of what can be done in a publicly funded institution can emerge. It is our hope that the vivid contrast between two very different institutional contexts will generate such further inquiry.

NOTES

1. Our research reveals similar findings for both Latino and African American students, so Latinos are included where appropriate.
2. The community colleges tended to employ faculty-status and other "counselors" for academic and other advising, while the occupational colleges preferred to use the term academic "advisors."

REFERENCES

Adelman, C. (1995). *The new college course map and transcript files*. Washington, DC: U.S. Department of Education.

Apling, R. N. (1993, July/August). Proprietary schools and their students. *Journal of Higher Education, 64*, 379–416.

Bailey, T., Badway, N., & Gumport, P. (2002). *For-profit higher education and community colleges*. Stanford, CA: Stanford University, School of Education.

Bishop, J. (1988). *Vocational education for at-risk youth: How can it be more effective?* (Working Paper 88–11). Ithaca, NY: New York State School of Industrial and Labor Relations, Cornell University.

Brewer, D. J., & Gray, M. (1999). Do faculty connect school to work? Evidence from community colleges. *Educational Evaluation and Policy Analysis, 21*, 405–416.

Cicourel, A., & Kitsuse, J. (1964). *The educational decision-makers*. Indianapolis: Bobbs-Merrill.

Clark, B. (1973). The cooling out function in higher education. In R. R. Bell & H. R. Stub (Eds.), *The sociology of education* (pp. 362–371). Homewood, IL: Dorsey.

Coleman, J. S. (1988). Social capital in the creation of human capital. *American Journal of Sociology, 94*, S95–S120.

Deil-Amen, R., & Rosenbaum, J. (2002). The unintended consequences of stigma-free remediation. *Sociology of Education, 75*, 249–268.

Deil-Amen, R., & Rosenbaum, J. (2004). Charter building and labor market contacts in two-year colleges. *Sociology of Education, 77*, 245–265.

Dougherty, K. (1994). *The contradictory college: The conflicting origins, impacts, and futures of the community college.* Albany: State University of New York Press.

Granovetter, M. (1995). *Getting a job: A study of contacts and careers* (2nd ed.). Chicago: University of Chicago Press.

Grubb, W. N. (1996). *Working in the middle.* San Francisco: Jossey-Bass.

Hamilton, S. F. (1989). *Apprenticeship for adulthood: preparing youth for the future.* New York: Free Press.

Hecker, D. J. (2001). Occupational employment projections to 2010. *Monthly Labor Review, 124*(11), 57–84.

Heckman, J. (1999, Spring). Doing it right: Job training and education. *Public Interest,* 86–107.

Heckman, J., & Lochner, L. (2000). Rethinking education and training policy: Understanding the sources of skill formation in a modern economy. In S. Danziger & J. Waldfogel (Eds.), *Securing the future: Investing in children from birth to college* (pp. 47–86). New York: Russell Sage Foundation.

Holzer, H. (1996). *What employers want: Job prospects for less-educated workers.* New York: Russell Sage Foundation.

Jacobs, J. A., & Winslow, S. (2003). Welfare reform and enrollment in postsecondary education. *Annals of the American Academy of Political and Social Science, 586,* 194–217.

Joseph, L. B., & Lynn, L. E. (1990). Introduction. In L. B. Joseph (Ed.), *Creating jobs, creating workers: Economic development and employment in metropolitan Chicago* (pp. 1–17). Chicago: University of Illinois Press.

Lin, N., Ensel, W., & Vaughn, J. (1981). Social resources and strength of ties. *American Sociological Review, 46,* 393–405.

Moss, P., & Tilly, C. (2000). *Stories employers tell: Race, skill and hiring in America.* New York: Russell Sage Foundation.

Neckerman, K. M., & Kirschenman, J. (1991). Hiring strategies, racial bias, and inner-city workers. *Social Problems, 38,* 801–815.

Oakes, J. (1985). *Keeping track: How schools structure inequality.* New Haven, CT: Yale University Press.

Orfield, G. (1990). Wasted talent, threatened future: Metropolitan Chicago's human capital and Illinois public policy. In L. B. Joseph (Ed.), *Creating jobs, creating workers: Economic development and employment in metropolitan Chicago* (pp. 129–160). Chicago: University of Illinois Press.

Orfield, G. (1997). Going to work: Weak preparation, little help. *Advances in Educational Policy, 3,* 3–32.

Orfield, G., & Paul, F. G. (1994). *High hopes, long odds: A major report on Hoosier teens and the American dream.* Indianapolis: Indiana Youth Institute.

Person, A. E., & Rosenbaum, J. E. (in press). Labor-market linkages among two-year college faculty and their impact on student perceptions, effort, and college persistence. In D. Neumark (Ed.), *The school-to-work transition.* New York: Russell Sage Foundation.

Peterson, T., Spaorta, I., & Seidel, M. L. (2000). Offering a job. *American Journal of Sociology, 106,* 763–816.

Rosenbaum, J. E. (1976). *Making inequality: The hidden curriculum of high school tracking*. New York, NY: Wiley.

Rosenbaum, J. E. (2001). *Beyond college for all: Career paths for the forgotten half*. New York: Russell Sage Foundation.

Rosenbaum, J. E., & Kariya, T. (1989). From high school to work: Market and institutional mechanisms in Japan. *American Journal of Sociology, 94*, 1334–1365.

Rosenbaum, J. E., Miller, S., & Krei, M. (1996). Gatekeeping in an era of more open gates. *American Journal of Education, 104*, 257–279.

Rosenbaum, J. E., Miller, S., & Krei, M. (1997). What role should counselors have? *Advances in Educational Policy, 3*, 79–92.

Rothstein, R. (2002). *Out of balance: Our understanding of how schools affect society and how society affects schools*. Retrieved January 5, 2005, from www.spencer.org/publications/conferences/traditions_of_scholarships/traditions_of_scholships.pdf

Schneider, B., & Stevenson, D. (1999). *The ambitious generation: America's teenagers, motivated but directionless*. New Haven, CT: Yale University Press.

Sewell, W. H., & Shah, V. P. (1968). Parents' education and children's educational aspirations and achievements. *American Sociological Review, 33*, 191–209.

Shaw, K. M., & Rab, S. (2003). Market rhetoric versus reality in policy and practice: The workforce investment act and access to community college education and training. *Annals of the American Academy of Political and Social Science, 586*, 172–193.

U.S. Department of Education. (2002). *Digest of education statistics, 2001*. Washington, DC: National Center for Education Statistics.

Wegener, B. (1991). Job mobility and social ties. *American Sociological Review, 56*, 60–71.

Wilms, W. W. (1974). *Public and proprietary vocational training: A study of effectiveness*. Berkeley, CA: Center for Research and Development in Higher Education.

Wilson, W. J. (1987). *The truly disadvantaged: The inner city, the underclass, and public policy*. Chicago: University of Chicago Press.

Wong, M., & Rosenbaum, J. (2002, August). *Changes in the educational attainment process over four decades*. Paper presented at the annual meeting of American Sociological Association, Chicago.

6

Diversity on Campus

Exemplary Programs for Retaining and Supporting Students of Color

DEAN K. WHITLA
CAROLYN HOWARD
FRANK TUITT
RICHARD J. REDDICK
ELIZABETH FLANAGAN

Educating students for a pluralistic society requires that colleges have ethnically diverse student bodies, as it is a well-documented fact that all students gain substantial benefits, both cognitive and social, from regular, positive interactions with others outside their own ethnic peer group (Antonio, 2001; Chang, 2001; Gurin, Dey, Hurtado, & Gurin, 2002; Hu & Kuh, 2003). Our own research at law and medical schools has found that white students who have diverse peer interactions develop the capacity to communicate effectively with clients or patients from different cultures. Furthermore, student ethnic diversity clearly enhances both classroom and out of classroom experiences for all students (Orfield & Whitla, 1999; Whitla et al., 2003).

These findings are particularly salient in the context of an increasingly diverse college-age student population (see Kurlaender & Flores, this volume). Over the past 20 years, college enrollment for Latinos has more than tripled; for African Americans, it grew by 56 percent; and among Native Americans it grew by 80 percent (Harvey, 2002). However, underrepresented minority students (i.e., African American, Latino/a, and Native American students) are disproportionately enrolled in two-year or less-selective colleges. Furthermore, once enrolled, these students are not being retained at the same rates as their white and Asian peers (NCES, 2002). The college experience for a number of these students has been characterized by the struggle to simply graduate, rather than the exhilaration of high achievement: to survive rather than thrive (Feagin, Vera, & Imani, 1996).

In an attempt, then, to address inequities and better educate a more pluralistic society, targeted admissions and retention policies have been used by colleges and universities to increase minority student enrollment.[1] While recognizing the importance such efforts have had in recruiting and enrolling underrepresented students, this chapter, based on data from the National Campus Diversity Project (NCDP) located at the Harvard Graduate School of Education, describes other strategies colleges use to improve minority achievement and student satisfaction. Specifically, we 1) identify diversity programs that have been models for improving the racial climate on campuses and 2) locate programs that have markedly improved minority student academic achievement. To be successful, campus initiatives cannot be balkanized or exist in a vacuum, but instead need to be woven into campus life (Hurtado, Milem, Clayton-Pederson, & Allen, 1999; Smith, 1997). As the importance of educational opportunity becomes exceedingly high, this study highlights methods that can successfully transform institutions of higher education to serve a changing society.

With seed support from the Ford Foundation and expanded support from Atlantic Philanthropies, the NCDP launched a search for highly effective diversity programs.[2] Programs designed to promote and enhance a diverse campus fall into three major categories: 1) programs and activities that enhance curricula for all students, as well as specific academic programs designed to support minority and female student achievement in science, mathematics, engineering, and technology, which we will refer to as the *educational* capital of a school; 2) programs influenced by the organizational behavior of a school with respect to promoting diversity, or the school's *institutional* capital; and 3) programs aimed at increasing the structural diversity of a school and the direct efforts in place to recruit, admit, and retain minority students, faculty, and staff, which we will refer to as the school's *human* capital. We will use the three major areas as an outline for this chapter. This categorization of activities frames what other researchers have noted about diversity efforts: Successful efforts tend to have an impact on more than one area of the school, and such overlap provides mutual reinforcement of these efforts (Chang, 2002; Hurtado et al., 1999).

The educational capital of a school, for the purpose of this chapter, refers to the inclusiveness of curriculum, pedagogy, and special academic initiatives for minority students and women in science and mathematics. Our student interviews yielded information on curriculum transformation linked to academic achievement, and faculty interviews yielded information on specific classroom strategies to engage all students more effectively. Programs that appeared to be the most portable and yielded the greatest measured results were those specifically designed to promote academic achievement for minorities and women in science, mathematics, engineering, and technology. Therefore, we will focus on these programs for the section on educational capital.

Broadly speaking, looking at the institutional capital of a school means looking at the behavior of the presidents, vice presidents, deans, and academic chairs (Berger, 2002). The institutional capital of a school directly affects diversity activities because high-level administrators are primarily responsible for programmatic and policy decisions that affect the entire campus over periods of time (Berger, 2000). Along with tenure-track faculty, these people are the keepers of the school's institutional memory. The institutional capital also encompasses the administrative offices of diversity, school mission statements, and whether or not a school has adopted a long-term strategic plan to address issues of diversity or formed a commission to investigate diversity issues. We found campus evaluation, conducting campus cultural climate assessments, sharing outcomes of these with the campus community, and developing strategies to address concerns to be very significant for enhancing a positive environment for diversity.

The human capital of a school with respect to diversity includes the admissions, recruitment, and retention of minority students, faculty, and staff. A review of recruitment and admissions strategies was a large piece of our research, but is beyond the scope of this chapter. We therefore will focus specifically on issues of underrepresented minority student development, retention, cross-cultural discussions, and student leadership activities. Students from our focus groups mentioned that these cross-cultural activities play a vital role in how minority students thrive, rather than merely survive, on campus. Throughout our interviews, students described the people who direct these activities (assistant deans, multicultural affairs directors, even graduate students) as lifelines, and as integral to student success. The human capital of a school involves not just diversity programs, but also the staff who run these programs, and the degree of respect with which students and high-level administrators hold such staff.

Only a few schools were able to leverage all three areas—educational, institutional, and human capital. Through our interviews, Occidental College and Mount Holyoke College stand out qualitatively as examples of schools that have been able to use the capital from all three areas of campus influence to create environments that are inclusive and welcoming for minority students. Compared with the other 26 schools we visited, students at these schools appeared to be the most satisfied with their campus cultural climate, as well as the depth and breadth of diversity programming on their campus (Stanford University students of color ranked a close third in terms of satisfaction). However, there are a variety of excellent programs across the campuses we visited, at large state institutions as well as smaller private colleges and universities. Therefore, to broaden our discussion and include schools much larger than Mount Holyoke and Occidental, we have highlighted a few model programs that have proven portable and replicable from other campuses in each of the areas listed above. The primary limitations of this research are the narrow window of time involved in data collection and the fact that pre/post evaluations could not be conducted on some of the initiatives described in the institutional and human capital sections of the chapter. Influences on minority student retention rates and campus climate are numerous and variable. This chapter, as an exploratory study, therefore primarily serves to highlight some programs that study participants felt improved campus climate, enhanced minority achievement, or improved minority student retention rates within the major discipline.

EDUCATIONAL CAPITAL:
ACADEMIC ENHANCEMENT PROGRAMS FOR UNDERREPRESENTED MINORITY STUDENTS

Efforts to break down the isolation of minority groups offer promising strategies for supporting their academic achievement. Some researchers suggest that among African American males, academic achievement is considered a "white" activity, and the social cost of such achievement either discourages African American males from applying themselves or prevents them from exhibiting academic strength (Hrabowski, Maton, & Greif, 1998). Minority youth who achieve academically in such a culture are often isolated.

Stanford psychologist Claude Steele has identified "stereotype threat" as yet another impediment for students of color (1999). Steele's concept of stereotype threat suggests that the most academically motivated minority students are most susceptible to the threat of being negatively stereotyped in the academic environment. These students internalize societal messages about their ethnic group, which in turn leads to a diminished performance in academics. Steele suggests that the best approach to reducing stereotype threat is for an instructor to explicitly state that high standards are the criteria for success, and that students' earlier efforts lead the instructor to believe that they can meet the standard. Using this tactic, Steele noted that students performed in line with their ability.

Uri Treisman, whose research evolved into one of the most common programs addressing minority student underperformance, surveyed faculty members on their perceptions of students of color in the 1970s. He found that faculty assumed underrepresented minority students were not as motivated as Asian and white students, that they were inadequately prepared for college, that their families did not support their foray into higher education, and that low family income, not ethnicity, was the dominant variable in predicting student difficulty (Treisman, 1992). His research, however, disproved each of these presumptions. Beginning with Treisman's work and how it has been implemented at the University of Texas at Austin, we will review several science, mathematics, engineering, and technology programs that not only create academically successful minority peer groups, but also provide networks of faculty mentors and connections with professionals in their chosen fields.

Emerging Scholars Program at UT Austin

The work of Uri Treisman at the University of California, Berkeley, highlighted how black and Latino students could become high achievers in introductory calculus courses by changing their study habits. Treisman found that the African American students in his math classes were not performing nearly as well as his Asian students. However, transcript and test-score data on incoming freshman taking Treisman's classes indicated that African American students were as able as the Asian students to do well in calculus. It is, in fact, tough to get into UC Berkeley, and even tougher to get into the math department, so Treisman decided to observe the way his students studied. When he visited the Asian students he found that they first studied individually and then gathered together to discuss their work. They then separated and worked alone again. However, when Treisman visited his African American students he found that they usually worked alone rather than in groups. Treisman encouraged his African American students to study in groups, which they agreed to do, and their grades improved dramatically. It was a great educational experiment, for it produced a marked change in behavior and an increase in achievement. Using this technique, underrepresented minority students achieved at the same rates as their peers and often created a "common culture of mathematics" (Treisman, 1992). Treisman presented his work at Berkeley in what are now known as his Professional Development Program Workshops. Similar workshops were developed at the University of Michigan and UT Austin, where Treisman holds a distinguished chair in mathematics.

The Emerging Scholars Program (ESP) at UT Austin, which was initiated by Efraim Armendariz in mathematics (using Treisman's model), has met with great success. Students participate in six hours weekly of group discussion outside of class. During these discussions they break into groups in which they are challenged with active problem-solving by graduate teaching assistants. Twenty-one students participated in the pilot of ESP in 1988, and as of 2001, 950 students had enrolled.

A ten-year review of ESP found that more than 70 percent of the students participating earned grades of B or better. Overall, students participating in ESP earned grades one-half to one full grade point higher than their non-ESP counterparts. Finally, ESP students were more likely to enroll in a second semester of calculus than were non-ESP students. Because ESP provides social support and faculty mentoring for students, it does not have the attrition of female and minority students that other mathematics programs do (Moreno & Muller, 1999). Training for instructors has been central to ESP's success. It is intense, and offers a background in cooperative learning techniques as well as diverse learning methods.

Among our small college cohort, students often mentioned positive faculty engagement as an outgrowth of diversity initiatives. Most of these schools have well-evaluated science and/or math programs aimed at promoting the achievement of underrepresented students and women. A few of these are based on Treisman's model for math scholarship, while others (at Mount Holyoke, Williams, and Wellesley) are centered on college chemistry programs. In addition to faculty mentoring, students learn about participation in research labs for summer internships and funded opportunities for graduate study. One particular program at Rice University stood out among faculty, students, and administrators as a model program.

Rice University: Spend a Summer with a Scientist

Nationally known computer scientist Richard Tapia was the first Latino professor at Rice University. He sits on the President's Council and is one of the most vocal advocates for increasing student diversity in the sciences. Tapia began the Spend a Summer with a Scientist (SaS) program in 1989 with the ultimate goal of increasing the number of underrepresented students in mathematics, engineering, and the computational sciences. His intent was to give these students experience in academic research that would help them gain confidence in their research skills, in the hope that they would attend graduate school. By 1992, the focus of the program had shifted to address the retention of Rice's minority graduate students. By 1995, Tapia included white female participants, and now the program consists of a multiyear summer research experience, mixing Rice graduate students with undergraduates from all over the United States. Students are encouraged to return each summer, moving from undergraduate to graduate science work within the same research community.

The program has six essential supporting goals that work to meet the ultimate goal of increasing the number of underrepresented students in math, computer science, and engineering: 1) developing a community that supports students with caring people who make time to socialize every Friday afternoon; 2) acculturating students to the professional research community by discussing expectations and professional codes of conduct; 3) getting students involved in research by working with a faculty mentor and developing a high-quality product by the end of the summer; 4) providing professional development; 5) providing financial support; and 6) providing academic support. The academic support piece is particularly innovative, as it addresses different levels of undergraduate and graduate academic preparation.

By 1998, SaS had been formally evaluated and had achieved admirable results: of undergraduate participants who had graduated from college, 62 percent enrolled in graduate school, 33 percent were employed in a science- or mathematics-related field, and only 5 percent (one student) were unemployed by that summer (Alexander, Foertsch, & Daffinrud, 1998). Our focus group of students, across disciplines in math and sciences, mentioned the extensive support they receive from Tapia. He is highly regarded as a leader and innovator in the field. Thus, researchers Richardson and Skinner (1990) noted 15 years ago what holds true today: In addition to academic preparation, personal contact with faculty members in the major is a key factor in academic success. Furthermore, students who become "planted" in their major early on seem far more likely to graduate.

These programs represent a fraction of those discussed across our campus visits. Carnegie Mellon, Mount Holyoke, Northwestern, Occidental,

Stanford, the University of Florida, the University of Miami, Wellesley, Williams, and Yale all have specific, very successful science, mathematics, engineering, and technology programs for underrepresented students. Programs following a model of sustained community, directed by tenured professors who have nurtured and evaluated program strengths, appear to be successful and replicable. Both majority and minority tenured professors direct these programs—having a minority director does not appear to be a prerequisite for success. However, all directors must have an explicit interest in the needs of and support networks required for underrepresented students.

In all the programs, the faculty involved have articulated and acted on a deep interest in minority student success and have taken it upon themselves personally to discover the components of success. Once that is clear, all of these faculty members have managed to critically evaluate their programs, make changes where necessary, and lobby successfully for institutional or departmental dollars to keep the programs running, in some cases for more than a decade.

INSTITUTIONAL CAPITAL:
VISION AND TRANSFORMATION

The research literature notes the importance of an administration's institutional vision and how it may positively or negatively influence campus climate with respect to diversity (Chang, 2002; Hurtado et al., 1999; Ibarra, 2001; Smith, 1997). When the administrative leaders of a predominantly white institution decide that they will not only increase diverse student enrollment and diverse faculty hires but also invest in support and success of these constituents, everyone benefits. And, when these administrative efforts are made explicit to the student population, it appears that the effects are amplified. In our research, we asked students about middle- and high-level administrative support for diversity programming on campus. When averaging comments from all students on diversity programs at small private campuses, five top themes emerged in this order: 1) the existence of good or excellent diversity programming; 2) administrative support for diversity initiatives; 3) the burden of being a minority on campus (in terms of having to educate others, or having to be "perfect" as one does not have the advantage of "blending in"); 4) positive faculty engagement (either through special initiatives described below, or because faculty have taken the role of mentor very seriously); and 5) negative administrative responses to protests or events (where students felt that the administration could have done more to prevent the event or ameliorate the aftermath of a crisis). However, at those small schools where students appear to be most satisfied with campus climate, the order of themes mentioned most often shifts to the following: 1) existence of good or excellent diversity programming; 2) positive administrative support; 3) positive faculty engagement; 4) positive minority mentoring (provided by staff or faculty); and 5) the burden of being a minority on campus. Furthermore, at these campuses, mentions of negative administrative response to incidents drops from number five to number 30 on a list of the 42 most frequently discussed. At state universities where student satisfaction was high, positive administrative support was the most frequently mentioned theme. As Ted Mitchell, president of Occidental College, stated, with model programs we should be finding schools where issues of diversity recruitment, admission, and retention of faculty and students are central to decisions regarding the growth of the institution (personal communication, April 16, 2002).

Leadership, vision, financial resources, college institutional research and evaluation, and the interaction among these items combine to form the institutional capital of the college. Many would argue that leadership and vision are most important, as these will drive components of human capital, such as faculty hires and student admissions. Surprisingly, the magnitude of institutional financial resources in our cohorts does not appear to play a major role. Occidental and Mount Holyoke, for example, exhibit the highest levels of institutional capital yet are the two colleges with the fewest monetary resources among the private institutions we examined (NCES, 2001). In other words, the idea that incorporating diversity throughout the campus culture is expensive, or that schools need a high faculty salary scale to hire excellent faculty of color, has not been supported by our research.

The most effective strategic plans for diversity involve the following elements: 1) a mission that defines the purpose of the institution; 2) assessment of the future and external environment; 3) examination of institutional strengths and weaknesses to sharpen focus of attention; and 4) a decision to provide the resources to make things happen (Shirley, 1988; Smith, 1997). Nearly all of our investigated schools had mission statements promoting diversity attached to a strategic plan or a commission updating such a plan. For example, the opening of Occidental College's (2005) Mission Statement reads: "The mission of Occidental College is to provide a gifted and diverse group of students with a total educational experience of the highest quality—one that prepares them for leadership in an increasingly complex, interdependent and pluralistic world." Occidental's strategies supporting their mission are discussed further in this chapter. All of our schools had assessed various strengths and weaknesses of their campus climates, either through participation in national or consortium surveys or through their own internal surveys. Supportive, vocal presidents have specific task forces, commissions, or, better yet, administrative offices dedicated to follow through on strategic-planning initiatives.

At a few schools, students are pushing the awareness of individual student needs and gaps in services. Sometimes they push to the point of protest when it appears that few administrators are responding to their demonstrated needs. At times, administrators appear to be aware of issues but have little idea of how to introduce effective programming to deal with them. As student populations evolve a campus needs to change, and tasks associated with change require ongoing dialogue if an administration wishes to be ahead of the curve rather than always confronted by yet another student protest (Ingle, 2001).

During the course of our data collection, over half of our selected schools were trying to move from a merely responsive to a proactive system with respect to diversity. Two of the schools—Mount Holyoke and Occidental College—could be considered highly proactive or high performing. Both schools have administrators who positively shape the environment regarding diversity rather than being reactive (such as to a student protest) or simply anticipatory.

Mount Holyoke College

During 2001–02, of the 28 schools we investigated, Mount Holyoke College had the sixth largest group of full-time minority faculty on a percentage basis (19.2%), after the University of Miami, Occidental, Pomona, Tulane, and Emory, respectively. Given the geographic advantages of the other schools in terms of recruiting, Mount Holyoke, the only New England school in the group, has done well. Indeed, Mount Holyoke is very strategic when it comes to staff and faculty hiring, and these plans are connected with ongoing institutional research and evaluation. Holyoke's vision is to infuse the administration and the campus community with the goals of its Office of Diversity and Inclusion: "Affirming Identity, Building Community, and Cultivating Leadership"—on campus, otherwise known as the "ABCs." This office was created in 1989 but has its roots in a faculty committee that was formed in the late 1960s.

Faculty members at Mount Holyoke seek diversity among new hires, despite pressure to immediately fill faculty posts. Searches are "failed" if the pool of applicants is not adequately diverse. With such practices, the college maintains the highest percentage of full-time minority faculty in the cohort of women's schools we investigated. Minority students we interviewed were aware of this fact, which in some cases affected their college choice, and they also noticed that both the dean and the assistant dean of the college at the time of our visit were African American women. As one student noted, "Mount Holyoke has some outstanding professors who are very in tune with a positive climate." Another student explained that "faculty are supportive and also willing to learn. I've seen stuff happen in classes outside of Holyoke that would never happen here." And a third student said, "The dean and the assistant dean make the ALANA [African American, Latino/a, Asian, and Native American] groups feel very important. We have an oasis with them" (personal communications, February 19, 2002). Beverly Tatum, who also was the acting president of Mount Holyoke when we visited (in 2002) and is recognized as an expert in race relations, used her positions as faculty member and dean of the college to bring diversity into daily dialogues with students and staff. She and her other administrative leaders systematically engaged all departments in dialogues about cross-cultural differences and how to manage these dialogues across staff and student lines. For example, Dean Tatum and the assistant dean, Rochelle Calhoun, specifically hired outside consultants to conduct staff and faculty training on diversity.

The consultants' work was grounded in creating a community, permitting a dialogue about race relations on campus, and partnering. Staff members found the training particularly useful in giving them a vocabulary to discuss and learn from difference. Discussions with new staff during their orientation focus on the fact that they are joining a multicultural community, and individual departments have mission statements expressing their commitment to this community.

Occidental College

Occidental College was the private college in our group of schools with the fewest financial resources, yet at that time it had the second largest percentage of full-time minority faculty (22.6%) of all of the schools we initially investigated. Occidental also had the largest group of tenured full-time minority faculty (21.7%) of all our selected schools; Pomona had the second-largest group (18.8%; NCES, 2003). Occidental hired an institutional research team in 2001 to evaluate diversity activities and, according to our interviews, the team had the full support of the campus community. Such support for evaluation activities is not typical on many college campuses.

Our qualitative data in terms of student, faculty, and staff focus groups indicate that Occidental appears to be farther along than most of our visited schools in terms of following institutional vision. At Occidental, student satisfaction in areas of positive faculty engagement, positive campus climate with regard to race and ethnicity, positive campus engagement with respect to diversity issues, and perceived positive administrative support for diversity was significantly higher than the peer schools studied. Occidental's president Ted Mitchell gives us some reasons why:

> At Occidental [we] talk about diversity in the context of nearly everything that we do. Unlike other places where diversity is an add-on or a program, diversity is *the* conversation that we have here. You'll hear people talk about the college's multicultural mission, or use the code words "equity and excellence." Occidental has a mission statement that is also its mission, and people know it. So, big and small decisions that we make come up against our mission as a mirror and we're able to ask about faculty hiring, about reconfiguring dorms, about athletic programs, about the library, about technology. Questions start with "How does this serve our self-conscious attempt to promote a diverse student body and a multicultural approach to the liberal arts?" That's the foundation. It's interesting about your comment about the notion that it comes from the top. I would argue that you *should* be finding that in institutions where issues of diversity and culture are central to the educational project. (personal communication, April 16, 2002)

Occidental uses a minority scholar in residence program as a successful faculty recruitment tool. Faculty members mentioned in our interviews that the dean of the college makes a concerted effort to welcome that scholar in an attempt to keep him or her on board. According to our interviews, faculty and staff of color at Occidental are delighted with the campus climate in terms of diversity and with the efforts being made by the upper administration.

The conversation from student focus groups at Occidental and Mount Holyoke echoed much of the conversation held with administrators and faculty with regard to diversity. Students in both groups were aware of their college's mission supporting diversity and articulated how college programs supported ethnic identity and cross-cultural interaction (both colleges have cross-cultural dialogue groups). At both schools, students rattled off names of faculty and administrators who were regular sources of support, as well as programming that was academically and socially helpful. Students at Occidental discussed the many forums, opportunities, and administrators or faculty available for support at great length. Students of color at these schools described some areas of white student ignorance of or apathy toward the issues, but appeared to feel neither exhausted nor overtly frustrated by that apathy. As one African American student in our focus group noted:

> I think this [Occidental] is a really safe environment to talk about diversity and multiculturalism, it's incredibly safe because that's what they promote. I'd agree that some students show indifference or apathy, but the structure itself, the school, the programming really does promote multiculturalism. That's why I came here. That's what it's known for. (personal communication, April 16, 2002)

These schools are small (fewer than 2,000 students) and highly student-centered, and Mount Holyoke is a women's school. They differ from many of the other schools we visited in that the president of each has taken a highly active, vocal stance in support of diversity and moved an existing proactive system into the area of a high-performing system. These schools have ongoing courses, staff education, and leadership that improve campus climate and transform underlying issues consistent with explicit campus values. Each school also has an office or advisory group whose mission is to shape culture and climate: Mount Holyoke's Office of Diversity and Inclusion has been in place for over a decade, and Occidental's Committee on Multiculturalism has been in place for more than two. At both schools, the people who work in those areas see their job as infusing the values of a welcoming, diverse campus throughout the community. One African American female student at Occidental describes her experience:

> I think that the college does an excellent job of promoting racial and ethnic diversity on this campus and I think we have a strong support system at this college. I've been involved with culture clubs since I began here as a freshman, and I think that the ICC, which was previously the Cultural Resource Center, is an excellent place for people to start learning about issues of diversity, and gender, and race. I can find people from the Right to argue with me and to engage in dialogue with me, and more importantly, I think that we do so on this campus with a certain level of respect. And I think, obviously, there are certain people that fall out of that, both on the Right or on the Left, but I think what's

exciting is that we can engage one another in discussion while being civil to one another. (personal communication, April 16, 2002)

Students are affected by the organizational culture of their school. This is especially true for students who sit on multicultural advisory boards or are leaders within their affinity groups. Administrators who assume authoritarian and hierarchical leadership styles find such styles often lead to negative or reactive strategies, and possible student backlash. Colleges and universities lacking institutional leadership in diversity initiatives tend to be reactive and ad hoc in their approaches to crises and challenges, rather than aware and flexible. One likely result of a reactive rather than a strategic approach is minority student and faculty attrition. As Ingle (2001) stresses, another possible net result of reactive leadership is the corrosive mixed message it sends to faculty, staff, and students regarding civility and climate issues ("lip service" rather than action or strategic planning). Institutional capital often drives the human capital of a school with respect to diversity; however, sometimes when leadership regarding diversity is lacking, diverse members forming the human capital of a school (middle management and line staff as well as students) come together to address this void.

Smaller liberal arts colleges have more capacity for increased communication among students, administrators, and faculty; researchers have noted that this increased interaction leads to increased student satisfaction (Astin, Keup, & Lindholm, 2002). Larger schools can find ways of making the store small by layering supports throughout the levels of associate and assistant deans. Successful schools, both large and small, that improve campus climate with regard to race relations consistently monitor the atmosphere with assessments. Research also suggests that institutional efforts in creating inclusive, diverse environments positively influence sense of community, cultural awareness, racial understanding, and college satisfaction among white students as well as students of color (Tanaka, 2002).

HUMAN CAPITAL: STUDENT AND
LEADERSHIP DEVELOPMENT PROGRAMS

Minority student retention is one of the most important challenges that college and university administrators face today. Researchers note the positive relationship between warm and welcoming campus climates and increased minority student retention (Chang, 2000, 2001; Ibarra, 2001; Swail, Redd, & Perna, 2003). As Swail and his colleagues note, campus climate is not some intangible, abstract concept that just happens. More accurately stated, campus climate is the development of the beliefs and practices of the administration, faculty, staff, and students belonging to that institution. Therefore, it can be created and, to some degree, controlled. To develop a positive campus climate supportive of learning and human development, campuses should promote diversity on campus and extol the virtues of shared culture. . . . [P]roviding social opportunities for students to forge new friendships and build trust with their fellow classmates are examples. (p. 107)

Beyond the academic support that all of the schools in our cohorts provide, these schools offer social supports and cultural opportunities, typically through their offices of student affairs. Supports include funds for cultural affinity organizations and culturally themed weeks or months; safe spaces or havens for cultural groups that allow closed meetings where students can freely express support for each other; residential experiences that can be multicultural or culturally themed by design to allow students an immersion experience; multicultural centers where students of different cultures meet regularly for programmed events; and intercultural or cross-cultural dialogue groups that are specifically designed and facilitated to help students discuss differences in safe, civil environments. Schools that had avenues for cultural support and safety (requiring closed meetings and separate spaces) as well as facilitated cross-cultural contact and multicultural events had the most satisfied students.

The positive effects of diversity programming cannot be overstated. Among all of our school cohorts (small private schools, midsized private schools, Ivy League schools and flagship state schools), the number one theme mentioned by students was positive diversity programs and their role in minority student success. Satisfied students from all backgrounds praised programs aimed at cross-cultural interaction. When majority students became more educated about diversity, students of color told us they felt less of a burden to be "the teacher of all things multicultural" or the "representative of their race." At schools where focus groups were characterized by low student satisfaction with their school regarding diversity efforts, there were far fewer positive programs mentioned. However, at some schools where students were less satisfied with upper administration regarding diversity efforts, the existent diversity programming (and people running these programs) often were cited as the "life-lines" for students of color or the major support in helping them graduate. Recognizing that all avenues for cultural contact support and safety are important at schools, for purposes of this chapter we will focus on practices that facilitate cross-cultural interaction.

Leadership and Sustained Dialogue at Princeton University

What Princeton University students mentioned with pride and enthusiasm during our focus group was their program known as the Sustained Dialogue, which is an organization of roughly 40 students committed to improving campus race relations. It was founded in 1999 when students at a retreat heard a speech by Princeton alumnus Harold Saunders, who was involved with the Camp David peace negotiations during the Carter administration. He developed a methodology for conflict resolution that involves a five-stage discussion. This begins with members sharing personal experiences and leads to an understanding of the roots of the problem (in this case, racial discord or disunity), then works to find solutions (Saunders, 1999). It is a gradual process involving relationship-building among members, and the content of the dialogues is confidential.

As part of Sustained Dialogue, students are invited to meet every two weeks over a long dinner (sometimes three hours) to discuss race relations in small groups. Moderators (either trained students, faculty, or administrators) run these groups to guide conversations and keep members on topic. One concern students had with the organization is the difficulty in recruiting members who differ from the ideological and philosophical make-up of most group members. However, students in the focus group agreed that the organization does get students talking about difficult subjects and helps foster stronger relationships across racial lines. As one student mentioned, "With Sustained Dialogue, you talk about race issues in general and race issues on campus. You form a bond or a relationship with these people, and you get comfortable [enough] to really discuss what you feel and think" (personal communication, May 2, 2001). Sustained Dialogue appears to be a powerful force in establishing lines of communication across student racial and ethnic groups and has been successfully implemented at other campuses, including Harvard University and the University of Virginia.

Student Housing and Intercultural Activities at Stanford University

Stanford University has a strong residential education component that incorporates multicultural cocurricular programming under the direction of the multicultural educator. This educator trains and informs staff, students, alumni, and even board members about the benefits of a diverse campus and how to make it a place where everyone can thrive. As a result, Stanford has a number of themed student residence houses. However, the African American, Asian American, Native American, and Latino houses (Ujamaa, Okada, Muwekma, and Casa Zapata) each have a requirement in which 50 percent of students in the house must be from the theme group, and 50 percent are a mix of other students. Stanford students described both the housing and the programming as integral to the success of the diversity initiatives. As one Stanford student mentioned:

> I think one of the best things about the Stanford campus is the themed dorms. It is one of the best ways to promote diversity within a campus because you are constantly living with other people and you are exposed to a wide range of different ethnicities. The fact that they are 50 percent of the themed race or ethnicity and 50 percent of all different ethnicities allows a variety of people to get exposed to, and learn from, that themed culture and ethnicity. (personal communication, February 21, 2003)

One cannot be a passive participant in the Stanford culturally themed residences, and the programming is designed with regular, facilitated intercultural communication. Stanford residence assistants regularly work with METrO, Stanford's Multicultural Education Training Organization, to host a variety of programs taken from the Core Diversity Programs Menu. For example, Stanford's version of sustained dialogue is the Stanford Dialogues, a series of facilitated student groups that meet throughout the year to discuss a variety of issues. These groups of eight to 16 people meet in one-hour sessions for six weeks. The facilitators from METrO's staff include deans, assistant deans, directors of cultural centers (Stanford has nine), and other volunteers. Stanford also has a credit-bearing program known as the Stanford Race Dialogues that runs for ten weeks. The Stanford students from our focus groups were among the most satisfied with their diversity initiatives, as well as with the cross-cultural interaction on campus, of the colleges we visited.

CONCLUSION

Schools that have excellent diversity programming typically have a number of initiatives aimed at the three major areas of campus life: educational, institutional, and human capital. When diversity efforts in these three areas work together, the outcomes are quite remarkable for all students. Open assessment of campus climate and responsiveness to findings, as well as transparency of findings, can move campus systems from reactive to responsive modes and from crises to positive events. Planning and education can move leadership from responsive to proactive modes.

The students we interviewed hailed school structures that encouraged intergroup involvement as models for diversity planning. Biweekly meetings among all group leaders or a multicultural council were recommended. The intention behind all of these activities is to celebrate difference and work with the complexity of plurality. With such support, students understand that they can build coalitions across groups without a sense of assimilation or loss of self.

Predominantly or historically white campuses that have successfully funded initiatives, with rare exceptions, have successfully educated majority campus constituents, board members, and alumni. Developing such an educational component is critical to improving minority student retention. As mentioned earlier, Stanford University has a design where a full-time multicultural educator is charged with exactly that type of activity—from educating students and staff about issues of race and ethnicity (including white privilege) to educating the board members and alumni. Such education moves a campus into a proactive rather than a reactive stance, especially when it comes to incidents of bias. Furthermore, the community becomes interested in, rather than resistant to, ethnic affinity organizations and residences when they are educated about the desirability of such enclaves. Race and ethnicity courses produce considerable gains in openness and awareness. Intergroup dialogue programs in which students are given opportunities for structured discussion about difficult topics are particularly effective.

There are a number of colleges not included in this study doing excellent work in diversity programming (Columbia, Duke, Georgetown, New York University, Syracuse University, the University of Southern California, and Wesleyan, to name just a few). As such, future work should broaden our school sample and complete an analysis of current campus climate surveys. Also, pre- and post-analyses of some of the student development initiatives mentioned under our section on human capital, such as the Sustained Dialogue, including how they affect student retention and the life choices of alumni, would be useful.

As diversity programming continues to evolve to meet the changing needs of changing student populations, we applaud the work of the diligent campus presidents, vice presidents, deans, associate and assistant deans, faculty, human relations workers, and most important, the students, who allowed us a glimpse into their work and world. The effects of the *Grutter*

(2003) decision on such efforts remain to be seen (see Ancheta, this volume), although early indications suggest that programs exclusively focused on certain racial and ethnic groups should do so with caution. Universities will need to consider the policy implications that may arise from the need to review or modify such programs as they remain committed to maximizing the learning experiences of all students. Furthermore, in states where the ability to consider race in the decision-making process has been removed (e.g., California), continued creative energy will need to be spent conceptualizing and implementing opportunities that maximize the benefits of an increasingly diverse student body and ultimately work toward the removal of the color line in higher education.

NOTES

1. When affirmative action admissions policies came under attack, business leaders and higher education researchers successfully mounted a "diversity defense" in the 2003 Supreme Court cases *Grutter v. Bollinger* and *Gratz v. Bollinger* (Green, 2004) expressing the benefits of educating a diverse student population.
2. For a complete description of our methodology, please contact the authors at National Campus Diversity Project, Harvard Graduate School of Education, Larsen Hall, Suite 409, Appian Way, Cambridge, MA 02478.

REFERENCES

Alexander, B. B., Foertsch, J., & Daffinrud, S. (1998). *The Spend a Summer with a Scientist Program: An evaluation of program outcomes and the essential elements for success.* Madison: University of Wisconsin–Madison, Learning through Evaluation, Adaptation and Dissemination (LEAD) Center.

Antonio, A. (2001). The role of interracial interaction in the development of leadership skills and cultural knowledge and understanding. *Research in Higher Education, 42,* 593–617.

Astin, A. W., Keup, J. R., & Lindholm, J. A. (2002). A decade of changes in undergraduate education: A national study of system "transformation." *Review of Higher Education, 25,* 141–162.

Berger, J. B. (2000). Organizational behavior and student outcomes: A new perspective on college impact. *Review of Higher Education, 23,* 177–198.

Berger, J. B. (2002). The influence of the organizational structures of colleges and universities on college student learning. *Peabody Journal of Education, 77*(3), 40–59.

Chang, M. J. (2000). Improving campus racial dynamics: A balancing act among competing interests. *Review of Higher Education, 23,* 153–175.

Chang, M. J. (2001). Is it more than about getting along? The broader educational relevance of reducing students' racial biases. *Journal of College Student Development, 42*(2), 93–105.

Chang, M. J. (2002). Preservation or transformation: Where's the real educational discourse on diversity? *Review of Higher Education, 25,* 125–140.

Feagin, J. R., Vera, H., & Imani, N. (1996). *The agony of education: Black students at white colleges and universities.* New York: Routledge.

Gratz v. Bollinger, 539 U.S. 244 (2003).

Green, D. O. (2004). Justice and diversity: Michigan's response to *Gratz, Grutter,* and the affirmative action debate. *Urban Education, 39,* 374–393.

Grutter v. Bollinger, 539 U.S. 306 (2003).

Gurin, P., Dey, E. L., Hurtado, S., & Gurin, G. (2002). Diversity and higher education: Theory and impact on educational outcomes. *Harvard Educational Review, 72,* 1–21.

Harvey, W. B. (2002). *Minorities in higher education, 2001–2002: Nineteenth annual status report.* Washington, DC: American Council on Education.

Hrabowski, F., Maton, K., & Greif, G. (1998). *Beating the odds: Raising academically successful African American males.* New York: Oxford University Press.

Hu, S., & Kuh, G. (2003). Diversity experiences and college student learning and personal development. *Journal of College Student Development, 44,* 320–344.

Hurtado, S., Milem, J., Clayton-Pederson, A., & Allen, W. (1999). *Enacting diverse learning environments: Improving the climate for racial/ethnic diversity in higher education* (ASHE-ERIC Higher Education Report, 26). Washington, DC: George Washington University, Graduate School of Education and Human Development.

Ibarra, R. A. (2001). *Beyond affirmative action: Reframing the context of higher education.* Madison: University of Wisconsin Press.

Ingle, G. (2001, July). *Strategies for improving civility and campus climate.* Presentation for Senior Administrators Staff Development Day at Brown University, Providence, RI.

Moreno, S. E., & Muller, C. (1999). Success and diversity: The transition through first-year calculus in the university. *American Journal of Education, 108*(1), 30–57.

National Center for Education Statistics. (2001). [Raw data from the Integrated Post Secondary Data System, including statements of financial position.] Retrieved August 21, 2004, from http://nces.ed.gov/ipedspas/

National Center for Education Statistics. (2002). [Raw data from the Integrated Post Secondary Data System, including statements of financial position.] Retrieved August 21, 2004, from http://nces.ed.gov/ipedspas/

National Center for Education Statistics. (2003). [Raw data from the Integrated Post Secondary Data System, including statements of financial position.] Retrieved August 21, 2004, from http://nces.ed.gov/ipedspas/

Occidental College. (2005). *Occidental College mission statement.* Retrieved February 15, 2005, from http://www.oxy.edu/x2640.xml

Orfield, G., & Whitla, D. K. (1999). Diversity and legal education: Student experiences in leading law schools. In G. Orfield (with M. Kurlaender) (Eds.), *Diversity challenged: Evidence on the impact of affirmative action* (pp. 143–174). Cambridge, MA: Harvard Education Publishing Group.

Richardson, R. C., & Skinner, E. F. (1990). Adapting to diversity: Organizational influences on student achievement. *Journal of Higher Education, 61,* 485–511.

Saunders, H. H. (1999). *A public peace process: Sustained dialogue to transform racial and ethnic conflicts.* New York: St. Martin's Press.

Shirley, R. C. (1988). Strategic planning: An overview. *New Directions for Higher Education, 64,* 5–14.

Smith, D. G. (with Gerbick, G. L., Figueroa, M. A., Watkins, G. H., Levitan, T., Moore, L. C., Merchant, P. A., Beliak, H. D., & Figueroa, B.). (1997). *Diversity works: The emerging picture of how students benefit.* Washington, DC: Association of American Colleges and Universities.

Steele, C. (1999, August). Thin ice: "Stereotype threat" and black college students. *Atlantic Monthly, 284*(2), pp. 44–54.

Swail, W. S., Redd, K. E., & Perna, L. W. (2003). *Retaining minority students in higher education: A framework for success* (ASHE-ERIC Higher Education Report). Hoboken, NJ: Wiley.

Tanaka, G. K. (2002). Higher education's self-reflexive turn. *Journal of Higher Education, 73,* 263–296.

Treisman, U. (1992). Studying students studying calculus: A look at the lives of minority mathematics students in college. *College Mathematics Journal, 23,* 362–372.

Whitla, D., Orfield, G., Silen, W., Teperow, C. A., Howard, C., & Reede, J. (2003). Educational benefits of diversity: A survey of medical school students. *Academic Medicine, 78,* 460–466.

7

Potential or Peril

The Evolving Relationship between Large-Scale Standardized Assessment and Higher Education

CATHERINE L. HORN

Large-scale standardized tests have been a commonplace accountability mechanism for both students and schools at the K–12 level for more than 30 years (Heubert & Hauser, 1999). While many have noted the limitations of using such measures as the primary criteria upon which to judge educational achievement (e.g., Joint Committee on Testing Practices, 2004; Linn, 2000; National Commission on Testing and Public Policy, 1990; Orfield & Kornhaber, 2001), assessments have become a ubiquitous policy tool aimed at reforming public education and ultimately improving the life chances of all students. At both the state and federal levels, test scores have been used to make decisions ranging from student promotion and graduation to institutional and district rewards and sanctions. Most recently, the 2001 passage of the No Child Left Behind Act (NCLB) required that every school make "adequate yearly progress (AYP)" toward 100 percent of its students at designated grade levels reaching proficiency on reading and mathematics assessments within 12 years. Assuming that a system of test-based accountability would "create performance pressures for schools to improve student proficiency . . . and narrow achievement disparities based on student background characteristics" (Kim & Sunderman, 2004, p. 9), NCLB mandates both an "absolute performance standard" for all students and required improvement among federally defined subgroups in grades 3–

8. Schools that do not meet AYP goals are subject to sanctions ranging from school restructuring to school reconstitution (Kim & Sunderman, 2004).

Until the 1998 reauthorization of the Higher Education Act (HEA), similar large-scale test-based accountability at the higher education level had not been as prevalent.[1] Some individual institutions, systems, and states had considered and/or implemented programs that use standardized test scores to make competency judgments (e.g., the University of Texas system, Utah State Board of Regents, and Massachusetts Board of Higher Education), but the commonplace use of such exams at the national level had not permeated the broad higher education landscape (Burd, 2003). With its reauthorization however, HEA required that all states provide accountability data on teacher-training programs. Specifically, states had to "rank colleges according to the percentage of their teacher-education students who pass certification exams, to describe state standards, and to identify those teacher-training programs considered 'low performing'" (Basinger, 2001, p. 26). The teacher education accountability provision thus "became the vehicle for an expanded federal role in quality assurance, through mandates of state approaches to public accountability for results" (Wolanin, 2003, p. 140).

This small but important federal test-based intervention at the postsecondary level is worth considering, then, for several reasons. First, it serves as a case study for assessing the extent to which such policies may either alleviate or compound racial inequities in higher education. Further, it questions whether institutions are raising standards or simply distorting policies in the name of meeting accountability goals. Finally, it highlights the underlying testing principles fundamental to such interventions. If such technical considerations are not made with attention to race, validity may be lessened and negative social consequences increased. While test-based accountability has not taken hold at the postsecondary level in the same way it has in K–12, it is still worth carefully thinking about the issue.

In this chapter I first provide a brief history of the HEA, and then present the already documented disparate performance of traditionally underrepresented students on mandated tests currently being used for federal accountability at the postsecondary level, as defined by that act.[2] I then discuss the possibilities and pitfalls of using such a form of federal quality assurance to achieve more equitable educational opportunities that lead to better outcomes for all students. Finally, I suggest ways that a viable accountability system for higher education might be achieved, keeping such goals in mind.

FEDERALLY MANDATED TEST-BASED ACCOUNTABILITY IN HIGHER EDUCATION: A BRIEF HISTORY

The new rules for teacher-training programs imposed with the 1998 reauthorization of the HEA were not the federal government's first attempt to place test-based accountability mechanisms on institutions of higher education. Building up to those changes, in 1993 the National Education Goals Panel recommended that the federal government create a test to measure students' critical thinking, communications, and problem-solving skills. Then education secretary Richard Riley (a Clinton appointee) supported the resolution, arguing that higher education needed to be held more accountable for student learning (Zook, 1993b). Preliminary steps were subsequently taken to create a voluntary National Postsecondary Student Assessment intended to evaluate whether students were developing the analytical skills needed for the workplace (Zook, 1993a). While the implementation of such an assessment never came to fruition, it opened up a dialogue about tying available monies to federally defined, large-scale, test-measured standards of postsecondary educational quality that ultimately manifested in the 1998 reauthorization (discussed in detail later in the chapter).

In the HEA reauthorization slated to take place in 2005, Republican lawmakers in particular have called for more accountability measures to be put in place and have continued to consider the role of large-scale testing in that process. In a hearing before Congress, for example, the chair of the University of Texas System Board of Regents, Charles Miller, testified that universities should test students in their first two years of college to create a measure of student learning on "core curriculum" across institutions (Burd, 2003). Whether and/or how such a test-based accountability mechanism might be incorporated into the 2005 reauthorization remains to be seen. If trends in federal elementary and secondary legislation are any indication, however, large-scale standardized test-based accountability for higher education will remain fodder for serious discussion.

TEACHER-TRAINING PROGRAMS

The 1998 HEA reauthorization in some ways marked the culmination of a multiyear effort to ratchet up postsecondary accountability mechanisms through federal legislation. Arguing that the 1998 amendments "respond to the Nation's critical need for high-quality teachers by enacting much of the Clinton Administration's proposal to improve the recruitment and preparation of new teachers" (U.S. Department of Education, 2002a), the law laid out new provisions requiring states and institutions of higher education "to report on information related to the quality of their teacher education programs [as defined by performance on state teacher exams] and to require the information to be disseminated to students and others" (Higher Education Act, 1998). Further, the law said that schools with poor student pass rates on state-mandated standardized tests would have to improve or face punitive consequences. With this, the federal government directly inserted itself into the process of defining and monitoring "quality" teacher preparation.

The provisions added in 1998 are being revisited in the 2005 reauthorization process. According to critics, "loopholes in the rules, mandated in the 1998 reauthorization of the Higher Education Act, allowed colleges to avoid reporting how many of their students failed the state teacher-licensure tests" (Basinger, 2003, p. A25). As part of efforts to close those loopholes, the U.S. House of Representatives education subcommittee approved HR 2211, the Ready to Teach Act, in 2003, specifically intended to amend Title II of the HEA.[3] The guidelines describe several new or revised accountability mechanisms with which states and individual institutions must comply. First, states receiving federally funded teacher-preparation grants must submit an annual accountability report to the U.S. Secretary of Education detailing the extent to which progress has been made in meeting the following goals:

- Increasing the percentage of highly qualified teachers (as defined in NCLB)
- Increasing student academic achievement for all students as defined by the eligible state
- Raising the state academic standards required to enter the teaching profession as a highly qualified teacher
- Increasing success in the pass rate for initial state teacher certification or licensure, or increasing the numbers of qualified individuals being certified or licensed as teachers through alternative programs
- Decreasing shortages of highly qualified teachers in poor urban and rural areas
- Increasing opportunities for enhanced and ongoing professional development
- Increasing the number of teachers prepared effectively to integrate technology into curricula and instruction (Ready to Teach Act, 2003)

If it is determined that the state is not making "substantial progress" in meeting these goals and objectives by the end of the second year of a grant, funds will be subsequently withheld (Ready to Teach Act, 2003).

Similarly, states are required to submit an annual report detailing the quality of teacher preparation. Those report cards, which include all institutions receiving teacher preparation grants, are to provide:

> effective data on the number of students passing state certification requirements, with improved reporting requirements that will prevent "gaming" of data that leave results without meaning. Additionally, institutions must compare both pass rates and average scores of their program participants with those of other programs in the state, making effective comparison data available to measure program quality. (House Education and the Workforce Committee, n.d.)

Institutions that lose state approval or funding because of low performance become ineligible for any federally funded grants for teacher professional development training and cannot accept or enroll any student who receives federal financial aid (Ready to Teach Act, 2003). The test-based guidelines laid out in the 1998 bill and being revised in 2005, then, could have potentially serious effects on teacher-training programs. Further, the institutional impact notwithstanding, literature documenting differential performance by race/ethnicity on many large-scale standardized tests in general and teacher licensure tests in particular suggests that the effects on the pool of potential black and Latino teachers may be profound. It is to this latter issue that I now turn.

Implications of Test-Based Accountability Mechanisms for Students of Color

At both the institutional and individual levels, students of color in teacher-training programs have been adversely affected by postsecondary test-based accountability relative to their white and Asian counterparts. At the institutional level, for example, among the 14 schools identified as being at risk of being classified as low performing or identified as low performing in 2001, four were historically black colleges and universities or Hispanic-serving institutions (U.S. Department of Education, Office of Postsecondary Education, 2002).[4] Additionally, two schools (Long Island University–Brooklyn and City University of New York–York College) had student bodies that were more than 80 percent nonwhite. While only descriptively related, the fact that almost half of the institutions most at risk for sanctions based on test-based accountability mechanisms have majority nonwhite student bodies is salient, as it suggests that such colleges and universities may face consequences at disproportionately higher rates. (And, at the very least, it highlights the importance of more systematically tracking impact.)

There are also many documented cases of black and Latino teacher candidates being disproportionately and/or incorrectly denied licensure because of test scores (Flores & Clark, 1999; Ludlow, 2001; Rhoades & Madaus, 2003). One of the best-known instances happened in Alabama during the 1980s, when four black plaintiffs, in *Allen v. Alabama Board of Education*, charged that the Alabama Initial Teacher Certification Test (AITCT) had an adverse racial impact on black students and colleges. During the course of the lawsuit, psychometricians discovered poorly written and miskeyed items in eight administrations of the AITCT, in addition to evidence of disparate impact.[5] One of the miskeyed items, for example, led to at least 355 candidates being incorrectly failed (Rhoades & Madaus, 2003).[6] As part of the settlement reached, both because of the evidence of disparate impact and because of the failure to meet appropriate test-development standards, Alabama was subsequently required to provide a new teacher certification process (Ludlow, 2001).[7]

A Board on Testing and Assessment (BOTA) report further highlights the potentially disparate impact of the concentrated use of licensure tests, in this case the Praxis Pre-Professional Skills Test (Praxis I), one of the more common licensure exams used nationally (Mitchell, Robinson, Plake, & Knowles, 2001).[8] Table 1 shows the differential passing rates among African Americans, Asian Americans, Hispanics, and whites on the reading test in 1998–99.[9] While only half of black candidates passed the exam, more than 86 percent of whites met the same standard. Further, the authors note that, while striking, such differences are not unique to the Praxis I test:

> The pattern in these results is similar to the patterns observed between minority and majority examinees on the National Board for Professional Teaching Standards (NBPTS) assessments. Certification rates of slightly over 40 percent for white teachers have been reported. . . . The reported certification rate for African American teachers was 11 percent, some 30 percent lower than the passing rate for white teachers. (p. 104)

A study by Gitomer, Latham, and Ziomek (1999) explores the academic and demographic characteristics of the prospective teacher pool and the impact prescreening testing has on that pool. Also using data from the nationally administered Praxis I test, the researchers found similarly stark differences in the passing rates of blacks and Latinos compared to whites and Asians (Table 2).

For example, of the white and Asian Praxis I test-takers who also took the SAT, 82 percent and 76 percent, respectively, passed at the state stan-

TABLE 1
Passing Rates on the Praxis I Test (Reading)
by Racial/Ethnic Group, 1998–99

Ethnicity	*N*	*Percentage Passing (%)*
African American	3,874	50
Asian American	670	59
Hispanic	375	65
White	21,944	86

Source: Mitchell et al. (2001).

TABLE 2
Passing Rates on the Praxis I at Low, State,
and High Passing Standards by Race/Ethnicity
and SAT/ACT Taker Status[1]

	% Passing at Low Standard (SAT Takers/ ACT Takers)	*% Passing at State Standard (SAT Takers/ ACT Takers)*	*% Passing at High Standard (SAT Takers/ ACT Takers)*
All Candidates	91/95	77/88	47/62
African American	67/76	46/63	17/28
Asian American	92/89	76/77	45/54
Hispanic	86/93	69/83	34/54
Native American	84/92	64/81	28/48
White	94/92	82/89	51/64
Other	87/93	71/84	46/61

Source: Gitomer et al. (1999).

[1]The second and fourth columns present data analyzing the effects of several hypothetical cut points for passing and will be discussed later in the chapter.

TABLE 3
Passing Rates for the CBEST by Population Group, 1995–96 Cohort

Ethnicity	*First-Time Passing Rates Percentage Passing (%)*	*Eventual Passing Rates Percentage Passing (%)*
African American	41	73
Asian American	66	87
Mexican American	51	88
Latino or Other Hispanic	47	81
White	79	94

Source: Mitchell et al. (2001).

dard. Only 46 percent of black and 69 percent of Latino test-takers had the same result. Similar patterns exist among Praxis I test-takers who took the ACT. These data raise concerns that, given the prevalent use of Praxis I, the exam may be having at least a marginally negative effect on the racial/ethnic diversity of the teacher-training program completers.

Differential performance has also manifested among state-specific licensing exams. Table 3 presents the first-time and eventual passing rates on the California Basic Educational Skills Test (CBEST) of the 1995–96 population of test-takers.

Again, the differences across racial/ethnic groups are substantial: A 32 percentage-point gap exists between Latino and white first-time test-takers, a 38 percentage-point gap between blacks and whites. Even in the context of much higher eventual passing rates, differences still remain; a 21-point pass-rate disparity exists among blacks relative to their white counterparts, for example, on the CBEST. These and the other data presented here paint a picture of an accountability system that may be unevenly affecting traditionally underrepresented students and the schools that serve them.

The 1998 HEA provisions have also led to research tracking the unintended effects of such types of policy on the pipeline of students flowing to the point of program completion and licensure. In particular, scholars have begun to study the ways large-scale test-based accountability has led to institutional changes to program prescreening policies that might (intentionally or unintentionally) improve performance on accountability measures. The next section presents some of what has been learned from those studies.

Program Policy Changes

As a result of the 1998 HEA reauthorization (or in some cases, preemptively), states and institutions have begun to modify standards for entrance into or completion of teacher-education programs (Lively, 1998). These efforts have come in several forms, including modified admission and completion standards (such as passing a required test to complete the program) and candidate prescreening. In the extreme, these types of policy shifts may result in radically inflated pass rates, because the screening mechanisms have, in essence, insured a population highly likely to score well on the required tests.

A study by the American Association of State Colleges and Universities (AASCU) resulted in a report to Congress explaining the reasons behind 100 percent pass rates reported by 308 institutions in 2002 (n.d.). They found that many of these reported rates were the result of changes in meaning of the term "program completer" (although not all changes were directly tied to the 1998 HEA Title II provision). Among the responding institutions, 75 percent indicated that test passage is a prerequisite (as defined by the state or the institution) for program completion. The state of Michigan, for example, has a long-standing policy requiring all preservice students to take basic skills and subject-area tests during their time in approved teacher-preparation programs. In 1998, for the purposes of Title II reporting, Michigan used that policy as a basis for defining "program completer" as someone who had passed all required tests in addition to the required coursework (AASCU, n.d.). Additionally, some states and institutions have used the test itself as a prescreening tool for admission into the program. In 1997, for example, the state of Alabama instituted a policy requiring all colleges and universities to use a passing score on the Alabama Basic Skills Test as a prerequisite for admission to teacher-preparation programs.[10] As a result, all pass rates in Alabama were 100 percent in 2001 (AASCU, n.d.).

At the institution level, Ludlow, Shirley, and Rosca (2002) found that many colleges and universities in Massachusetts have begun to concentrate on early identification of at-risk students, and in some cases freshmen were required to take the Praxis I test to serve as a kind of pretest for teacher candidates. A study by the Alliance for Equity in Higher Education found that even some minority serving institutions, which graduate a significant proportion of minority teacher education students, have begun to deny admission into teacher education programs "for those students whose previous academic performance—as measured by high school GPA and ACT, SAT, and Praxis I scores—'predicts' poor future performance on teacher licensure exams" (2000, p. 26). Williford (1993) surveyed deans and department chairs of the 46 state-approved North Carolina schools and education departments to determine the impact of state-imposed regulations on teacher-training program development and implementation efforts. She found that respondents, particularly those from historically black colleges and universities, felt the required minimum National Teacher Exam (NTE) score for formal admission had an adverse effect on traditionally underrepresented students.

As states and institutions come under potentially increasing pressure to improve outcomes—that is, the percentage of students passing licensure exams—there is incentive to winnow the pool at earlier stages in order to ensure more favorable end results. While such practices are facially neutral in that they do not explicitly discriminate on the basis of race/ethnicity (and are certainly beneficial to institutions and states under the watchful eye of

Title II requirements), as evidenced by the data in Tables 1 and 2, as well as a large body of research documenting the differential performance on standardized tests, in general the effects of using test-based screening and completion mechanisms are potentially devastating to the number of traditionally underrepresented students present in the final pool of teachers.

Such policies may result specifically in selection system bias. They make the assumption, absent any additional information, that students who perform poorly on the standardized tests would perform poorly in the classroom relative to those students with higher scores (Jencks, 1998). Without consideration of other relevant attributes that may contribute to becoming a proficient teacher in the classroom, blacks and Latinos may be siphoned out before ever having the opportunity to go through appropriate training.

The scope of this chapter does not allow for a full discussion of the cumulative impact barriers to college (e.g., unequal opportunities to learn, standardized tests for promotion and graduation) may have on the racial/ethnic diversity of the eventual pool of potential teachers. It is, nevertheless, important to acknowledge those disparities in understanding the context of test-based accountability mechanisms at the postsecondary level. In her dissenting opinion in *Gratz v. Bollinger*, Justice Ginsburg notes,

> We are not far from an overtly discriminatory past, and the effects of centuries of law-sanctioned inequality remain painfully evident in our communities and schools. In the wake "of a system or racial caste only recently ended," . . . large disparities endure . . . African American and Hispanic children are all too often educated in poverty-stricken and underperforming institutions. (2003, pp. 298–301)

In particular, the gaps in performance on state-mandated tests for K–12 promotion and graduation and on college entrance exams have been well documented (e.g., Bishop & Mane, 2001; Gitomer et al., 1999; Horn, 2003; Madaus & Clarke, 2001). Given the strong reliance on such assessments for high-stakes decisionmaking at the secondary level and in college admissions (Heubert & Hauser, 1999; Nettles, Perna, & Millet, 1998), these large-scale, standardized gatekeepers are critical to consider.

THE LINKS BETWEEN HEA AND NCLB

Educational accountability at the federal level has indelibly linked higher education to the K–12 sector through NCLB's promise of "highly qualified teachers" in every classroom. NCLB requires that states develop plans to achieve the goal that all teachers of core academic subjects be highly qualified by the end of the 2005–06 school year. Further, annual, measurable objectives that each local school district and school must meet in moving toward the goal must be self-defined according to federal guidelines (U.S. Department of Education, n.d.).

This connection is important for several reasons. First, implementers of NCLB can learn from the lessons of the teacher-training accountability mechanism of the 1998 HEA reauthorization. Foreshadowing many of the complexities that have already arisen with the testing component of NCLB, implementation of the HEA mechanism has proven problematic. For example, the requirements for program entrance, completion, and licensure for prospective teachers vary across states, making it difficult to gather the required data. The timing of administrative and institutional requirements attached to certification exams (e.g., passage for graduation) and a lack of a consistent definition of "low performing" also make comparisons across institutions or states virtually impossible (Basinger, 2001). As HEA is reauthorized and the potential for a new version of NCLB seems imminent, interested parties should take the opportunity to learn from the collective successes and failures of the current acts.

Second, and perhaps more importantly, the direct tie between the two pieces of federal legislation codifies the tangled relationship between K–12 and postsecondary education in achieving more equitable educational outcomes for all students, and highlights the complexity of using a test-based accountability system to aid in that process: "Without addressing the inadequate academic preparation that many minorities receive at the K–12 level, using higher test scores as a gatekeeper will reduce significantly the pool of minority teacher candidates" (Alliance for Equity in Higher Education, 2000, p. 26). The "chicken and egg" nature of the relationship between elementary and postsecondary constituencies suggests that explicit partnerships may prove important, and that test scores may simply complicate rather than enhance those connections.

THE TECHNICAL REALITIES OF TEST-BASED ACCOUNTABILITY[11]

Underlying the use of large-scale standardized tests for accountability purposes is the assumption that they provide valuable information, which, at their best, they do. Well-constructed and utilized standardized assessments can provide stakeholders with a snapshot of how individuals or groups are performing, relative to a set of predetermined standards or objectives. Attendant results can highlight strengths and flag areas where growth is needed at various instructional levels of interest, thus acting as one component in the diagnosis and ultimately the improvement of educational achievement for all students. Testing, however, is, by definition, a sociocultural phenomenon and always an imperfect and incomplete tool (Madaus & Horn, 2000).

In understanding the potential and the pitfalls of large-scale standardized tests, Crocker and Algina (1986) note four measurement problems common to all assessments: 1) no single approach is collectively accepted; 2) they are typically based on a limited sample of content; 3) measurement scales lack well-defined units; and 4) the measurement obtained is subject to error. While each of these presents a unique set of psychometric complexities, this chapter focuses exclusively on the last of these issues: error.

All tests contain error; the degree to which it exists, however, varies depending on the quality of test construction, administration, and score interpretation. In minimizing the influence of error, the twin peaks of reliability and validity become paramount. Reliability is the consistency between two measures of the same phenomena. Many factors can affect the reliability of a test. For example, all other things being equal, a test that is longer, not rigidly limited by time, and administered to a heterogeneous group will produce more reliable results than one that neglects one or more of these criteria. Especially important for standardized tests purported to assess students' mastery of standards is assurance that the content domain taught matches the content domain measured.

Validity represents the meaningfulness, adequacy, and accuracy of the inferences being made from test scores. As with reliability, many factors, some of which overlap, may influence the various components of validity. Messick (1989) outlines four kinds of validity evidence that are needed—construct, content, criterion, and consequential—and notes that any responsible use of test scores requires that inferences being drawn for the intended purpose with such evidence are justifiable. Each of these validity types is necessary unto itself, but the overall extent to which validity exists is more than simply the sum of the parts. In order to understand the implications of such technical realities on test-based accountability at the postsecondary level, consider the example below that illustrates the influence that one process interrelated to reliability and validity—cut score setting—can have.

Cut Score Setting: Error and Subjectivity Meet

On many large-scale standardized tests used to measure achievement, a minimum threshold (or several) is set to mark a predetermined score needed to indicate proficiency or "passing." A person scoring at or above that point is assumed to have demonstrated the desired level of competence in the area of interest; those scoring below are presumed deficit. Such a point—a cut score—is based on underlying assumptions about the reliability, and particularly the validity, of the measure and the inferences made from it. In understanding how such cut scores may affect traditionally underrepresented students, consider first that each state sets its own qualifying scores, either on the commonly used Praxis I or on a uniquely developed instrument (Educational Testing Service, 1998). The determination of competency or qualification, then, is a subjective one that varies widely.

Perhaps more importantly, this variation can have substantial effects on the racial/ethnic makeup of the qualifying group. Gitomer et al. (1999) show that the establishment of a cut score at any of various points on a scale can lead to drastic differences in the racial/ethnic composition of the student pool (Table 2). Across racial/ethnic groups, blacks had a 50 percentage point and Latinos a 52 percentage point difference in the passing rates, depending on where the cutoff standard was placed. So, for example, where 46, 69, and 82 percent of black, Hispanic, and white SAT takers, respectively, would pass the Praxis I exam at a state-determined cut point, only 17, 34, and 51 percent, respectively, would meet the same standard at an arbitrarily higher point. As illustrated, then, where a cut score is placed can have profound effects both within and across racial/ethnic groups (Horn, Ramos, Blumer, & Madaus, 2000).

Gene Glass (1978), a pioneer in psychometric research, writes:

> Interpretations and decisions based on absolute levels of performance on exercises will be largely meaningless, since these absolute levels vary unaccountably with exercise content and difficulty, since judges will disagree wildly on the question of what consequences ought to ensue from the same absolute level of performance, and since there is no way to relate absolute levels of performance on exercises to success on the job, in higher levels of schooling or in life. (p. 259)

The arbitrary nature of cut-score setting coupled with all tests' ever-present error makes the use of an absolute performance criterion for high-stakes decisionmaking risky. In Massachusetts, for example, the cut score for the communication and literacy skills test for educational licensure was set after intense debate and charges of political interference. The Board of Education first adopted a score under which 44 percent of test-takers in the first administration would have failed. Under pressure from the governor, however, they changed the cut score and set a higher standard, resulting in 59 percent of test-takers failing (Lively, 1998). As states continue to come under pressure based on institutions' test scores, as in Massachusetts, the technical realities may run squarely into the political realities of large-scale assessment. Unfortunately, many states have chosen to forge ahead, disregarding or downplaying the problems.

A NEW MODEL OF ACCOUNTABILITY

Federally mandated, large-scale test-based accountability at the postsecondary level is small but unlikely to diminish any time in the near future. Whether or not such perceptions are accurate, such policy "helps to restore public confidence related to standards of admission for teacher training programs" (Freeman & Schopen, 1991, p. 279). There is a fundamental assumption that tests provide objective and infallible information that can be trusted, which reflects a broader sentiment about test-based accountability in general and postsecondary education more specifically. Although the technical and social realities of test construction, administration, and interpretation make this assumption fundamentally untrue, the ubiquity of standardized tests has made them an entrenched part of the current definition of accountability at every level (e.g., the student, institution, and state).

The importance of increasing the numbers of highly qualified teachers of color is undeniable. Research has shown the value of having underrepresented teachers in the classroom in order to reach such goals as realizing important achievement gains among minority students (Dee, 2001) and providing role models (e.g., Ladson-Billings, 1994). Further, these findings come in the context of estimates that suggest that minority students will become the majority of the school-age population by 2050 (Orfield & Lee, 2004). Currently, however, black and Latino students account for only 15 percent of the enrollment in teacher education programs (Alliance for Equity in Higher Education, 2000). Further, the National Collaborative on Diversity in the Teaching Force (2004) notes that 90 percent of all teachers currently in classrooms across the country are white. Given the fact that the data presented in this chapter suggesting that federally mandated test-based accountability at the postsecondary level might in fact exacerbate these disparities, the reauthorization of the HEA provides an opportunity to think about broader accountability measures that might be added.

Using accountability to increase racial/ethnic diversity requires a fundamental shift in the way accountability is both conceptualized and actualized. "Current accountability systems in higher education do not and cannot provide data that are reflective of the status of African Americans and Latinos and thus prevent policy makers from considering equity as a policy goal or taking into account the potential effects of policymaking on the state of equity" (Bensimon, Hao, & Bustillos, in press). The use of test-based accountability is having unintended negative consequences on many colleges and universities, particularly those that graduate a large percentage of minority teacher candidates. The definition of relevant inputs and outcomes ought to be expanded to include factors affecting the racial/ethnic composition of the student body.

Several scholars are already working on new models of accountability. At the K–12 level, Oakes, Mendoza, and Silver (in press) write about the College Opportunity Ratio (COR), which constructs indicators about the status of college access and the distribution of K–12 schooling conditions critical to making college accessible. Similarly, Bensimon, Hao, and Bustillos (in press) recommend an Academic Equity Scorecard, which lays out four concurrent perspectives on institutional performance in terms of equity in educational outcomes for students: access, retention, institutional receptivity, and excellence. The Alliance for Equity in Higher Education (2000) offers other considerations for an incentive structure that might be included in a federal accountability system more focused on equity:

> Bonus grants based on a broad set of criteria related to institutional commitment to addressing the teacher crisis could be awarded to high-performing institutions. Eligibility requirements for such bonus grants could include a number of factors—for example, the population of students served; improvement in pass rates using each institution's individual baseline; and the percentage of graduates who remain in teaching and/or teach in high-need areas. (pp. 42–43)

In all of these accountability models, traditional measures of achievement are combined or revisited in ways that make them far more useful for assessing the extent to which equity is being achieved. Such models also highlight the fact that a range of information rather than a single measure proves most useful in making accountability assessments. A more radical shift away from such traditional measures altogether, however, may ultimately be necessary to accurately hold schools accountable for the extent to which racial/ethnic diversity in the teaching force is actually being achieved. The likelihood of convincing a skeptical public of the value of "devaluing" test scores in lieu of attention to harder and more costly to measure constructs of good teaching, however, is tenuous.

CONCLUSION

NCLB is right in that its regulations imply that good teachers matter. But equally important is the fact that good traditionally underrepresented teachers matter. Current accountability rhetoric has overtaken a related access and equity discussion without really improving the quality of the teacher workforce. As Angrist and Guryan (2003) insist, "Testing has acted more as a barrier to entry than as a quality screen" (pp. 15–16). As the data presented in this chapter have shown, black and Latino students—and often the institutions that have historically served them—are being punished by a mechanism that imposes a simplified structure onto a complex undertaking. Additionally, institutions have gamed the accountability policy by distorting their admissions, retention, and graduation practices in the name of higher standards.

Extending these sorts of policies without careful consideration of the social consequences tied to them will likely compound the problem of the lack of minority graduates entering the teaching workforce. To this end, the disparate impact Title II of the 1998 HEA has had on students of color is a warning note. If institutions of higher education enact further policy without thinking explicitly and coherently about racial inequalities, the end result will likely be an artificial raising of standards but an increased exclusion of people.

The nation faces an unprecedented teacher shortage over the next decade which will disproportionately negatively affect poor and minority students (Murphy, DeArmond, & Guin, 2003). Given the importance of a racially/ethnically diverse teacher workforce to a diversified student body (Darling-Hammond, 1994), the disparities between the number of students of color in the K–12 system and the number of teachers of color ready to educate them are both striking and troubling. Without serious attention to increasing the black and Latino teacher workforce, the beneficial outcomes such teachers bring to a diverse classroom will be lost. This point is important in its own right and in the context of broader postsecondary concerns about a diverse student body. In her concluding statement in *Grutter v. Bol-*

linger, U.S. Supreme Court Justice O'Connor postulates, "It has been 25 years since Justice Powell first approved the use of race to further an interest in student body diversity in the context of higher education. Since that time, the number of minority applications with high grades and test scores has indeed increased. We expect that 25 years from now, the use of racial preferences will no longer be necessary to further the interest approved today" (*Grutter,* 2003, p. 344). If elementary, secondary, and postsecondary education truly hope to work toward such a goal, efforts must include actively addressing key issues, such as a shortage of teachers of color. In considering ways to shrink that gap from a federal perspective, this chapter has suggested that imposing test-based accountability will likely have little success. The technical realities of assessment burden its use in postsecondary accountability in much the same way they encumber other large-scale standardized measures of achievement at the K–12 level.

Accountability, more broadly defined and cognizant of the range of institutional missions and constituencies served by those missions, however, may increase black and Latino representation among the teacher workforce. Bensimon et al. (in press) write, "It is said that what gets measured gets noticed. We are well aware that accountability systems in and of themselves will not solve the problem of inequality, but we believe that it is important to make visible the inequitable outcomes that are not currently addressed in accountability reports." By pushing for an expanded view of accountability to include issues of racial/ethnic equity, states and the country as a whole ideally reap the benefits.

As a group of retired military officers intimate in an amicus curiae brief submitted on behalf of the University of Michigan in both *Gratz* and *Grutter* (Brief of the Retired Military Officers, 2003), the classroom and the workplace of the 21st century will require diverse leadership:

> Based on decades of experience, amici have concluded that a highly qualified, racially diverse officer corps educated and trained to command our nation's racially diverse enlisted ranks is essential to the military's ability to fulfill its principal mission to provide national security. ... [I]ncreasing numbers of officer candidates are trained and educated in racially diverse educational settings, which provides them with invaluable experience for their future command of our nation's highly diverse enlisted ranks. (pp. 5–7)

The importance of holding institutions and states accountable for the production of a diverse leadership, then, is paramount. Ultimately, with all of these accountability measures, the point is to use them as a means of reaching the end goal of improved academic achievement for all students. Increasing the amount of useful and useable information available to make accountability assessments is essential in aiding those efforts. Data that allow for accurate tracking of key considerations such as graduation rates increase the opportunity at the federal level to make meaningful policy decisions based on sound, data-driven debates.

Finally, beyond simply broadening the definition of accountability, channeling federal resources to programs with high potential for increasing the number of black and Latino teachers is important. One such promising effort is the Centers for Excellence provision in the 2003 Ready to Teach Act. Under the provision, grants are administered to traditionally minority-serving institutions in order to establish centers that

1. help recruit and prepare teachers, including minority teachers, to meet the national demand for a highly qualified teacher in every classroom; and
2. increase opportunities for Americans of all educational, ethnic, class, and geographic backgrounds to become highly qualified teachers. (Ready to Teach Act, 2003, pp. 49–50)

Other opportunities, such as certification programs focused on the art of being in the classroom as much as on knowing the content, may bear fruit as well. By empowering rather than punishing the institutions training the majority of black and Latino teachers, racial/ethnic representation in the teaching profession may improve over the long term. Equally important, achievement at the K–12 level leading to college may, in turn, increase. As the federal government and institutions of higher education together and individually consider how to ensure highly qualified teachers, specifically, and a well-educated work force more broadly, access needs to be an integral component within the defined parameters of accountability.

NOTES

1. The Higher Education Act was introduced by President Lyndon Johnson and first passed in 1965. Its primary function was to provide financial assistance as a means of expanding educational opportunity. It has subsequently been reauthorized to include a broader set of topics including, most recently, teacher preparation, recruitment, and development; international education; and graduate programs (U.S. Department of Education, 2002b).
2. For the purpose of this chapter, the descriptors "underrepresented," "minority," and "of color" are used interchangeably and include blacks and Latinos. Also, the

terms "Latino" and "Hispanic," and "black" and "African American," will be used interchangeably.

3. Title II of the HEA was added in 1998 to address the recruitment of teachers and the quality of their preparation.

4. The 14 institutions include: Jackson State University (MS); Central Methodist College (MO); Missouri Valley College (MO); Boricua College (NY); City University of New York–York College (NY); Long Island University–Brooklyn (NY); Shaw University (NC); Heidelberg College (OH); Lake Erie College (OH); Denison University (OH); Urbana University (OH); Central State University (OH); Notre Dame College (OH); University of Wyoming (WY).

5. The term "disparate impact" is used in the law to indicate a differential negative effect on a protected class resulting from a facially neutral policy or practice. In this case, the exam being used to screen teacher applicants was disproportionately screening out black applicants from the pool.

6. In December 2004, the Alabama Board of Education approved an amended consent decree to require subject matter testing for preservice teachers. It awaits final federal court approval (State of Alabama, 2004).

7. Two similar cases have been tried unsuccessfully (*Association of Mexican American Educators v. State of California*, 2002, and *United States v. South Carolina*, 1977). In both instances, "courts ruled that the tests were consistent with business necessity and that valid alternatives with less disparate impacts were not available" (Mitchell et al., 2001, p. 112).

8. Praxis I, which measures basic reading, writing, and math skills, screens students for entry into teacher training programs and is currently used by 36 states (Alliance for Equity in Higher Education, 2000). The Praxis II is generally taken at the end of college or after graduation and measures subject area knowledge and ability to teach that subject (Alliance for Equity in Higher Education, 2000).

9. It should be noted that data for Hispanic and Asian Americans were not further delineated by ethnic subgroup, which may mask further disparities among candidates in these racial/ethnic categories.

10. Interestingly, Alabama universities had previously used a fixed cutoff score on the American College Test (ACT) for admission to undergraduate teaching programs. This practice was struck down, however, in the 1991 decision, *Groves v. Alabama State Board of Education* (Heubert & Hauser, 1999).

11. This section is modified from Horn (in press).

REFERENCES

Allen v. Alabama State Board of Education, 612 F. Supp. 1046 (M.D. Ala. 1985).

Alliance for Equity in Higher Education. (2000). *Educating the emerging majority: The role of minority-serving colleges & universities in confronting America's teacher crisis*. Washington, DC: Institution for Higher Education Policy. Retrieved October 21, 2004, from http://www.ihep.org/Pubs/PDF/FinalTeacherED.pdf

American Association of State Colleges and Universities. (n.d.). *Validity of 100 percent pass rate scores: Report to Congress*. Retrieved February 2, 2005, from http://www.aascu.org/passrateReport/

Angrist, J., & Guryan, J. (2003). *Does teacher testing raise teacher quality? Evidence from state certification requirements. National Bureau of Economic Research* (Working Paper 9545). Cambridge, MA: National Bureau of Economic Research. Retrieved February 1, 2005, from http://www.nber.org/papers/w9545

Association of Mexican American Educators v. State of California, 231 F.3d 572 (U.S. App. 2000).

Bensimon, E., Hao, L., & Bustillos, L. (in press). Measuring the state of equity in higher education. In P. Gándara, C. L. Horn, & G. Orfield (Eds.), *Leveraging promise: Expanding opportunity in higher-education policy.* Albany: State University of New York Press.

Bishop, J., & Mane, F. (2001). The impacts of minimum competency exam graduation requirements on college attendance and early labor market success of disadvantaged students. In G. Orfield & M. Kornhaber (Eds.), *Raising standards or raising barriers: Inequality and high stakes testing in public education* (pp. 51–83). New York: Century Foundation.

Brief of the Retired Military Officers as *Amici Curiae* in Support of Respondents, *Grutter v. Bollinger,* 123 S. Ct. 2325 (2003) and *Gratz v. Bollinger,* 123 S. Ct. 2411 (2003).

Burd, S. (2003, May 23). Republican lawmakers call for more accountability in higher education. *Chronicle of Higher Education,* p. A23.

Crocker, L., & Algina, J. (1986). *Introduction to classical and modern test theory.* New York: Harcourt Brace Jovanovich College.

Darling-Hammond, L. (with Green, J.). (1994). Teacher quality and equality. In J. Goodlad & P. Keating (Eds.), *Access to knowledge: The continuing agenda for our nation's schools* (pp. 237–258). New York: College Entrance Examination Board.

Dee, T. (2001). *Teachers, race, and student achievement in a randomized experiment* (Working Paper 8432). Cambridge, MA: National Bureau of Economic Research. Retrieved February 16, 2005, from http://www.nber.org/papers/w8432

Educational Testing Service. (1998). *The use of Praxis pass rates to evaluate teacher education programs.* Washington, DC: Author.

Flores, B., & Clark, E. (1999, Fall). High-stakes testing: Barriers for prospective bilingual education teachers. *Bilingual Research Journal, 21,* 335–356.

Freeman, B., & Schopen, A. (1991). Quality reform in teacher education: A brief look at the admissions testing movement. *Contemporary Education, 62,* 279–282.

Gitomer, D., Latham, A., & Ziomek, R. (1999). *The academic quality of prospective teachers: The impact of admissions and licensure testing.* Princeton, NJ: Educational Testing Service. Retrieved October 21, 2004, from http://www.ets.org/research/dload/RR-03-35.pdf

Glass, G. (1978). Standards and criteria. *Journal of Educational Measurement, 15,* 237–261.

Gratz v. Bollinger, 539 U.S. 244 (2003).

Groves v. Alabama State Board of Education, 776 F. Supp. 1518 (M.D. Ala. 1991).

Grutter v. Bollinger, 539 U.S. 306 (2003).

Heubert, J., & Hauser, R. (Eds.). (1999). *High stakes: Testing for tracking, promoting, and graduation.* Washington, DC: National Academy Press.

Higher Education Act of 1998, Pub. L. No. 105–244 (1998).

Horn, C. L. (2003). High stakes testing and students: Stopping or perpetuating a cycle of failure? *Theory into Practice, 42*(1), 30–41.

Horn, C. L. (in press). The technical realities of measuring history. In S. G. Grant (Ed.), *Measuring history: Cases of high-stakes testing across the states*. Greenwich, CT: Information Age.

Horn, C. L., Ramos, M., Blumer, I., & Madaus, G. (2000). *Cut scores: Results may vary*. Chestnut Hill, MA: Boston College, National Board on Educational Testing and Public Policy.

House Education and the Workforce Committee. (n.d.) The Ready to Teach Act: HR 2211. Retrieved October 21, 2004, from http://edworkforce.house.gov/issues/108th/education/highereducation/2211billsummary.htm

Jencks, C. (1998). Racial bias in testing. In C. Jencks & M. Phillips (Eds.), *The black-white test score gap* (pp. 55–85). Washington, DC: Brookings Institution.

Joint Committee on Testing Practices. (2004). *Code of fair testing practices in education*. Washington, DC: American Psychological Association.

Kim, J., & Sunderman, G. (2004). *Large mandates and limited resources: State response to the No Child Left Behind Act and implications for accountability*. Cambridge, MA: Civil Rights Project at Harvard University.

Ladson-Billings, G. (1994). *The dreamkeepers: Successful teachers of African American children*. San Francisco: Jossey-Bass.

Linn. R. (2000). Assessments and accountability. *Educational Researcher, 29*(2), 4–16.

Lively, K. (1998, July 31). States move to toughen standards for teacher-education programs. *Chronicle of Higher Education*, p. A27.

Ludlow, L. (2001, February 22). Teacher test accountability: From Alabama to Massachusetts. *Education Policy Analysis Archives, 9*(6). Retrieved October 21, 2004, from http://epaa.asu.edu/epaa/v9n6.html

Ludlow, L., Shirley, D., & Rosca, C. (2002, December 12). The case that won't go away: Besieged institutions and the Massachusetts teacher tests. *Education Policy Analysis Archives, 10*(50). Retrieved October 21, 2004, from http://epaa.asu.edu/epaa/v10n50.html

Madaus, G., & Clarke, M. (2001). The adverse impact of high-stakes testing on minority students: Evidence from one hundred years of test data. In G. Orfield & M. Kornhaber (Eds.), *Raising standards or raising barriers: Inequality and high stakes testing in public education* (pp. 85–106). New York: Century Foundation.

Madaus, G., & Horn, C. (2000). Testing technology: The need for oversight. In A. Filer (Ed.), *Assessment: Social practice and social product* (pp. 47–66). London: Routledge Farmer.

Messick, S. (1989). Validity. In R. L. Linn (Ed.), *Educational measurement* (3rd ed., pp. 13–103). New York: Macmillan.

Mitchell, K., Robinson, D., Plake, B., & Knowles, K. (Eds.). (2001). *Testing teacher candidates: The role of licensure tests in improving teacher quality*. Washington, DC: National Academy Press.

Murphy, P., DeArmond, M., & Guin, K. (2003, July 31). A national crisis or localized problems? Getting perspective on the scope and scale of the teacher shortage. *Education Policy Analysis Archives, 11*(23). Retrieved February 1, 2005, from http://epaa.asu.edu/epaa/v11n23/

National Commission on Testing and Public Policy. (1990). *From gatekeeper to gateway: Transforming testing in America.* Chestnut Hill, MA: Boston College, National Commission on Testing and Public Policy.

Nettle, M., Perna, L., & Millet, C. (1998). Race and testing in college admissions. In G. Orfield & E. Miller (Eds.), *Chilling admissions: The affirmative action crisis and the search for alternatives* (pp. 97–110). Cambridge, MA: Harvard Education Publishing Group.

Oakes, J., Mendoza, J., & Silver, D. (in press). California opportunity indicators: Informing and monitoring California's progress toward equitable college access. In P. Gándara, C. L. Horn, & G. Orfield (Eds.), *Leveraging promise: Expanding opportunity in higher-education policy.* Albany: State University of New York Press.

Orfield, G., & Kornhaber, M. (Eds.). (2001). *Raising standards or raising barriers? Inequality and high-stakes testing in public education.* New York: Century Foundation Press.

Orfield, G., & Lee, C. (2004). *Brown at 50: King's dream or* Plessy's *nightmare?* Cambridge, MA: Civil Rights Project at Harvard University.

Ready to Teach Act of 2003, H. Rep. 2211, 108th Cong. (2003). Retrieved October 21, 2004, from http://thomas.loc.gov/

Rhoades, K., & Madaus, G. (2003). *Errors in standardized tests: A systemic problem.* Chestnut Hill, MA: National Board on Educational Testing and Public Policy.

State of Alabama. (2004, December 9). Governor Riley and Alabama board of education approve teacher testing agreement. Retrieved February 2, 2005, from http://www.governorpress.alabama.gov/pr/pr-2004-12-09-01-teachertesting.asp

United States v. South Carolina, 445 F. Supp. 1094 (U.S. Dist., 1977).

U.S. Department of Education. (n.d.). Introduction: No Child Left Behind. Retrieved October 17, 2004, from http://www.ed.gov/nclb/overview/intro/index.html#fn1

U.S. Department of Education. (2002a). Improving teacher quality, recruitment, and preparation. Retrieved October 21, 2004, from http://www.ed.gov/offices/OPE/PPI/Reauthor/tch1016.html

U.S. Department of Education. (2002b). Major topics of HEA. Retrieved February 14, 2005, from http://wdcrobcolp01.ed.gov/CFAPPS/OPE/HEA/index.cfm

U.S. Department of Education Office of Postsecondary Education. (2002). *Meeting the highly qualified teachers challenge: The secretary's annual report on teacher quality.* Washington, DC: Author. Retrieved February 1, 2005, from www.ed.gov/about/reports/annual/teachprep/2002title-ii-report.pdf

Williford, L. (1993). *Perceived impact of state rules and regulations on teacher education programs.* Chapel Hill: North Carolina Educational Policy Research Center.

Wolanin, T. (Ed.). (2003). *HEA: Reauthorizing the Higher Education Act, issues and options.* Washington, DC: Institute for Higher Education Policy. Retrieved October 17, 2004, from http://www.ihep.org/Pubs/ReAuthHEA.pdf

Zook, J. (1993a, March 24). A national test of students' analytical skills. *Chronicle of Higher Education.* Retrieved March 1, 2005, from http:chronicle.com/prm/che-data/articles.dir/articles-39.dir/issue-29.dir/29a02302.htm

Zook, J. (1993b, August 4). Panel asks government to measure college learning. *Chronicle of Higher Education,* Retrieved March 1, 2005, from http://chronicle.com/prm/che-data/articles.dir/articles-39.dir/issue-48.dir/48a2001.htm

8

After *Grutter* and *Gratz*
Higher Education, Race, and the Law

ANGELO N. ANCHETA

For most of the nation's history, America's leading colleges and universities enrolled very few racial minority students. Because of overt segregation and the creation of racially defined public universities and colleges in nearly 20 states, as well as historic discrimination and admissions procedures that yielded low minority enrollments, selective universities across the country remained virtually all white. The civil rights reforms of the 1960s recognized that the changing legal landscape and the growth in minority populations required affirmative, race-conscious efforts to overcome both historical and contemporary barriers to equal educational opportunity. Colleges in the South were required to implement race-conscious admissions plans because of their past discrimination, while most elite colleges in other parts of the country adopted policies voluntarily. Programs designed to remedy the present effects of past discrimination and to increase the diversity of university student bodies led to significant progress in the racial integration of higher education and the workforce—but never without great controversy. Legal challenges to race-conscious programs in higher education admissions, as well as in employment and government contracting, have severely limited the types of affirmative action programs that institutions can employ to address discrimination and to promote diversity, and the future of affirmative action remains uncertain, even with the U.S. Supreme Court's recent rulings in the University of Michigan affirmative action cases.

In *Grutter v. Bollinger* (2003) and *Gratz v. Bollinger* (2003), the Supreme Court upheld the basic rationale for race-conscious admissions in higher education, reaffirming the ruling 25 years earlier in *Regents of the University of California v. Bakke* (1978) that promoting diversity in higher education is a constitutionally compelling interest and that the flexible use of race in a carefully crafted admissions policy can survive constitutional challenge. Yet, while settling several important questions of law, the Court's rulings did little to alleviate the contentiousness of the affirmative action debate, and challenges to race-conscious policies—not only in admissions, but in related areas such as financial aid, recruitment, and faculty and staff hiring—will no doubt occupy the agendas of both policymakers and litigators for many years.

In this chapter I address some of the key legal and research questions that have arisen in the aftermath of the University of Michigan decisions. I summarize the constitutional standards that apply to race-conscious policymaking in higher education and examine the Supreme Court's rulings in *Grutter* and *Gratz*. I then analyze the major areas of race-conscious policymaking in higher education left unaddressed by the Supreme Court, including the appropriate use of race in outreach and recruitment, financial aid, and faculty hiring. I conclude by discussing areas of research that are likely to inform future policy debates and litigation involving race-conscious policies in higher education.

THE CONSTITUTIONAL LIMITS OF RACE-CONSCIOUS ADMISSIONS

The University of Michigan cases underscored the Supreme Court's basic requirement that all race-conscious policymaking—even if designed to benefit members of racial minority groups—is subject to "strict scrutiny," which is an exacting standard used by the courts to evaluate the legality of policies under the Equal Protection Clause of the Fourteenth Amendment (*Adarand Constructors, Inc. v. Peña*, 1995; *City of Richmond v. J. A. Croson*, 1989).[1] Because the Supreme Court has also held that Title VI of the Civil Rights Act of 1964, the federal statute prohibiting racial discrimination by recipients of federal funding, is "coextensive" with the Equal Protection Clause, the same constitutional standard that applies to public institutions also applies to private institutions receiving federal dollars; thus, almost every college and university in the country is bound by the constitutional strict scrutiny requirement.

Under strict scrutiny, the courts address two fundamental questions that evaluate the ends and the means employed in race-conscious policymaking: First, is the goal of the policy sufficiently important to constitute a "compelling interest"? Second, if the policy is in fact compelling, is it "narrowly tailored"—that is, is it closely fitting and necessary to advance the stated interest? Strict scrutiny is an exacting standard, but it is not inflexible. As the Supreme Court stated in *Grutter v. Bollinger*, "Context matters when reviewing race-based governmental action under the Equal Protection Clause" (p. 327). Applying strict scrutiny within the context of an inclusive higher education policy, the Supreme Court ruled in *Grutter v. Bollinger* that colleges and universities do have a compelling interest in creating a diverse student body. In applying its narrow tailoring requirements to each of the admissions policies at issue in the University of Michigan cases, the Court upheld the university's law school admissions policy in *Grutter*—a whole-file review policy that considered race as one of many admissions factors—but struck down the University's undergraduate policy in *Gratz*—a point-system policy that automatically assigned a fixed number of points to underrepresented minority applicants—because it lacked the required flexibility and holistic consideration of applicants.

The Compelling Interest in Student Body Diversity

Prior to *Grutter* and *Gratz*, the University of Michigan, like many of the selective colleges and universities throughout the country, had relied on Justice Powell's opinion in the 1978 case of *Regents of the University of California v. Bakke* as legal support for its admissions policies. In *Bakke*, a divided Supreme Court struck down the special admissions policy at the medical school of the University of California, Davis, but overturned a lower court's ruling that race could not be considered at all in admissions. Justice Powell's controlling opinion stated that a university's interest in promoting educational diversity—and not just racial diversity—within its student body is grounded in traditional academic freedoms and constitutes a compelling interest that can justify the use of race in admissions. Drawing on the undergraduate admissions policy at Harvard College as an example, Justice Powell went on to distinguish an unconstitutional policy such as the Davis medical school plan, in which white applicants were excluded from competition for specified seats in the entering class, from a legal policy in which race is a "plus" factor among many factors employed in a competitive process in which all applicants are eligible to compete for seats in the entering class.

In *Grutter v. Bollinger*, Justice O'Connor's majority opinion wholly endorsed Justice Powell's conclusion in *Bakke* that creating a diverse student body is a compelling interest for a college or university. In doing so, Justice O'Connor drew significantly on Justice Powell's recognition that institutions of higher learning are entitled to a high degree of deference by the courts because of academic freedoms rooted in the First Amendment: "Our holding today is in keeping with our tradition of giving a degree of deference to a university's academic decisions, within constitutionally prescribed limits. . . . We have long recognized that, given the important purpose of public education and the expansive freedoms of speech and thought associated with the university environment, universities occupy a special niche in our constitutional tradition" (p. 329).

The *Grutter* Court also presumed good faith on the part of colleges and universities when selecting their student bodies: "Our conclusion that the Law School has a compelling interest in a diverse student body is informed by our view that attaining a diverse student body is at the heart of the Law School's proper institutional mission, and that 'good faith' on the part of a university is 'presumed' absent 'a showing to the contrary'" (p. 329). Unlike the Court's compelling interest analysis in earlier cases involving policies containing race-conscious remedies, where the Court required that an institution present a "strong basis in evidence" to document its compelling interest in remedying the present effects of past discrimination, the *Grutter* Court imposed no special evidentiary requirement on colleges and universities and granted significant deference to the university in establishing its diversity interest.

The *Grutter* opinion offered an especially strong endorsement of the value of student body diversity in promoting several benefits, including 1) concrete educational benefits; 2) assisting in the breakdown of racial and ethnic stereotypes; and 3) the development of a diverse, racially integrated leadership class and democracy. Relying on both expert testimony and research studies documenting the educational benefits of diversity, the *Grutter* opinion recognized that diversity leads to benefits for *all* students, including the promotion of cross-racial understanding, improved classroom discussions, and enhanced preparation for a diverse workforce and society. In addition, the Court concluded that diversity "helps to break down racial stereotypes" (p. 330) and that "diminishing the force of such stereotypes is both a crucial part of [an institution's] mission, and one that it cannot accomplish with only token numbers of minority students" (p. 333).

The *Grutter* Court also recognized that colleges and universities—and law schools in particular—provide the training ground for many of the nation's leaders. According to the Court, "In order to cultivate a set of leaders with legitimacy in the eyes of the citizenry, it is necessary that the path to leadership be visibly open to talented and qualified individuals of every race and ethnicity" (p. 332). Access to higher education "must be inclusive of talented and qualified individuals of every race and ethnicity, so that all members of our heterogeneous society may participate in the educational institutions that provide the training and education necessary to succeed in America" (pp. 332–333).[2]

Although the Supreme Court's deference in *Grutter* to academic freedoms suggests that higher education may provide a unique context for upholding a compelling interest in diversity, the Court's language supporting the value of diversity throughout the educational system and in other institutions implies that the *Grutter* Court's ruling may be applied more broadly. For instance, the Court stated, "We have repeatedly acknowledged the overriding importance of preparing students for work and citizenship, describing education as pivotal to 'sustaining our political and cultural heritage' with a fundamental role in maintaining the fabric of society" (p. 332). Language such as this may be influential in future cases involving challenges to diversity-related policies in K–12 education, in employment, and in higher education outside of admissions.

Narrow Tailoring

Under the narrow tailoring requirement of strict scrutiny, the courts measure the "fit" between a compelling interest and the policy used to advance that interest. The Supreme Court has not developed a single test for narrow tailoring, and the standards employed in *Grutter* and *Gratz* draw on guidelines from a variety of earlier cases. In *Bakke*, Justice Powell discussed two elements of narrow tailoring specific to admissions policies: First, an admissions policy cannot rely on quotas or separate tracks that insulate racial minorities from competitive review, and second, race must be employed as only one of many factors in a competitive process that evaluates individual applicants. In another line of cases involving policies designed to remedy the present effects of past discrimination by public institutions, the Supreme Court has looked at several narrow tailoring factors, such as the necessity of the policy and availability of race-neutral alternatives; the flexibility and duration of the policy; and the impact of the policy on third parties (*U.S. v. Paradise*, 1987).

The Supreme Court's narrow tailoring test in *Grutter* combined elements from *Bakke* and the Court's remedial cases into the following basic inquiries:

1. Does the program offer a competitive review of all applications (i.e., are there quotas or separate tracks for minorities)?
2. Does the program provide flexible, individualized consideration of applicants so that race is only one of several factors being considered?
3. Has the institution considered workable race-neutral alternatives to its program?
4. Does the program unduly burden nonminority applicants?
5. Is the program limited in time, so that it has a logical end point?

The *Grutter* Court applied all five of these inquiries and upheld the University of Michigan Law School's admissions policy. The *Gratz* Court focused on the second inquiry and found that the university's undergraduate admissions policy lacked the necessary flexibility and individualized consideration needed to satisfy narrow tailoring. Because of the importance of the narrow tailoring requirement in future legal challenges in higher education admissions and other areas of race-conscious policymaking, each of these inquiries is discussed in detail below.

Competitive Review

Both *Bakke* and *Grutter* prohibit the use of quotas, set-asides, or separate tracks for minority applicants in order to advance an interest in student body diversity.[3] However, as the *Grutter* Court made clear, *quotas* are distinct from *goals*:

> Properly understood, a "quota" is a program in which a certain fixed number or proportion of opportunities are "reserved exclusively for certain minority groups." . . . In contrast, "a permissible goal . . . require[s] only a good-faith effort . . . to come within a range demarcated by the goal itself," and permits consideration of a "plus" factor in any given case while still ensuring that each candidate "compete[s] with all other qualified applicants." (p. 335)

Thus an admissions policy that uses race as a plus factor, even if it gives more weight to race than other factors, is not the equivalent of a quota. Nor does "some attention to numbers" necessarily change a flexible system into a quota. A goal that seeks racial minority enrollments beyond a token number but does not establish a fixed number or percentage of admittees can be an appropriate objective for colleges and universities.

Accordingly, the *Grutter* Court upheld the law school's use of a "critical mass" of minority students as a flexible goal that established targets for minority enrollments, and found that no quota was in place. The critical mass concept was never defined as a fixed number or percentage, and it was used to establish a flexible goal of achieving minority enrollments beyond token numbers that would lead to the educational benefits consistent with a diverse student body.

Flexible and Individualized Consideration

Taken together, the *Grutter* and *Gratz* cases suggest that the most important inquiry into whether an admissions policy is narrowly tailored is whether it is flexible and provides sufficient individualized consideration of all applicants. According to the *Grutter* Court, "a university's admissions program must remain flexible enough to ensure that each applicant is evaluated as an individual and not in a way that makes an applicant's race or ethnicity the defining feature of his or her application" (p. 337).

Race therefore cannot be the exclusive or predominant factor in an admissions decision. Institutions are entitled to some degree of deference in defining the composition of their student bodies, but a race-conscious policy must consider at least some nonracial factors to ensure that all the factors that can contribute to student body diversity are considered along with race. The *Grutter* Court endorsed an admissions policy that "seriously weighs many other diversity factors besides race that can make a real and dispositive difference for nonminority applicants as well" (p. 338).

On the other hand, an admissions policy that employs a mechanistic or automatic assignment of a benefit based on race is not sufficiently flexible to satisfy narrow tailoring. Nor is a policy that offers such a heavy advantage to minority applicants that it virtually guarantees their admission. According to the *Gratz* Court, a flexible admissions program does not "contemplate that any single characteristic automatically ensure[s] a specific and identifiable contribution to a university's diversity. . . . [Instead] each characteristic of a particular applicant [is] to be considered in assessing the applicant's entire application" (p. 271). The *Gratz* Court struck down the University of Michigan undergraduate admissions policy because it concluded that the 20 points (out of a maximum of 150) assigned to underrepresented minority group members lacked the necessary flexibility to be narrowly tailored and virtually guaranteed admission to minority students.

Race-Neutral Alternatives

Narrow tailoring, according to the *Grutter* Court, also requires "serious, good faith consideration of workable race-neutral alternatives that will achieve the diversity the university seeks" (p. 339). However, the consideration of alternatives does not require that an institution exhaust every possible alternative; instead, the requirement focuses on the documentation of good faith efforts to develop effective and *workable* solutions that can advance the interest in diversity. As the *Grutter* Court recognized, race-neutral alternatives such as a lottery system could compromise a school's parallel interest in selectivity and could actually impair diversity by precluding individualized review. Nor are policies such as "percent plans" that guarantee admission to all students in the state who graduate from their high school with a class ranking above a given threshold (e.g., the top 10%) truly workable alternatives at many universities, particularly at graduate and professional schools.[4]

Undue Burden on Nonminorities

In addition, "a race-conscious admissions program must not 'unduly burden individuals who are not members of the favored racial and ethnic groups'" (p. 341). Although a denial of admission can impose a burden on an applicant, the burden at issue in a selective admissions process revolves around fairness in the admissions *process*, not a rejection per se. Indeed, selective institutions are often in the business of rejecting more highly qualified applicants than they accept, and no student involved in a truly competitive admissions process has an entitlement to attend a selective school. A fair and flexible admissions process that considers both racial and nonracial factors allows nonminorities to be competitive with minorities, and will not impose an undue burden.

Time Limits

A final narrow tailoring inquiry focuses on the duration of an admissions policy. Although an institution can have a permanent interest in obtaining a diverse student body, the use of race to advance that goal is subject to time limits. "The requirement that all race-conscious admissions programs have a termination point 'assure[s] all citizens that the deviation from the norm of equal treatment of all racial and ethnic groups is a temporary matter, a measure taken in the service of the goal of equality itself'" (p. 342). However, fixed or absolute time limits are not essential. According to the *Grutter* Court, the durational requirement can be satisfied by sunset provisions or by periodic review that evaluates whether a race-conscious policy is still needed to attain a diverse student body.

There is also language in the *Grutter* opinion that some have interpreted to impose a fixed end date for all race-conscious affirmative action programs in higher education: "We expect that 25 years from now, the use of racial preferences will no longer be necessary to further the interest approved today" (p. 343). The better reading of this passage is not that race-conscious affirmative action terminates in 2028, but that the *Grutter* Court was expressing, by reference to the passage of time since the *Bakke* decision, its aspiration that there should be enough progress in equal educational opportunity to make race-conscious policies unnecessary in the future. Moreover, the Court's statement in no way undercuts the lasting nature of the compelling interest in diversity; the Court's language clearly expresses an understanding that even if race-conscious measures will not be needed, student body diversity itself will be no less important in 25 years.

Dissenting Opinions

Justices O'Connor, Stevens, Souter, Ginsburg, and Breyer formed the five-member majority in *Grutter*, upholding the law school's admissions policy. In *Gratz*, Chief Justice Rehnquist and Justices O'Connor, Scalia, Kennedy, and Thomas, joined by Justice Breyer, who concurred in the judgment of the Court, formed the six-member majority voting to strike down the undergraduate admissions policy. Several concurring and dissenting opinions were issued in the cases, but a number of the dissenting opinions are especially important because they provide insights into future affirmative action cases and may prove significant if the voting alignment of the Court shifts as new Justices are appointed.

Justice Kennedy's dissenting opinion in *Grutter* indicated that he agreed in theory with the majority's holding that promoting student body diversity is a compelling governmental interest. His dissent focused on the majority's narrow tailoring analysis and the strictness of the Court's review in finding the law school's policy constitutional. Justice Kennedy wrote approvingly of "the use of race as a factor in the admissions process," and that "[i]n the context of university admissions the objective of racial diversity can be accepted based on empirical data known to us" (p. 388). Although these and other passages in the Kennedy dissent do not guarantee positive votes in the future, there appear to be at least six members of the current Court who may support other diversity-based policies, such as nonadmissions policies in higher education or voluntary desegregation policies in K–12 public education.

Justice Kennedy's and Chief Justice Rehnquist's dissents in *Grutter* were highly critical of the majority's narrow tailoring analysis, having argued that the majority's analysis was far too lax and that the law school violated the prohibition on quotas and separate tracks for minority students. In particular, the dissents criticized both the theory and the application of the critical mass concept, and argued that actual admissions data proved that critical mass established not only goals but de facto quotas at the law school. Nevertheless, the *Grutter* majority upheld the critical mass concept and rejected the dissents' arguments because of significant variations in minority enrollments at the law school over several years. Whether critical mass will continue to be subject to litigation is not entirely clear. The university never fully defined critical mass or specified it in numerical terms; indeed, excessive precision might imply the use of an admissions quota. Nonetheless, as long as critical mass is used as a flexible goal and not as a functional quota, the courts are likely to uphold its use, even without greater specificity in its definition.

Justice Scalia's opinion in *Grutter* disagreed fundamentally with the majority's strict scrutiny analysis, but his opinion is instructive for its listing of potential claims that might be raised in the aftermath of the University of Michigan decisions:

> Some future lawsuits will presumably focus on whether the discriminatory scheme in question contains enough evaluation of the applicant "as an individual," . . . and sufficiently avoids "separate admissions tracks" . . . to fall under *Grutter* rather than *Gratz*. Some will focus on whether a university has gone beyond the bounds of a "good faith effort" and has so zealously pursued its "critical mass" as to make it an unconstitutional *de facto* quota system, rather than merely "a permissible goal." . . . Other lawsuits may focus on whether, in the particular setting at issue, any educational benefits flow from racial diversity. . . . Still other suits may challenge the bona fides of the institution's expressed commitment to the educational benefits of diversity that immunize the discriminatory scheme in *Grutter.* (Tempting targets, one would suppose, will be those universities that talk the talk of multiculturalism and racial diversity in the courts but walk the walk of tribalism and racial segregation on their campuses—through minority-only student organizations, separate minority housing opportunities, separate minority student centers, even separate minority-only graduation ceremonies.) And still other suits may claim that the institution's racial preferences have gone below or above the mystical *Grutter*-approved "critical mass." Finally, litigation can be expected on behalf of minority groups intentionally short changed in the institution's composition of its generic minority "critical mass." (pp. 348–349)

On their face, some of these claims may be unconvincing to the courts. For instance, the *Grutter* opinion does not require that the educational benefits of diversity must be documented at every institution that employs race-conscious admissions, nor does the existence of minority organizations or student centers mean that universities are acting in bad faith when they promote diversity through admissions. Moreover, the omission of any racial minority group from a critical mass does not imply that race cannot still be a factor in an applicant's individual review or that any given applicant bears an undue burden. Nevertheless, some of Justice Scalia's potential claims do implicate the strong legal boundaries established by *Grutter* and *Gratz*, such as converting a flexible goal into a quota, or adopting race-conscious procedures that do not provide enough individualized review.

UNANSWERED QUESTIONS: THE LEGALITY OF HIGHER EDUCATION POLICIES BEYOND ADMISSIONS

Despite the split decisions in the University of Michigan cases, the *Grutter* and *Gratz* opinions provide clear guidance to institutions on the constitutional boundaries of race-conscious admissions policies. The cases confirm that admissions quotas and separate tracks for minorities are illegal, as are admissions systems that assign benefits on the basis of race that automatically lead to the admission of minority students. Policies that are flexible and holistic and that consider race as one of many factors should be constitutional, as long as they comply with the Court's additional narrow tailoring requirements addressing race-neutral alternatives, undue burdens, and limited duration. Goals such as reaching a critical mass of underrepresented minority students are permissible, as long as they advance the interest in diversity and do not employ fixed admissions numbers or percentages.

Nonetheless, the Supreme Court did not directly address the legality of race-conscious policies in higher education outside of admissions. For example, it is not clear whether scholarships or other competitive forms of financial aid that employ race as a factor are necessarily constitutional, even if designed to promote student body diversity. In particular, programs that employ race in a more significant way—such as minority-targeted scholarships or minority-only support programs—are not clearly constitutional or unconstitutional. What is clear, however, is that the interest in obtaining the benefits of student body diversity is constitutionally compelling and should serve as a legal justification for other types of race-conscious policies in higher education—such as recruitment and outreach, financial aid, and retention programs. The legality of programs outside of admissions, if they are justified by the same interest in student diversity, would turn on whether they satisfy the Court's narrow tailoring requirements.

Related higher education policies, such as affirmative action programs designed to promote diversity in the faculty or staff at a university, would probably face a different set of challenges. Although one might be able to demonstrate a relationship between faculty hiring and the diversity of the student body, the relationship might not be sufficiently strong to convince a court that a hiring policy for faculty was necessary to promote diversity among the students. However, a distinct interest in faculty diversity—with its expected benefits in promoting the intellectual life of the university, improving classroom learning, creating new research, and other benefits—could be documented and satisfy the compelling interest requirement independent of the related interest in student body diversity.

And, in some areas of university policymaking, judicial deference to university decisionmaking may not be appropriate at all. For instance, when a university decides to employ race-conscious affirmative action in granting contracts for construction and improvement of its physical plant, the academic freedom argument that underlies the *Grutter* reasoning becomes misplaced. In this example, a university is really no different than any other institution seeking to have a new building constructed on its property, and would probably have to articulate some other compelling interest, such as remedying its own past discrimination, in order to satisfy strict scrutiny.

Some of the strengths and weaknesses of potential challenges to race-conscious policies outside of higher education admissions are discussed below.

Race-Conscious Financial Aid

The receipt of financial aid often determines whether a student can attend a university at all (see Heller, this volume), so the linkage between financial aid and the interest in creating—and retaining—a diverse student body is clear. By analogy to admissions, a competitive financial aid program that considers race as one factor among several factors would likely be upheld as constitutional if it is designed to promote the interest in student body diversity and it is narrowly tailored. A selective financial aid program that awards aid through a process that requires individualized consideration of both racial and nonracial factors, does not insulate minority students from competitive review or provide them with automatic and determinative benefits, and complies with other narrow tailoring requirements should be constitutional under the Supreme Court's guidelines in *Grutter*.

However, selective scholarship programs may weight race more heavily, and some programs have been designed so that they benefit only one minority group (or a selected few) and restrict the application process to minority students. There is little case law on these types of programs, and the rulings in *Grutter* and *Gratz* cast some doubt on their legality. A case decided by a federal appeals court in the mid-1990s, *Podberesky v. Kirwan* (1994), struck down the University of Maryland's Benjamin Banneker program, a competitive scholarship program that restricted its awards to African American students. However, the basis for the court's ruling grew largely out of the inadequacy of the evidence—the university lacked a "strong basis in evidence" to document its interest in remedying the present effects of its past discrimination against African Americans. The university thus advanced a remedial interest but did not advance a diversity interest, and the *Podberesky* case could be distinguished from new litigation on these grounds.

Because *Grutter* and *Gratz* prohibit quotas or separate tracks for minority students in admissions, a court might draw a parallel with a race-conscious scholarship program to argue that a minority-only program fails to satisfy narrow tailoring. A court might rule that a minority-only program (or a program heavily weighting race) imposes an undue burden on nonminority students, lacks sufficient flexibility, and, as a practical matter, virtually guarantees that minority students receive scholarship monies. On the other hand, a university might be able to counter these arguments by documenting the necessity of employing a race-targeted program because it creates strong incentives for minority students to attend the university and by demonstrating that nonminority students are also able to obtain scholarships and other forms of financial aid that will allow them to attend the university. Thus there is no undue burden on nonminority students because they can also access scholarship dollars within the larger pool of financial aid. How a court might rule in this type of case remains to be seen.

Challenges to minority-exclusive scholarships also raise questions about the legality of ethnic- or ancestry-targeted scholarships—for example, scholarships that are only available for, say, Italian Americans, or scholarships intended only for the descendants of a particular group with specific roots in a city or region of another country. It is not uncommon for private donors to provide specific funds to universities for these purposes, and some funds have been in existence for many decades without having been challenged legally. The same constitutional analysis applicable to a minority-targeted scholarship program could be applied to an ancestry-based program to render it unconstitutional as well.

A related legal question is the viability of race-conscious scholarship programs that are not administered by universities themselves, but by other entities such as nonprofit foundations. Constitutional requirements such as strict scrutiny may not apply to private foundations because they are not governmental entities and do not receive federal funding. However, a number of federal civil rights statutes, including some dating back to the Reconstruction era,[5] do prohibit racial discrimination in contracts and in the transfer of property, so that a race-targeted scholarship might be subject to challenge under these laws, even if the monies are held and administered by entirely private sources. Again, the law is not clear in this area, but there may be litigation that will provide more guidance in the future.

Race-Conscious Outreach and Recruitment

As an element of the process of enrolling a diverse student body, colleges and universities typically employ race-conscious outreach and recruitment to encourage minority applicants to apply for admission. Any legal analysis of these types of programs should track the *Grutter* and *Gratz* analyses, but because recruitment and outreach do not impose the same types of burdens that a selective admissions process can create, a strict scrutiny analysis may not be appropriate. An unfair admissions process can lead to a denial of admission, but no one is discouraged from applying to a university and is not disadvantaged in the admissions process itself because of a race-conscious recruitment process that targets minority applicants. Of course, one could argue that an applicant who does not receive the same treatment as a minority applicant is bearing a differential burden—and one could go further and argue that a nonminority applicant might not be aware of a college or university and never even apply if she did not receive the same form of recruitment and outreach—but such arguments probably stretch *Grutter* and *Gratz* beyond their logical limits.

Lower court rulings prior to *Grutter* and *Gratz* in the area of recruitment and outreach point strongly in the direction of upholding race-conscious programs. Indeed, a number of courts have proposed that strict scrutiny need not even be employed when examining race-conscious recruitment policies. For example, in *Weser v. Glen* (2002), a case involving a challenge to a public law school's comprehensive affirmative action program, a federal court concluded that "[r]acial classifications that serve to broaden a pool of qualified applicants and to encourage equal opportunity, but do not confer a benefit or impose a burden, do not implicate the Equal Protection Clause" (p. 399). The court made clear that "[e]ven if the Law School's recruiting and outreach efforts were 'race conscious' in being directed at broader recruiting of minorities . . . such efforts would not constitute discrimination" (p. 399). Similarly, the court in *Honadle v. University of Vermont* (1999), a case involving the recruitment of minority faculty, stated: "A public university may be racially 'aware' or 'conscious' by . . . encouraging broader recruiting of racial and ethnic minorities without triggering the equal protection clause's strict scrutiny review. These activities do not impose burdens or benefits, nor do they subject individuals to unequal treatment" (p. 428).

However, some courts have held, in the context of public employment and contracting, that recruitment and outreach programs that confer significant benefits or "preferences" may go beyond the simple dissemination of information and trigger strict scrutiny. For instance, the Washington, D.C., federal appeals court applied strict scrutiny to strike down federal rules promoting equal employment opportunity in the broadcasting industry because of the pressure that a federal agency can impose on stations to limit their hiring pools developed through targeted, race-conscious recruitment efforts (MD/DC/DE Broadcasters Association, 2001). Nevertheless, a university's outreach and recruitment efforts, as long they are broad and inclusive of both minority and nonminority students, and simply explain the basic opportunities available to all students in applying to the university, should fall within the boundaries of the law.

Race-Conscious Support Programs

Even before the Supreme Court delivered its decisions in the *Grutter* and *Gratz* cases, many academic support programs for minorities were already being challenged as illegal. Many of these programs are designed to provide special environments or preparatory settings for minority students, especially those students in academic arenas with especially low enrollments of minority students, such as the sciences and engineering. A common example is a summer program designed to prepare first-year minority students for the rigors of a new environment by providing academic training and adjustment to a university setting, as well as counseling and peer support.

Because of their race-exclusive programs, several universities have been contacted in recent years by anti-affirmative-action organizations such as the Center for Equal Opportunity and the American Civil Rights Institute that have threatened litigation or investigations by the federal government. The courts have provided almost no guidance in this area, and after the

Grutter and *Gratz* decisions, a number of colleges and universities decided to change their minority-only programs to programs that factor in a student's race, but do not make race determinative, and that incorporate several race-neutral criteria such as economic hardship and past educational disadvantage into the selection criteria (Schmidt, 2004).

Minority-only programs may still be defensible, but to comply with a strict scrutiny analysis, universities would have to carefully document their program's unique benefits in order to overcome the arguments that there are less restrictive alternatives and that nonminority students are unduly burdened by their exclusion from the program. For instance, evidence showing that a minority-only program increased student retention and provided concrete benefits that are available only through a special learning environment would support the argument that there is a tight fit between the program's design and the university's interest in student body diversity. A university could further argue that nonminority students are not at all disadvantaged by being excluded from the programs and have the full opportunity to participate and excel in the regular curriculum.

Faculty and Staff Diversity

When a university is acting as an employer, it is bound by both constitutional standards and federal (and state) employment discrimination laws. Because the strict scrutiny standard is more exacting than the affirmative action rules under Title VII of the Civil Rights Act of 1964, a university that satisfies strict scrutiny should also be complying with Title VII, although this is an area of the law that still needs greater clarification by the courts. *Grutter* and *Gratz* are certainly relevant to affirmative action in university employment, but additional issues arise because of the different institutional roles that a university can play (educator versus employer) and because of the different interests that may be advanced to justify an affirmative action program (student body diversity versus faculty or staff diversity).

A university might be tempted to justify a race-conscious faculty employment policy on the basis of its interest in student body diversity—thus automatically completing one-half of the strict scrutiny test—but it may be more sound for a university to advance a separate interest in promoting the diversity of its faculty. Student body diversity could very well be improved because of a more diverse faculty: For instance, the presence of minority faculty and courses taught by those faculty could provide incentives for students to attend the university. However, some of the Supreme Court's analyses in pre-*Grutter/Gratz* affirmative action cases have frowned upon looking at teachers as role models in order to justify race-conscious policies, and members of the current Court may be unreceptive to a line of argument that links the presence of minority faculty to student enrollment (Wygant, 1986).

But a separate and distinct interest in faculty diversity can be closely tied to a university's student diversity interest because of the parallel arguments favoring academic freedom, judicial deference to that freedom, and the educational benefits that accrue from having both a diverse faculty and diverse student body, including improved learning environments, greater cross-racial understanding, and the breakdown of racial and ethnic stereotypes. The Nevada Supreme Court recognized this in *University and Community College System of Nevada v. Farmer* (1997), when it upheld a race-conscious affirmative action plan under Title VII and stated that "the desirability of a racially diverse faculty [is] sufficiently analogous to the constitutionally permissible attainment of a racially diverse student body" (p. 97).

The U.S. Supreme Court has not determined whether a faculty diversity interest is a compelling interest, but there is a good chance that the federal courts would recognize such an interest, as long as it parallels the student diversity interest and is equally well documented. Of course, any policy would have to satisfy the narrow tailoring requirements of *Grutter,* and, as the Nevada Supreme Court also recognized in *Farmer,* in order for an employment policy to be legal, "race must be only one of several factors used in evaluating applicants" (p. 97).

Another wrinkle in university employment is the question of whether the courts should grant the same degree of deference to universities when they are acting as employers versus when they are acting in their role as educators and academic decision makers who are creating diverse student bodies and faculties to promote educational benefits. Nonfaculty staff members can also make important contributions to the intellectual life and learning environments of a university, so a distinct interest in staff diversity could also be articulated and documented in order to justify a race-conscious employment policy. Still, some types of university employment might have less direct effects in creating the educational benefits that accrue from diverse student bodies and diverse faculties. For example, a university-run hospital might want to employ a race-conscious affirmative action policy in hiring and promotions for its administrative and clerical staff, but whether the same educational benefits accrue from the diversity of those particular staff, as compared to the faculty of the medical school, is another question.

Contracting

One area in which race-conscious policymaking by a college or university may be subject to standards entirely different from *Grutter* and *Gratz* is in contracting. It is not unusual for a public institution to establish a race-conscious affirmative action policy that grants additional benefits to minority-owned business enterprises, but the typical justification for the policy is the remediation of the present effects of past discrimination by the institution against minority contractors. The academic freedom arguments articulated in Justice Powell's *Bakke* opinion and in *Grutter* seem inapposite to a university's decisionmaking to establish bidding rules and to create contracts. If a university decides to employ race-conscious measures in hiring contractors to construct new buildings on its campus, it is difficult to see a significant difference between a university and any other public institution seeking to have a new building developed on its property.

Judicial deference to university prerogatives is thus considerably less compelling in the contracting area, and any interest in contractor "diversity" seems far more difficult to justify. Instead, a university would have to articulate and document, through a strong basis in evidence, some other compelling interest such as remedying the present effects of its own past discrimination in order to satisfy strict scrutiny.

IMPLICATIONS FOR HIGHER EDUCATION POLICY AND RESEARCH

The *Grutter* and *Gratz* decisions immediately led to the revision of many admissions policies across the country, particularly among state universities that employed race-conscious point systems in order to process large numbers of applicants. Many universities, including the University of Michigan, converted their undergraduate admissions systems to whole-file review processes, added new inquiries to their applications, and hired additional staff to augment their existing resources for screening applications. But the inclusion of multiple narrow tailoring requirements in *Grutter,* requirements that Justice Powell did not articulate in *Bakke,* also has forced universities to further document their consideration of race-neutral alternatives, to carefully monitor their admissions and enrollment numbers, and to develop periodic review systems.

In addition, colleges and institutions must be attentive to potential challenges to both their admissions policies and to other types of policies that employ race as a criterion. Schools in Texas, for example, that had adopted "race-neutral" policies because of pre-*Grutter* court rulings have been criticized for reinstalling race-conscious policies after the University of Michigan decisions; the University of Michigan itself continued to be engaged in litigation over whether applicants who were denied admission to their undergraduate program should receive monetary damages. As schools move forward in the post-*Grutter*/*Gratz* era, it will be essential for them to document institution-specific practices and to turn to research studies on the benefits of diversity, the linkages between race-conscious policies and diversity interests, and the overall effectiveness of their policies. Some of the more salient areas of policymaking and research are discussed below.

Research to Comply with *Grutter* and *Gratz*

Large numbers of research studies documenting the educational benefits of student body diversity were introduced in *Grutter* and *Gratz* through the trial court records and through amicus curiae briefs submitted to the Supreme Court. The *Grutter* Court itself cited several studies, as well as an amicus brief filed by the American Educational Research Association and other leading groups highlighting many of the recent empirical findings documenting the benefits of diversity. Notwithstanding Justice Scalia's suggestion in his *Grutter* dissent that the benefits of diversity need to be repeatedly documented, such a burdensome requirement is not essential to defend every race-conscious affirmative action program at every campus. Yet, research into the benefits of student body diversity is far from complete, and studies that demonstrate any detrimental effects in diverse student bodies may also arise and weaken the empirical basis for the Court's legal conclusion that diversity is constitutionally compelling. The Supreme Court is not likely to revisit the basic compelling interest question in the immediate future, but the empirical predicates for student body diversity need to remain strong in order for universities to defend their policies in arenas outside of admissions.

Individual institutions must, of course, conduct regular evaluations of their policies to comply with *Grutter,* and research into the various elements of narrow tailoring will be essential for universities seeking to defend their admissions policies. Some of this research could include addressing some of the following questions:

- Are there more specific and quantifiable definitions for critical mass, and how might these definitions influence the legal distinction between a goal and a quota? Is it possible to have multiple definitions of critical mass that apply to different minority groups?

- What race-neutral alternatives, if any, are as effective as race-conscious policies in attaining student body diversity? How effective are policies used in states such as California, Florida, or Washington, where race-conscious measures are prohibited by state law?
- Are there new race-conscious admissions models that are more effective than current models? For instance, public universities in Texas have been employing various models, including percent plans, non-race-conscious admissions, and aggressive minority recruitment efforts. Are these models desirable and replicable?
- Are there are other measures of "merit" that can be employed in admissions, particularly ones in which racial disparities are not accentuated (compared to other heavily used measures, such as standardized tests, where disparities are significant and may be detrimental to minority students)?
- Are there higher education policies that can influence equal educational opportunity in the K–12 system and narrow achievement gaps over the next 25 years?

Nonadmissions Policies and Additional Compelling Interests

As noted earlier, the Supreme Court has not resolved several important legal questions outside the area of university admissions. The narrow tailoring inquiries established in the admissions context in *Grutter* are applicable to most race-conscious financial aid and support programs, and these policies must be substantiated, even when clearly designed to promote student body diversity. For example, there is limited empirical research documenting the effectiveness of minority-only programs, and supportive studies will be needed if universities intend to defend scholarship or academic support programs that limit participation to members of racial minority groups. Similarly, the burdens on nonminority students arising from their exclusion from race-conscious scholarship or academic support programs are not well established, and studies would be needed to undergird the defense of minority-only programs.

Additional compelling interests in the promotion of leadership development among minorities or in the promotion of specific community interests—such as providing competent health care within minority communities through the training of minority health professionals—might be documented to augment the compelling interest in student diversity. Potential compelling interests in faculty diversity or staff diversity, while logically flowing from the arguments favoring the compelling interest in student diversity, need to be more thoroughly documented as well. One would hypothesize that faculty diversity can provide concrete classroom benefits, promote the breakdown of stereotypes, assist in leadership development, and promote an expansion of the curriculum and research at the university, but all of these hypotheses should be tested systematically in order to satisfy constitutional standards, even if the Supreme Court does not insist on a strong basis in evidence requirement for colleges and universities.

In *Grutter v. Bollinger,* the Supreme Court offered a powerful statement on the importance of diversity and racial integration in the United States: "Effective participation by members of all racial and ethnic groups in the civic life of our Nation is essential if the dream of one Nation, indivisible, is to be realized" (p. 332). As colleges and universities move forward in a post-*Grutter/Gratz* era, they must certainly be mindful of the specific legal requirements imposed by the Supreme Court, but they should never lose sight of the basic moral imperatives that have animated affirmative action policies for the past 40 years. The pursuit of equal educational opportunity and fundamental notions of racial justice should guide our institutions of higher learning, just as much as the mandates of the law.

NOTES

1. The Supreme Court has employed a three-tiered model in reviewing the constitutionality of legislation under the Equal Protection Clause. Most legislation is subject to a deferential standard known as "rational basis" scrutiny, under which most legislation is upheld. "Strict scrutiny," the highest standard of review, is applied to legislation that establishes "suspect" classifications such as classifications based on race or national origin; legislation is presumed unconstitutional under the strict scrutiny standard and the government bears a heavy burden in overcoming that presumption. An "intermediate scrutiny" standard is applied in cases involving "semi-suspect" classifications, such as legislation involving gender classifications; legislation is presumed unconstitutional, but the courts impose lesser burdens on the government to demonstrate a statute's constitutionality.

2. The *Grutter* opinion also drew heavily on the importance of diversity in business and in the military to support the value of educational diversity. "[M]ajor American businesses have made clear that the skills needed in today's increasingly global marketplace can only be developed through exposure to widely diverse people, cultures, ideas, and viewpoints. . . . [A] 'highly qualified, racially diverse officer corps is essential to the military's ability to fulfill its principal mission to provide national security'" (pp. 330–331).

3. It is important to note that quotas or set-asides are not per se unconstitutional. Under *Grutter,* they may not be employed to advance the interest in educational diversity, but they may be used to advance the compelling interest in remedying the present effects of past discrimination; indeed, the Court approved the use of a hiring

quota in *United States v. Paradise* (1987), and the lower courts frequently have approved quotas or set-asides as short-term remedies for past discrimination.

4. The *Grutter* Court also cautioned that percent plans could "preclude the university from conducting the individualized assessments necessary to assemble a student body that is not just racially diverse, but diverse along all the qualities valued by the university" (p. 340).

5. For example, 42 U.S. Code section 1981, originally enacted following the Civil War, prohibits racial discrimination in the creation and implementation of contracts. Thus, a loan or grant that creates a contract between a student and the private foundation might be subject to the requirements of section 1981.

REFERENCES

Adarand Constructors, Inc. v. Peña, 515 U.S. 200 (1995).

City of Richmond v. J. A. Croson Co., 488 U.S. 469 (1989).

Gratz v. Bollinger, 539 U.S. 244 (2003).

Grutter v. Bollinger, 539 U.S. 306 (2003).

Honadle v. University of Vermont, 56 F. Supp. 2d 419 (D. Vt. 1999).

MD/DC/DE Broadcasters Association v. Federal Communications Commission, 236 F.3d 13 (D.C. Cir. 2001).

Podberesky v. Kirwan, 38 F.3d 147 (4th Cir. 1994), *cert. denied,* 514 U.S. 1128 (1995).

Regents of the University of California v. Bakke, 438 U.S. 265 (1978).

Schmidt, P. (2004, March 19). Just not for minority students anymore. *Chronicle of Higher Education, 50*(28), p. A17.

United States v. Paradise, 480 U.S. 149 (1987).

University and Community College System of Nevada v. Farmer, 113 Nev. 90, 930 P.2d 730 (1997), *cert. denied,* 523 U.S. 1004 (1998).

Weser v. Glen, 190 F. Supp. 2d 384 (E.D.N.Y.), *aff'd,* 41 Fed. Appx. 521 (2d Cir. 2002).

Wygant v. Jackson Board of Education, 476 U.S. 267 (1986).

9

From Strict Scrutiny to Educational Scrutiny

A New Vision for Higher Education Policy and Research

PATRICIA MARIN AND JOHN T. YUN[1]

The challenges racial and ethnic minorities face in achieving access to higher education are formidable. As discussed in previous chapters, the crisis of the color line in higher education will continue unless these issues of inequity are addressed. One way to move forward is to first look back and examine the historic U.S. Supreme Court's *Grutter* and *Gratz* decisions—an important crisis point that galvanized the higher education community. Focusing on lessons learned from this crisis and in preparing for the defense of affirmative action, including the legal framework of "strict scrutiny," may help institutions of higher education move to erase the color line and realize the goals set forth in their institutional missions.

With its 2003 *Grutter v. Bollinger* and *Gratz v. Bollinger* opinions, the U.S. Supreme Court affirmed the ability of colleges and universities to use race/ethnicity as one factor among many in admissions policies that provide a holistic, individualized review of applicants.[2] Achieving this victory, however, required a coordinated effort that included colleges and universities, attorneys and legal scholars, civil rights activists, business and military leaders, and social scientists. Those involved with the defense of affirmative action feared that without the use of race-conscious policies, racial and ethnic diversity on selective campuses would decline, thereby sharpening the existing color line in higher education.[3] Furthermore, such a decline would pre vent selective colleges and universities from attaining the diverse student body they believed necessary to achieve their educational goals and, ultimately, their institutional missions. As declared by Lee Bollinger and Nancy Cantor, president and provost, respectively, of the University of Michigan when the admissions lawsuits were filed in district court, "The country cannot afford to deprive institutions of higher education of the ability to educate generations of young Americans—minority and nonminority—in an environment that enables all to flourish, and understand each other, in a truly integrated society" (Bollinger & Cantor, 1998).

A critical component of the extensive efforts to defend affirmative action in higher education admissions involved compiling empirical evidence that examined the educational impact of a diverse student body. In order to be useful in court, this research employed a legal lens while taking care not to compromise the professional standards for empirical research. According to the legal framework, race-conscious policies are subject to strict scrutiny, which means they "will be upheld only where there is sufficient 'basis in evidence' to support the belief that the given program serves a 'compelling interest' and is 'narrowly tailored' to achieve that interest" (Palmer, 2001, p. 49). (See Ancheta, this volume, for a detailed discussion of the legal issues in *Gratz* and *Grutter*.) This framework of strict scrutiny, once understood by researchers, contributed to their thinking as they expanded their studies on the impact of racial and ethnic diversity on college campuses. Many studies later, the evidence compiled and submitted to the Supreme Court in the Michigan cases supported an educational rationale for the compelling interest colleges and universities have in student diversity (e.g., Antonio, 2001; Chang, 1999; Gurin, 1999; Marin, 2000; Moreno, 2000; Orfield & Whitla, 2001).[4]

In spite of the *Grutter* and *Gratz* opinions, challenges and reversals to race-conscious policies of all types continue. The Center for Equal Opportunity continues to challenge institutional affirmative action policies around the country (Clegg, 2005); the Michigan Civil Rights Initiative is attempting to add a measure banning affirmative action to Michigan's 2006 ballot (Brush, 2005); and some institutions, despite *Grutter* and *Gratz*, are dismantling their race-conscious policies instead of attempting to align them with the Supreme Court's opinions (Selingo, 2005). These actions suggest that the affirmative action battle is not over and that higher education institutions must continue to document their compelling interest in a diverse student body, as well as whether the means they are using to achieve that diversity are narrowly tailored.

It is equally important, however, for colleges and universities to evaluate policies, race-conscious and otherwise, in the absence of such challenges. Regular examination of policies and their rationales can improve practices by isolating those that no longer suit or promote the institutional mission. Specifically, in the case of race-conscious policies, such reviews can examine how, and even if, universities are using the diversity on their campuses effectively (e.g., Chang, 2002; Hurtado, Milem, Clayton-Pedersen, & Allen, 1999), and whether other university practices are at odds with the goal of achieving student diversity. In light of higher education's avowed compelling interest in educational diversity, ongoing policy review allows an institution to monitor and improve its own success in achieving, maintaining, and benefiting from a diverse student body and to prepare to meet new challenges. If institutions do not examine the racial/ethnic implications of their decisions for their own student body and, ultimately, the broader society, equitable access to higher education will remain elusive. This chapter presents the concept of educational scrutiny as a framework for conducting such an examination—an approach intended to replace the legal concept of "strict scrutiny" in the design of subsequent research beyond *Gratz* and *Grutter*, but respecting and incorporating the lessons learned defending the University of Michigan.

The concept of educational scrutiny is derived from the educational rationale for maintaining a diverse student body, but can be used more generally to study other university priorities and how they interact with one another. This educational framework can help arm institutions that may come under future attack; address issues of institutional autonomy in the face of the mounting accountability movement confronting higher education; improve institutional practices and outcomes; and address Justice O'Connor's expectations for the future of affirmative action outlined in *Grutter*.

The informational and cultural interchange between lawyers and social scientists during the legal battle for affirmative action has had an impact on the law, public debate, and social science. The legacy of those exchanges beyond the court cases, however, is still being determined. We are at a crossroads where freedom from the constraints of a legal framework allows us to use what we have learned from the law in shaping future research and policy agendas in higher education. The need for a new framework to help build the internal capacity of institutions has never been greater as the demographics of the United States are rapidly changing and institutions must adapt to this new environment. The *Gratz* and *Grutter* cases were examples of how colleges and universities can defend themselves and the capacities they must develop in order to do so. These cases have given higher education administrators an opportunity to think about issues they should have considered long ago. The proposed framework allows institutions to consider one pathway toward building the capacity to understand their own actions, assess the adequacy of existing institutional systems, and think long-term about issues of racial justice and equity. The framework presented in this chapter allows colleges and universities to look beyond *Gratz* and *Grutter* and engage in a new vision for higher education policy and research—one that recognizes the centrality of the diversity rationale institutions fought so diligently to defend, and one that increases institutions' capacity to defend the core values that they believe are vital to their missions.

PURSUING THE MICHIGAN DEFENSE: LESSONS FROM *GRUTTER*

In considering the possible lines of legal defense for the use of race-conscious policies, colleges and universities under challenge have two primary options: a remedial defense of affirmative action, which requires the documentation of the present effects of past discrimination at an institution, or a nonremedial defense, which focuses on an educational rationale. From the *Hopwood* (1996) case against the University of Texas at Austin to *Gratz* (2003) and *Grutter* (2003) against the University of Michigan, institutions being sued for race-conscious affirmative action policies have chosen to use a nonremedial defense, and attempt to document the educational benefits of a diverse student body and how they help achieve their institutional missions.

While educators have long believed that a racially/ethnically diverse student body is critical to the successful education of all students, before 1996 this belief was primarily documented in testimonials and not through social science evidence. In fact, the social science community could not provide research-based answers to the legal questions posed by attorneys regarding the relevance of racial and ethnic diversity to higher education—specifically, whether a racially/ethnically diverse campus was beneficial to *all* students. Following the 1996 *Hopwood* decision, researchers and institutions of higher education partnered with attorneys to better understand the relevant legal and empirical questions embodied in the legal standards of strict scrutiny and colleges' and universities' compelling interest in promoting a diverse student body because of its educational value. This collaboration across the boundaries of law and research allowed social scientists to provide a basis in evidence that addressed higher education's interests. Instead of regarding the need for a diverse student body as an end in itself, researchers focused on developing and testing a coherent theory of action for how structural diversity enhanced the educational experiences of students, and thus achieved the university's educational mission.

As researchers reconsidered how they studied the impact of racial and ethnic diversity on college campuses, they needed to develop research questions, consider educational outcomes that could be measured, identify methods to answer their questions, and pinpoint settings in which to conduct their research. This was all done with knowledge of the legal framework being used to defend affirmative action. For example, previous research examined why admitting racially/ethnically diverse students was beneficial for those students. The new research questions asked whether such diversity benefited *all* students. As educational outcomes were considered for measurement, researchers attempted to identify outcomes that were legally compelling, and especially whether they were aligned with the institutional mission. Researchers also had to consider whether the outcomes could be achieved through race-neutral means because, if they could, it would pose a challenge for defending the narrow-tailoring component of strict scrutiny. Finally, although some research (e.g., Astin, 1993) examined higher education broadly, the legal framework preferred institution-specific research that would establish findings relevant to the campus under investigation. Therefore, for the purposes of *Gratz* and *Grutter*, studies were conducted that focused on the University of Michigan. Developing this research agenda trained researchers to consider the law in their efforts and to look at policies in very different ways.

To help organize this research, Palmer (2001) offered a policy framework to reconceptualize this legal debate. He stated, "[I]n order to evaluate and make the case for affirmative action in higher education based on the diversity rationale, it is essential first to reconceptualize the legal debate into a policy-oriented framework" (p. 49). This framework considers policy development as a series of components, including "goals, objectives, strategy, and design, each of which is linked to the next by evidence and analytical presumptions" (p. 49). Specifically, Palmer highlights the evidence needed to demonstrate that the objective of having a racially diverse student body is linked to various compelling higher education goals, such as improving student learning and enhancing students' civic values. Ultimately, the legal rationale affirmed in *Bakke* (1978) and employed in the defense of the University of Michigan moved institutions toward more clearly articulating an educational rationale for their use of race-conscious policies and the centrality that such policies have in achieving institutional missions. This defense was critically important to the University of Michigan cases, and to higher education, since it shifted the discussion from the *assumption* that racial and ethnic diversity derived from race-conscious policies was important to the *need to examine* whether such a practice met an important component of a university's mission.

The Supreme Court ultimately agreed with the defendants' diversity rationale, stating that the research and expert testimony gathered and analyzed did provide evidence that diversity was indeed a compelling interest:

> As the District Court emphasized, the Law School's admissions policy promotes "cross-racial understanding," helps to break down racial stereotypes, and "enables [students] to better understand persons of different races." . . . The Law School's claim of a compelling interest is further bolstered by its *amici*, who point to the educational benefits that flow from student body diversity. In addition to the expert studies and reports entered into evidence at trial, numerous studies show that student body diversity promotes learning outcomes, and "better prepares students for an increasingly diverse workforce and society, and better prepares them as professionals." (*Grutter*, 2003, p. 330)

Because research was conducted using a legal framework, in court attorneys were able to successfully use the findings that investigated whether the educational benefits institutions claimed came from a diverse student body really were compelling, and whether those same benefits could be achieved through race-neutral means. In a post-*Gratz* and -*Grutter* world, however, institutions and researchers now have an opportunity to reconceptualize that evaluative framework to explore more effectively a theory of action by which racial/ethnic diversity leads to important educational outcomes and to design policies necessary to achieve the institutional mission.

EDUCATIONAL FRAMEWORK

What does an evaluative framework that uses educational scrutiny look like? Considering and adapting the work of various legal scholars (Coleman, 2001; Coleman & Palmer, 2004; Palmer, 2001), we offer a framework that calls for the alignment of institutional policy with the university's educational mission, and a simultaneous examination of the horizontal alignment of university policies that could affect the implementation of that mission. We propose that the framework incorporate some of the aspects of strict scrutiny, such as generating a basis in evidence that includes local data, and drawing from the ideal of narrow tailoring with its components of periodic review and time limits.[5] However, this framework is intended to serve as a guide for educational practice rather than a reaction to legal challenges. Most importantly, this framework places higher education's compelling interest in the educational benefits of diversity at the center and extends the idea of educational scrutiny beyond those policies that use race to all university policies that may have an impact on the ability of a university to achieve its various missions.

While the alignment of Michigan's race-conscious admissions policies to the mission of the institution was key in the legal defense in both *Gratz* and *Grutter*, others have argued that this alignment should be considered more broadly:

> What is important here is alignment—not only between an institution's educational interests in diversity and its admissions policy, but also between those interests and the institution's academic, cocurricular, residential, and other policies. Evidence in this context is intended to show that an institution is not paying mere lip service to the educational benefits of diversity. It must actively implement policies and practices to facilitate the "robust exchange of ideas" that diversity makes possible. (Coleman, 2001, p. 8)

Coleman's analysis suggests that a university's commitment to diversity should be reflected not only in admissions but in a multitude of programs and policies, and that an alignment of these policies with an institution's mission should be taken as a measure of its commitment to diversity. On the other hand, the absence of such alignment calls into question an institution's overall commitment to diversity, despite any arguments made by the university to the contrary. Absent such alignment one could argue that a stronger preference for goals other than diversity is revealed. Such horizontal alignment of policies across the university, or the lack thereof, could be conceptualized as a "revealed preference" for or against the educational benefits of diversity.

This line of reasoning is echoed by Justice O'Connor in the *Grutter* opinion when she writes,

> Our conclusion that the Law School has a compelling interest in a diverse student body is informed by our view that attaining a diverse student body is at the heart of the Law School's proper institutional mission, and that 'good faith' on the part of a university is "presumed" absent "a showing to the contrary." (*Grutter*, 2003, p. 329)

This discussion of "good faith" and its connection to revealed preferences raises important issues. It suggests that the institutional alignment of policies may be an important approach that an institution should pursue in order to document its good faith—whether attaining a diverse student body really is at the heart of an institution's mission and its reasoning for using race in admissions.

Chang (2002) also encourages an approach that broadens the examination of issues of diversity for the betterment of educational potential:

> If educators, particularly those in positions of leadership, fail to develop a fuller understanding and appreciation of campus diversity, their short-sightedness may both arrest educational potential and preserve the broader set of arrangements and institutional practices that diversity advocates seek to transform. (p. 136)

The fact that Chang and Coleman come to similar conclusions from two totally different frameworks (educational and legal) emphasizes the importance of operationalizing these concepts of policy-to-mission and horizontal alignment for consideration by institutions of higher education.

As we move forward to suggest a research/policy framework informed by the law, we make the assumption, along with that made by the Supreme Court in the *Grutter* opinion, that institutions claiming to have a compelling interest in a diverse student body sincerely care about racially/ethnically diverse campuses, that they believe in the importance of using race/ethnicity to achieve their goals, and that the efforts made to defend this ability indicate just how critical this is to higher education. However, we suggest that universities carefully examine all of their policies simultaneously to confirm that their beliefs and arguments are echoed across their campuses, and where they are not that they clarify the reasons for this misalignment. Ultimately, we believe that the questions raised in *Grutter* are not only about whether other policies also contribute to, or hinder, the goal of educational diversity, but also whether the legal scrutiny used to justify race/ethnicity should be used to justify other factors in admissions, and other policies across the university. This type of review has the potential to demonstrate whether an institution is truly operating in good faith—both legally and educationally—indicating a revealed preference for supporting a diverse student body.

Universities are complex organizations, and policies implemented by the leadership of an institution have far-reaching ramifications for the entire institution. This calls for a cross-policy evaluation component that examines how the pursuit of one policy may impede or enhance the functioning of others. The framework described below moves beyond justifying a policy on its own merits to evaluating its impact within the context of a specific educational mission, and of other policies that may enhance or detract from that mission.

While this framework for examining the internal consistency of university policies can provide important insights into how particular decisions can contradict and undermine the goals of creating and maintaining a diverse learning environment, it would be naive to assume that complex organizations like colleges and universities have only one important mission or a single way to achieve their missions, and that each choice a university makes will automatically support every institutional priority. There will be times when particular choices must be made that support one priority and undermine others. These tradeoffs are inherent in complex organizations.[6] However, this evaluation structure will allow reassessment of decisions as they become relevant, and will allow institutions to make informed choices based on data generated from research questions surfaced by our evaluation framework. Thus, universities that choose to follow one policy line over another will be able to clearly understand and articulate how their choices affect the university's chosen path toward achieving their institutional missions—making the revealed preferences of the university consistent with its stated preferences. This articulation will help them defend their decisions and provide a strong basis in evidence that may help to defend such policies and, as we argue later, should be required by governing agencies and the public.

To maximize clarity and applicability, we describe our framework broadly using race-conscious examples, and then provide a more specific example using the diversity rationale that guided the development of educational scrutiny. It is important to note, however, that even nondiversity-related university policies and processes must be evaluated in terms of how their pursuit will affect the diversity rationale. Our framework (Figure 1) has four main components. First, the components of the university's mission need to be explicitly stated. In Figure 1 this is shown by the boxes at the top representing missions A and B. Second, a policy-to-mission alignment must be performed that identifies university policies that in some way impact the diversity mission either positively or negatively. This policy identification is represented by the boxes labeled "University Policy 1–5" in Figure 1. As already discussed, individual policies may contribute to multiple goals or missions. This is represented in the figure by Policy 3 and its impact on both missions A and B. Third, a theory of action for how each policy can contribute to the fulfillment of the mission must be clearly delineated. It is the link between the policy and the university mission as shown in Figure 1. If the policy does not contribute to this mission, or in fact interferes with its completion, then this fact must be understood and investigated in the next step. Again note that it is not necessarily true that individual policies will have only one theory of action. Policy 3 in Figure 1 shows a situation where there may be separate theories of action for a single policy's impact on separate missions or goals. The fourth step allows universities to examine this cross-policy and cross-mission complexity by highlighting the horizontal alignment of policies, so those that work at cross purposes may be evaluated and judgments can be made about which direction to pursue, or in what ways interference between policies can be mitigated or, at a minimum, explained. This is represented by the box and connecting lines at the bottom of Figure 1, which represent the possible interactions between university policies. We now discuss each of these components in more detail.

Statement of the mission is extremely important. Without the clear identification of a mission, the outcomes of the identified policies cannot be adequately assessed. However, while stating the mission is essential, it is not always a simple thing to accomplish, particularly because there may be multiple missions for many institutions, some related to the academic well-being of the institution (promotion of student learning), others to the health of the organization (ensuring long-term growth for the endowment), etc. An understanding of multiple missions was expressed in *Grutter*, when Justice O'Connor indicated that the law does not "require a university to choose between maintaining a reputation for excellence or fulfilling a commitment to provide educational opportunities to members of all racial groups" (2003, p. 339). While institutions may not have to choose between multiple missions, they must mediate when such missions conflict with one another on institutional priorities, and publicly justify their actions so that stakeholders understand how and why such decisions were made.

The second component of the framework, identification of policies, is also critical. It connects policies to the missions they are expected to achieve. Without these explicit links, the institutional mission statements remain amorphous goals with no clear path to their realization. Another reason why this identification process is important is that it requires a survey of all policies currently operating across the university, many of which may have outlasted their usefulness. Without periodic accounting of this type, a component borrowed from strict scrutiny, many policies simply continue with-

FIGURE 1
General Framework for Educational Scrutiny

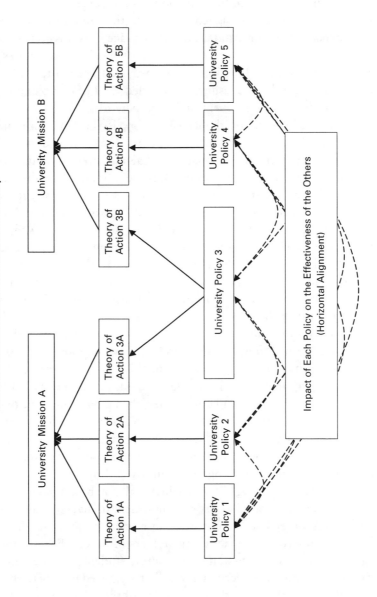

out being evaluated as to whether they still meet the needs of the changing institutional environment. However, as an added bit of complexity, it is important to acknowledge that one policy may achieve multiple missions or that multiple policies designed to achieve the same mission may interfere with one another. For instance, the use of race in admissions may be linked to the promotion of student learning and of civic responsibilities; the use of race and the SAT in admissions, both designed to promote student learning, may lead to conflicting results. This added level of complexity will be discussed in the final component of the framework.

The third piece, the theory of action, is the key component to this evaluative framework and to developing a "basis in evidence." It requires the institution to clearly articulate a causal mechanism that directly links the policy to the mission. These causal links are ultimately testable and form the foundation for data-based decisionmaking at the university level about the efficacy of institutional policies. This work, in large part, describes researchers' efforts in preparing for the Michigan cases. Instead of simply asserting the importance of student diversity, the researchers created and tested a theory of action as to how diversity contributed to the educational mission of the institution. As already discussed, such work was critical in the Court's ultimate decision. Most important to realize is that universities are uniquely suited to answer these questions, since they already have the built-in capacity to address them in the form of institutional researchers and faculty who have been trained to do such research and evaluations. Harnessing this internal capacity is critical to success in this evaluative framework. In fact, one might say that if such a model of continuous data-based monitoring cannot work in colleges and universities, then it has little hope of succeeding in other settings where the skills needed to perform such evaluations are not present to such a degree.

The final piece of the framework, the cross-policy evaluations, is essential for its useful functioning and is motivated by the promptings of Coleman (2001) and Chang (2002), which call for broadening the view with which we examine a university's commitment to diversity. Such policies, diversity and otherwise, do not work in a vacuum, and the effects of many policies can have an impact on the effects of others. For instance, let's assume the university's mission is to promote student learning and the university creates a policy to recruit nationally recognized faculty to the campus to meet this goal. However, the recruitment of these faculty actually competes for resources with campus initiatives to develop the teaching skills of existing faculty. So while focus on either policy would most likely contribute to

FIGURE 2
Example of Employing the Educational Scrutiny Framework for Higher Education

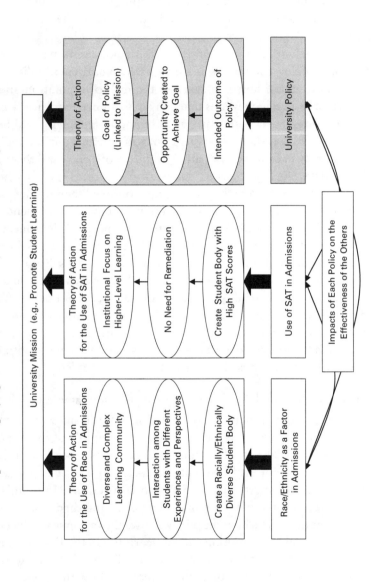

the overall mission, pursuit of both efforts may compromise the effectiveness of both policies. Such analysis must be included, if only to clarify the competing interests that do exist on campus, and clearly delineate the types of value choices that must be made to increase the effectiveness of all policies.

This evaluation framework for linking policies to particular university missions, and examining the process by which particular policies contribute to achieving those missions, clarifies the task of evaluation and generates important research questions that can be examined empirically by the institutions. In fact, each line (path) represented in Figure 1 could be a distinct research question that researchers both inside and outside the institution could pursue in order to evaluate the efficacy of policy and theory of action. This structure may also act to clarify for institutions exactly where policies are redundant, or where they have simply outlived their usefulness as conditions and contexts have changed in the university environment. Just as importantly, this framework incorporates all aspects of the educational scrutiny concept. For example, the idea of generating a basis in evidence is embedded in the framework with the testing of causal models for policy functioning. Local data must be used for these evaluations, since data from national databases, while generally informative, cannot be taken to apply to each institution. Finally, the idea of time limits to policies and periodic review are also addressed since this framework is well placed to identify policies that continue to meet their goals, and those that are outmoded or no longer serve the purpose for which they were intended.

The Use of Race and the SAT in Admissions: An Example

To provide a more concrete understanding of this framework in practice, we will use the context of a specific, simplified example of the pursuit of a diverse student body in admissions. Figure 2 describes how this structure could be used in the evaluation of two specific admissions policies—the use of race/ethnicity and the use of SAT scores as criteria for admissions decisions. The first two columns name each policy and then describe a theory of action that delineates how the policy allows the university to meet its overall mission or goal of promoting student learning. In the first column from the left we name the policy "Race/Ethnicity as a Factor in Admissions," then describe a simplified theory of action in terms of how this policy is translated into better learning outcomes. The middle column does the same for the use of the SAT in admissions. The third column shows the general structure of the model and suggests that many more policies could be aligned in this way.

For example, employing legacy admissions, preferential admissions for athletes, or early admissions policies could be inserted here. Each of these alternatives for an actual institution should be examined in a model like this and the collective impact studied. However, for the sake of brevity and as a demonstration case, we are only stepping through the model for the use of race and the use of the SAT in admissions.

The theory of action for the use of race in college admissions begins by assuming that the use of race will create a racially/ethnically diverse student body (represented by the first circle in the Theory of Action box in Figure 2). Given this initially attained diversity, one then has the chance to foster multiple interactions among students who may not otherwise have had the opportunity to meet and share their reflections, experiences, and thoughts with one another. The potential also exists for a more complex set of interactions to take place that may not have existed absent the racial/ethnic diversity that was created by the race-conscious admissions plan. Thus the policy of race-conscious admissions contributes to the overall goal/mission of the university, in this case by promoting student learning through the creation of an environment that can provide a "robust exchange of ideas." This theory of action is testable, and each of these outcomes is potentially measurable to answer the question, "Does our policy accomplish this goal/mission?"

In the second column of Figure 2 we similarly describe one possible theory of action for the use of the SAT in admissions, a common practice of selective colleges and universities. This example suggests that institutions using the SAT will preferentially admit students with higher SAT scores, thus there will be less of a need for remediation at the university. As a result, the institution will be able to focus more resources on higher-level learning skills that lead to the promotion of student learning. Again, each of these assumptions and suggestions can be tested and examined using locally obtained data from the institution, ultimately demonstrating whether or not this policy supports or hinders the goal of promoting student learning.[7]

Using the educational framework, we also are able to identify potential conflicts between policies. From previous research, we know that the SAT works at cross purposes to race-conscious admissions policies, insofar as SAT scores are strongly correlated with race such that African American and Latino students on average score lower than their white and Asian counterparts (Camara & Schmidt, 1999). Thus, if SAT scores are strongly weighted in the admissions process, there is the potential to hinder institutional efforts to achieve a racially/ethnically diverse student body because, on average, underrepresented minority students have lower test scores than their white and Asian counterparts. However, for the purposes of educational scrutiny, the important information is not what is true of the SAT and race overall, but what the situation is at the particular institution. There may be some institutions where there is little conflict—that is, the SAT scores of admitted classes are in a range in which there are ample numbers of minority students to fill their desire for a diverse student body. However, where this is not the case, it must be understood how these two policies can be reconciled. This type of analysis can put these differences into sharp relief and allow institutions to make informed choices between the benefits and costs for each policy they support. In fact, the short-run consequence of employing educational scrutiny could be the forced prioritization of mission components, privileging some at the expense of others, such that some of the policies and missions can be realized in whole, without the impediments that may have hindered their development prior to the analysis.

Value of the Framework

The concept of educational scrutiny supports the creation of strong internal accountability systems that demand justification for policy decisions. By using such a framework, institutions can insulate themselves from external accountability pressures and lawsuits on their own terms. Short of being able to analyze the question of policy effectiveness, if the institution can neither articulate its core missions nor describe how a policy is supposed to reach their goals, then this finding renders the importance of program effectiveness moot. Not until such a mechanism is understood and established can institutions begin to discuss effectiveness. Policies shouldn't exist that either no longer serve the institution's missions, or are too "expensive" in terms of efficiency because they block the impact of other programs directly related to the mission. This is an example of how educational scrutiny can act as an instrument of narrow tailoring by identifying policies and practices that have outlived their usefulness.

We believe this evaluative framework has value in a number of arenas. First, by constantly generating local, campus-specific evidence to explain its policies, an institution can better prepare itself for future legal challenges that will shake it out of its complacency and create an institutional policy environment that is more proactive than reactive. It is clear that legal challenges are not going away, so this type of preparation makes sense within this litigious reality, giving the university more time and structure to prepare for such occasions. Since this approach is based in the principles of strict scrutiny, many of the components of that legal framework are addressed in this more educational approach. This type of evaluation would also allow a university to preemptively modify any policies that could be legally questionable, thereby avoiding lawsuits, and develop such a strong basis in evidence for their practices that they would not be attractive targets for potential litigators.

Second, government agencies, many in the public, and some professionals in higher education have become increasingly interested in imposing more oversight of the ways institutions carry out their mission. This has been clear with the emergence of a stronger accountability movement in higher education (see Horn, this volume, for one example of this movement). In fact, critics of higher education have condemned institutions for, among other things, maintaining weak standards, wasting funds, caving to the political correctness movement, and accepting unqualified students in the name of affirmative action (Zumeta, 2001). Since "the measurement or assessment of outcomes from higher education is rudimentary at best" and "developing useful accountability systems for educational outcomes remains a difficult and challenging task" (Breneman, 2001, pp. viii–ix), this evaluation framework provides one model that could be considered an important step in the direction of such an institution-wide accountability system. The more data, and the stronger the rationale created by universities to defend their decisions as based in research and effective practice, the stronger their position to provide answers to their critics and preserve the autonomy that they value.

Our original motivation for the educational scrutiny framework was to build on the knowledge gained from *Gratz* and *Grutter* and use it to improve educational practices across the university. The lessons learned from the work that many higher education institutions did to defend affirmative action policies should not be forgotten as the urgency of the Supreme Court cases dissipates. Instead, it makes sense to take the best of the legal frameworks and transform them to make them most relevant to the educational development of higher education, moving toward what Chang (2002) calls a discourse of transformation. To this end we designed the framework to verify that an institution's policies are serving its missions, and that policies are working cooperatively to achieve those missions across the university.

That said, it is important to clarify two aspects of this framework. First, this framework is predicated on an institution's capacity to articulate its missions and the rationales for policies, and to answer the empirical questions raised by this exploration. It is clear that some institutions have much more capacity to pursue these studies than others. However, regardless of whether or not each of the research programs envisioned by such a framework could be realized, all institutions would benefit by the clarification of mission, policy, and theory of action. Second, this framework is designed to be a working model and can be applied to all levels of the institution. For example, it may be used to clarify how the institution's policy goals align to the mission of the university, or, as it is formulated in our example, how policies affect specific educational goals. In addition, it can be used within the institution at departmental and programmatic levels to address the unique goals/missions that they may have, and how their decisions interact with the larger institutional priorities.

The importance of the framework and the concept of educational scrutiny is the imperative to constantly assess the efforts of colleges and universities, based on their own internal criteria, while working to justify and evaluate each of their policy decisions and generate evidence for them. This approach is critical if an institution is interested in maximizing its intended outcomes outside of the legal framework of strict scrutiny which only applies to those policies that use race/ethnicity in their practices. Our intention is that educational scrutiny will extend to all policy functions of the university regardless of their use of race/ethnicity, suggesting that all policies should have a strong basis in evidence and a compelling interest to exist. Without such ongoing review, policies can become meaningless and even harmful to an institution's goals. This type of broad evaluation allows an institution to determine the best practices that work on its campus.

We believe that built into our framework, especially its periodic review component, are aspects that may help to address Justice O'Connor's expectation in the *Grutter* opinion: "We expect that 25 years from now, the use of racial preferences will no longer be necessary to further the interest approved today" (2003, p. 343). It is critical that institutions not wait 25 years to examine whether the use of race/ethnicity is still necessary. Instead, the constant self-examination advocated by our framework will allow institutions to document, through a strong basis in evidence, how successful they have been in eliminating the need for affirmative action. In fact, when a policy has outlived its usefulness, this process will automatically indicate that the practice should be discontinued. This seems to address the ideas put forth by Orfield, Horn, Marin, and Kurlaender (2003) after the release of the *Gratz* and *Grutter* opinions:

> It will be prudent for researchers and college officials to monitor the relevant trends, speak out on the necessary policies, develop multidi-

mensional assessments that better measure skills relevant to college success, and conduct research demonstrating what works to lower the gaps, what is a reasonable expectation of progress, and when equity has been achieved. If we adopt sound policies that effectively narrow gaps in achievement and assure all students fair access to competitive programs and schools, it is much more likely that we will move toward the desired goal. If we continue to increase segregation and inequality in educational experiences, however, these expectations are much less likely to be realized. (p. 3)

Of course, realizing Justice O'Connor's challenge is not only in the hands of higher education; however, higher education must begin documenting its contributions immediately in order to be prepared for the challenges to come.

CONCLUSION

Legal challenges to affirmative action pushed higher education to defend a policy it believed important to achieve its educational mission. We believe there are many lessons that can be taken from these efforts that should not simply be lost or forgotten, only to be relearned when another crisis arises. In fact, in combination with social science frameworks, these lessons have a great deal of promise for use by universities and researchers on many fronts. By employing our evaluation framework, which will allow institutions to monitor and justify current practices, universities are able to prepare a "strong basis in evidence" for all of their policies and build in a periodic review and implicit time limits on policy functions.

We recommend this evaluative framework with its educational scrutiny because we believe the levels of scrutiny that applied to race-conscious policies in *Gratz* and *Grutter* should similarly apply to other educational policies. In particular, higher education should be able to demonstrate that the use of a particular policy is in line with a compelling educational interest. While this is not required legally, we do believe that the value of the framework, discussed earlier, provides enough evidence for why such ongoing evaluation would be beneficial to higher education.

Although our intention is for this framework to be used broadly, it is important to note that it is derived from the defense of race-conscious policies. As such, we believe it is important that higher education institutions also use this framework to continue to demonstrate their commitment to such policies and to investigate those practices that work against achieving an institution's compelling interest in a racially/ethnically diverse student body. The policy decisions institutions make for other reasons may have an impact on their ability to deliver on the promise of the diversity rationale, thus calling their commitment to such outcomes into question. This framework may help institutions align their stated preferences with their revealed preferences, thus creating institutions that "practice what they preach," and pushing them toward a more active stance on the core values they say are important.

In the eyes of many observers, the *Gratz* and *Grutter* decisions represent a crisis averted. Some are tempted to believe that with the weight of the U.S. Supreme Court behind their choices, they are no longer in danger of losing what had been gained since the civil rights movement. However, the crisis in higher education, as documented in the other chapters in this book, is much more extensive than needing to defend the use of race in higher education admissions decisions. The authors in this book describe the larger context in which higher education must function. If institutions do not have the capacity to develop policies that reflect this context, examine the impact their choices have on their students' opportunities, and adapt to the changing society, then the existing inequalities in access to higher education will remain, or, worse, they will grow. In line with the title of this book, this framework of educational scrutiny can help build the needed capacity for an institution to document whether it is invested in erasing the color line and working toward college access, racial equity, and social change. Or, if not, it can force the clarification of an institution's reasons for moving away from this goal in the face of an increasingly diverse society that institutions of higher education are intended to serve.

NOTES

1. The authors wish to acknowledge the important contributions of José F. Moreno in the early stages of the conceptualization of this framework. We also thank Angelo N. Ancheta for his helpful comments on the legal aspects of this chapter. All errors and omissions are solely the responsibility of the authors.
2. Existing state law prohibits colleges and universities in California, Florida, and Washington from implementing race-conscious policies permitted under the *Gratz* and *Grutter* (2003) decisions.
3. Because race-conscious affirmative action is primarily an issue for selective colleges and universities, this chapter will focus on these institutions (Kane, 1998).
4. While the University of Michigan was specifically defending its right to use race/ethnicity in admissions decisions, the Supreme Court was clear that it was using the term *diversity* in the broadest sense.

5. Other aspects of narrow tailoring, such as the consideration of race-neutral alternatives and weighing the burden of the policies on nonminority students, could also be incorporated into the framework, particularly when this framework is being used to prevent or address future lawsuits.

6. See Bailey and Morest (2004) for a discussion of these tradeoffs in the educational context of community colleges.

7. There are, of course, other theories of action that could be tested and advanced for use of the SAT. However, the specific theory of action that we choose here is not as important as the process undergone by the institution and the use of a similar evaluation standard for non-race-conscious policies as those required for race-conscious policies. In fact, we argue that the idea of educational scrutiny should not be confined to the realm of race-conscious policies, but extended to all functions of the university. In some ways, other policies like the use of the SAT, early admissions policies, and legacy admissions may be in the same position as the use of race in admissions was after *Bakke*, demanding more research into their institutional uses, and whether those benefits outweigh the costs to other policies, such as race-conscious admissions policies.

REFERENCES

Antonio, A. L. (2001). Diversity and the influence of friendship groups in college. *Review of Higher Education, 25*(1), 63–89.

Astin, A. W. (1993). *What matters in college? Four critical years revisited.* San Francisco: Jossey-Bass.

Bailey, T. R., & Morest, V. S. (2004). *The organizational efficiency of multiple missions for community colleges.* New York: Teachers College, Columbia University, Community College Research Center.

Bollinger, L., & Cantor, N. (1998, April 28). The educational importance of race. *Washington Post.* Retrieved March 13, 2005, from http://www.umich.edu/~urel/admissions/statements/washpost.html

Brush, S. (2005, January 7). Activists file papers to put measure banning affirmative action on Michigan's 2006 ballot. *Chronicle of Higher Education.* Retrieved January 8, 2005, from http://chronicle.com/prm/daily/2005/01/2005010702n.htm

Camara, W. J., & Schmidt, A. E. (1999). *Group differences in standardized testing and social stratification* (College Board Report No. 99-5). New York: College Board.

Chang, M. J. (1999). Does racial diversity matter? The educational impact of a racially diverse undergraduate population. *Journal of College Student Development, 40,* 377–395.

Chang, M. J. (2002). Preservation or transformation: Where's the real educational discourse on diversity? *Review of Higher Education, 25,* 125–140.

Clegg, R. (2005, January 14). Time has not favored racial preferences. *Chronicle of Higher Education,* p. B10.

Gratz v. Bollinger, 539 U.S. 244 (2003).

Grutter v. Bollinger, 539 U.S. 306 (2003).

Gurin, P. (1999). Expert report of Patricia Gurin. In *The compelling need for diversity in higher education, Gratz et al. v. Bollinger et al. No. 97-75231 (E.D. Mich.) and*

Grutter et al. v. Bollinger et al. No. 97-75928 (E.D. Mich.) (pp. 99–234). Ann Arbor: University of Michigan.

Hopwood v. Texas, 78 F.3d 932 (5th Cir. 1996), *cert denied,* 518 U.S. 1033 (1996), *overruled in part by* Grutter v. Bollinger, 539 U.S. 306 (2003).

Hurtado, S., Milem, J., Clayton-Pedersen, A., & Allen, W. (1999). *Enacting diverse learning environments: Improving the climate for racial/ethnic diversity in higher education.* Washington, DC: U.S. Department of Education, Office of Educational Research and Improvement. (ERIC Clearinghouse on Higher Education, ED430513)

Kane, T. J. (1998). Misconceptions in the debate about affirmative action in college admissions. In G. Orfield & E. Miller (Eds.), *Chilling admissions: The affirmative action crisis and the search for alternatives* (pp. 17–32). Cambridge, MA: Harvard Educational Publishing Group.

Marin, P. (2000). The educational possibility of multi-racial/multi-ethnic college classrooms. In *Does diversity make a difference? Three research studies on diversity in college classrooms* (pp. 61–83). Washington, DC: American Council on Education and American Association of University Professors.

Moreno, J. F. (2000). *Affirmative actions: The educational influence of racial/ethnic diversity on law school faculty.* Unpublished doctoral dissertation, Harvard University, Cambridge, MA.

Orfield, G., Horn, C. L., Marin, P., & Kurlaender, M. (2003, June 25). *Researchers at The Civil Rights Project issue statement analyzing the implications of Supreme Court's decisions for higher education.* Retrieved January 15, 2005, from http://www.civilrightsproject.harvard.edu/policy/court/michiganre.php

Orfield, G., & Whitla, D. (2001). Diversity and legal education: Student experiences in leading law schools. In G. Orfield (with M. Kurlaender) (Eds.), *Diversity challenged: Evidence on the impact of affirmative action* (pp. 143–174). Cambridge, MA: Harvard Education Publishing Group.

Palmer, S. R. (2001). A policy framework for reconceptualizing the legal debate concerning affirmative action in higher education. In G. Orfield (with M. Kurlaender) (Eds.), *Diversity challenged: Evidence on the impact of affirmative action* (pp. 49–80). Cambridge, MA: Harvard Education Publishing Group.

Regents of the University of California v. Bakke, 438 U.S. 265 (1978).

Selingo, J. (2005, January 14). Michigan: Who really won? *Chronicle of Higher Education,* p. A21.

Zumeta, W. (2001). Public policy and accountability in higher education: Lessons from the past and present for the new millennium. In D. E. Heller (Ed.), *The states and public higher education policy: Affordability, access, and accountability* (pp. 155–197). Baltimore: Johns Hopkins University Press.

About the Contributors

Angelo N. Ancheta is assistant professor of law at the Santa Clara University School of Law and director of the Katharine & George Alexander Community Law Center. He is also an adjunct associate professor of law at the New York University School of Law. Ancheta was previously the director of legal and advocacy programs for The Civil Rights Project at Harvard University and a lecturer at Harvard Law School. His current research and writing center on constitutional law, voting rights, and immigrants' civil rights.

Regina Deil-Amen is a sociologist and assistant professor in the Educational Theory and Policy program at The Pennsylvania State University. Deil-Amen previously directed a study comparing subbaccalaureate career preparation at public and private two-year colleges; she is currently writing a book (with J. Rosenbaum) on the study's findings. Her expertise is sociology of education/higher education, inequality, community college students' aspirations and persistence, and race, ethnicity, and social class. Her latest research includes a qualitative study of urban, low-SES high school students' transition to community college.

Kevin J. Dougherty is associate professor of higher education at Teachers College, Columbia University. A sociologist by training, his research interests include student access to and success in higher education, the political origins of community colleges and their effects on students, the costs and benefits of government accountability requirements for higher education institutions, and the role of higher education institutions as sources of economic development. In 2003–04, he served as the chair of the Sociology of Education Section of the American Sociological Association.

Elizabeth Flanagan is executive assistant to the vice president for administration at Harvard University. She is a former staff member of the National Campus Diversity Project, and also worked previously as an admissions assistant at Harvard College and a development associate at the American Federation for the Arts. Flanagan's primary professional interest is the recruitment and admission of underrepresented minority students.

Stella M. Flores is a doctoral candidate at the Harvard Graduate School of Education, a research assistant at The Civil Rights Project at Harvard University, and a Spencer Research Training Grant recipient. Her research focuses on higher education policy and Latino educational attainment. She is coauthor of *Percent Plans in*

College Admissions: A Comparative Analysis of Three States' Experiences (with C. L. Horn, 2003), and coeditor of *Legacies of Brown: Multiracial Equity in American Education* (with D. J. Carter and R. J. Reddick, 2004).

Donald E. Heller is associate professor and senior research associate at the Center for the Study of Higher Education at The Pennsylvania State University. His research centers on higher education economics, public policy, and finance, with a primary focus on issues of access, choice, and persistence in postsecondary education. He is editor of *The States and Public Higher Education Policy: Affordability, Access, and Accountability* (2001) and *Condition of Access: Higher Education for Lower Income Students* (2002).

Catherine L. Horn is an assistant professor at the University of Houston. Her work addresses issues related to high-stakes testing, higher education access, affirmative action, and diversity. She has written on the effectiveness of alternative admissions policies in creating racially or ethnically diverse student bodies. Horn recently coedited (with P. Gándara and G. Orfield) a special volume of *Educational Policy* (2005) and *Leveraging Promise: Expanding Opportunity in Higher Education* (forthcoming), both of which analyze the educational access and equity crisis in California.

Carolyn Howard is the project manager for the National Campus Diversity Project and a former teaching assistant at the Harvard Graduate School of Education. Howard has worked for the past five years on research projects regarding racial/ethnic diversity at the professional school level (i.e., law and medical schools), as well as at the undergraduate level at a few small, private institutions. This research has included faculty development programs at tribal colleges, historically black colleges and universities, and small Midwestern colleges.

David Karen is associate professor of sociology at Bryn Mawr College. His research examines the social origins and destinations of students who attend different kinds of colleges and the political dynamics of college access, including the admissions process at elite colleges. Karen has also recently begun a series of projects on the links between social stratification and sports. As an elected school board member in his community, he focuses on K–12 education as well.

Michal Kurlaender is an assistant professor at the University of California, Davis. She is also a researcher with The Civil Rights Project at Harvard University. Her research interests focus on issues of educational stratification, specifically access to postsecondary schooling for underrepresented populations and K–12 school desegregation and integration. Her recent publications include "The Future of Race-Conscious Policies in K–12 Public Schools: Support from Recent Legal Opinions and Social Science Research" (with J. Ma) in *School Resegregation: Must the South Turn Back?* (edited by J. C. Boger and G. Orfield, forthcoming), and she collaborated on *Diversity Challenged: Evidence of the Impact of Affirmative Action* (edited by G. Orfield, 2001).

Patricia Marin is a higher education research associate at The Civil Rights Project at Harvard University. Her work focuses on issues of inclusion and equity in higher education, with a particular emphasis on policy. She has collaborated with social scientists, higher education administrators, association representatives, researchers, policy experts, attorneys, and government officials. She is coeditor of *Who Should We Help? The Negative Social Consequences of Merit Scholarships* and *State Merit Scholarship Programs and Racial Inequality* (with D. E. Heller, 2002, 2004), and coauthor of *Appearance and Reality in the Sunshine State: The Talented 20 Program in Florida* (with E. Lee, 2003).

Gary Orfield is professor of education and social policy at the Harvard Graduate School of Education and director of The Civil Rights Project at Harvard University, which he cofounded. He is interested in civil rights, education policy, urban policy, and minority opportunity, and on the impact of policy on equal opportunity for success in America. His recent work includes studies of changing patterns of school desegregation and of the impact of diversity on the educational experiences of law students. Orfield has also been involved with the development of government policy and has served as an expert witness in court cases related to his research. His numerous books include the recently published *Dropouts in America: Confronting the Graduation Rate Crisis* (2004).

Ann E. Person is a doctoral student in Human Development and Social Policy at Northwestern University. Her research examines students' college and career choices and the effects of institutional structures on student experiences with college and the labor market. She has previously worked as a teacher and an administrator in both K–12 and university settings.

Derek V. Price is an independent sociologist and higher education consultant. Before entering the consulting profession, Price was director of higher education research at Lumina Foundation for Education and an assistant professor of sociology at Morehead State University. He is the author of *Borrowing Inequality: Race, Class and Student Loans* (2004).

Richard J. Reddick is a doctoral student in Administration, Planning, and Social Policy at the Harvard Graduate School of Education, concentrating in higher education. His research focuses on the pedagogical and mentoring practices of professors educated at historically black colleges who are teaching at predominantly white institutions. He is also a research assistant with the National Campus Diversity Project at Harvard University. He is a coauthor of *A New Look at Black Families* (5th edition, with C. Willie, 2003) and *The Case for Black Colleges in the 21st Century* (with C. Willie and R. Brown, forthcoming).

James E. Rosenbaum is professor of sociology, education, and social policy at Northwestern University. His current research examines the institutional practices of public and private colleges. Rosenbaum's most recent books are *Crossing the*

Class and Color Lines (2000) and *Beyond College for All* (2001), which was awarded the Waller Prize in Sociology.

Frank Tuitt is assistant professor of higher education at the University of Denver. He was a research assistant with Harvard University's National Campus Diversity Project, served as a teaching fellow at the Harvard Graduate School of Education, and was cochair of the *Harvard Educational Review.* Tuitt is coeditor of *Race and Higher Education: Rethinking Pedagogy in Diverse College Classrooms* (with A. Howell, 2003).

Dean K. Whitla is a psychologist and psychometrician with a particular interest in assessment and evaluation. He has spent much of his professional life at Harvard University evaluating progress, development, and change in people and in institutions. His current major research effort is directing Harvard University's National Campus Diversity Project in a search for models of multicultural activities at colleges and universities. He also taught a seminar connected to the project at the Harvard Graduate School of Education. With Gary Orfield and others, Whitla conducted research on the effects of diversity in law schools and medical schools. The findings of the law school study were used by the University of Michigan in their Supreme Court affirmative action case.

Jill K. Wohlford is a program analyst at Lumina Foundation for Education. Her work focuses on student access to higher education, particularly as it relates to state policy and programmatic practice. She is coauthor of the report entitled *Assessing the Feasibility of Family Loans for Early Care and Education* (2001) and of *Unequal Opportunity: Disparities in College Access among the Fifty States* (2002).

John T. Yun is an assistant professor at the University of California, Santa Barbara. His research focuses on issues of equity in education, specifically patterns of school segregation; educational differences between private and public schools; the effects of funding, poverty, and opportunity on educational outcomes; and the educative/counter-educative impacts of high-stakes testing. He is coeditor of *The Complex World of Teaching* (with E. Mintz, 1999) and a former solicitations editor at the *Harvard Educational Review.*

Index

Information contained in figures and tables is indicated by an italic *f* and *t* respectively.